The Multinational Challenge
to Corporation Law

The Multinational Challenge to Corporation Law

*The Search for a New
Corporate Personality*

PHILLIP I. BLUMBERG

New York   Oxford
OXFORD UNIVERSITY PRESS
1993

Oxford University Press

Oxford   New York   Toronto
Delhi   Bombay   Calcutta   Madras   Karachi
Kuala Lumpur   Singapore   Hong Kong   Tokyo
Nairobi   Dar es Salaam   Cape Town
Melbourne   Auckland   Madrid

and associated companies in
Berlin   Ibadan

Published by Oxford University Press, Inc.
200 Madison Avenue, New York, NY 10016

Oxford is a registered trademark of Oxford University Press

Library of Congress Cataloging-in-Publication Data
Blumberg, Phillip I., 1919-
The multinational challenge to corporation law: the search for a
new corporate personality / Phillip I. Blumberg.
p.   cm.   Includes index.
ISBN 0-19-507061-5
1. International business enterprises—Law and legislation—United
States.   2. International business enterprises—Law and legislation.
3. Corporation law.   I. Title.
KF1419.B58   1993   346.73'066—dc20
[347.30666]   92-25046

9 8 7 6 5 4 3 2 1

Printed in the United States of America
on acid-free paper

To Ellen

Unending source of loving support and inspiration

Preface

Multinational corporations are challenging traditional concepts of corporation law and international law. Legal concepts fashioned to serve the needs of the largely agrarian society of yesterday, in which the role of business enterprise was both limited and local, have become archaic in a world where business is conducted worldwide by giant corporate groups, composed of affiliated companies organized in dozens of countries.

In response, the law is fashioning new doctrines of law, reformulating the outmoded doctrines inherited from a very different society to a dramatically changed world corporate economy. This volume examines the emerging enterprise law that is changing the traditional theory of the corporation based on the small local corporations of the nineteenth century to accommodate the reality of the modern world of corporate groups. It goes further and introduces for the first time a jurisprudential view of the legal personality of the corporate group.

The critical examination of the traditional jurisprudential foundations of corporation law is overdue. Corporation law evolved from early ecclesiastical roots over centuries of English legal development and had become firmly established by the time of Sir Edward Coke. The corporation was recognized as a separate juridical entity, created by an act of the sovereign, with rights and responsibilities separate and distinct from those of its shareholders. After the Revolution, the English law was incorporated intact into American law, and the traditional concepts prevail today.

Developed at a stage in legal evolution when a corporation could not acquire shares of another corporation unless expressly authorized by statute or its charter, traditional entity law matched the legal entity (the simple corporation) with the economic entity (its business). The corporation conducted the business, and the shareholders were investors. Legal obligations arising from the enterprise necessarily pertained to the corporation conducting it. The enterprise as a whole was responsible for its legal defaults. The doctrine of limited liability, emerging at a much later date, strongly reinforced entity law by expanding it to insulate the shareholders or investors from the liabilities of the business. Law served the needs of the economic society of the time.

When corporate groups emerged decades later, this simple model, in which legal concepts accurately reflected the economic realities that they were intended to govern, no longer fitted the new reality: business collectively conducted by dozens, or even hundreds, of affiliated corporations under common ownership and control.

Under traditional entity law, each component corporation of the group — whether parent, subsidiary, or affiliate — for legal purposes was still separate and distinct from every other corporation in the group, and its rights and responsibilities were separate from those of the other constituent companies of the group and were unaffected by them. Insofar as entity law insulated the ultimate investors or shareholders in the parent corporation from liabilities of the parent, the traditional concept continued to achieve its objective.

Entity theory and limited liability, however, did not apply only to the shareholder-investors of the parent. The parent itself was a shareholder in its subsidiaries. Accordingly, although the parent, unlike its public shareholder-investors, was part of the enterprise and engaged in the business, entity law and limited liability also insulated it from liability for the activities of its subsidiary companies. Corporate obligations imposed in accordance with entity law no longer pertained to the entire enterprise but only to the assets of the constituent corporation involved in the controversy. The remainder of the enterprise escaped liability.

Under traditional law, the fragmentation of an integrated business among a number of affiliated companies as a matter of legal form thus successfully achieves legal consequences of great importance. In sanctioning this result, the traditional law ignores the fact that despite the legal restructuring, only one business is involved — a business being conducted collectively by interlinked companies under common ownership and control.

Thus, with the application of traditional entity law to corporate groups, the older concept of the legal entity no longer matches the reality of the economic entity. The traditional law no longer reflects the society that it seeks to order, and implementation of the underlying policies of the law inevitably is gravely impaired. This is the nature of the challenge facing the legal systems of the world confronted by revolutionary changes in corporate structure and operation caused by the emergence of corporate groups, particularly multinational enterprises. Legal theory of the corporation still concerned with the small, local corporation of the nineteenth century must catch up with the reality of the modern world of giant, multinational groups.

The American legal system has been responding to the challenge presented by the legal interrelationships of the constituent companies of corporate groups. In a growing number of areas of the law — of which statutory law is the leading example but also including tort law and areas of procedural and bankruptcy law — the United States is making a surprising degree of progress. American law is moving from universal, indiscriminate reliance on entity concepts to formulating and utilizing new concepts of enterprise or group law where required to implement the underlying policies and objectives of the law in the area. This experience has already achieved a breadth of application of significant dimensions. At the same, however, in other areas — of which sections of property law and contract law, particularly contracts reflecting bargains over credit, are the prime examples — entity law shows little sign of erosion and appears to continue to serve effectively the society's needs.

Thus, application of enterprise principles that treat the constituent companies of a corporate group as a single unit depends on the particular nature of the legal problem at hand. Enterprise law is not a doctrine of universal application governing all of the legal interrelations of the constituent companies in the group. Instead, it is a selective doctrine, displacing entity law only in those particular legal areas where it appears to accomplish more effectively the underlying policies and objectives of the law than does continued reliance on traditional entity law doctrines. Further, even where they do prevail, enterprise concepts replace entity concepts only for the determination of the particular legal relationship of the parent and subsidiary in question, while entity law, with its traditional attributes, continues unchallenged for all other purposes.

In the five volumes comprising *The Law of Corporate Groups*, the author has comprehensively examined the increasing utilization by American courts and legislatures of enterprise principles, in place of traditional doctrines of entity law, in responding to the legal challenges presented by parent and subsidiary corporations. The availability of this extensive examination at last makes possible a further step in scholarly analysis. It is now feasible for scholars to consider the jurisprudential significance of the development, to reformulate the anachronistic older concepts of the corporate person (or legal unit) and the corporate personality (or the legal rights and attributes attributed to the unit), and to suggest a new conceptual framework for a major change in American law.

Although there has been an enormous amount of academic discussion of the jurisprudential nature of the corporate entity and corporate personality, American scholars have virtually ignored the realities of corporate and industrial organization in the contemporary world. American legal literature is almost exclusively concerned with the legal nature of the corporation of a century ago: the single corporation owned by shareholder-investors. Almost none of the discussion in the United States has recognized the reality of modern corporate structure, which makes this discussion essentially irrelevant. While European scholars have discussed the significance of corporate groups, they are essentially unfamiliar with the American experience with corporate groups, which offers the most fertile field of all for examination.

Finally, it must be recognized that the problem transcends national law. Today, multinational companies operating around the world are predominant in the world economy. The national enterprise law of one nation imposing obligations on foreign components of the group in dealing with the legal problems of in-country affiliates inevitably presents a serious risk of confrontation with other nation-states. The interrelationship between enterprise concepts and extraterritoriality adds a major dimension to an already serious jurisprudential problem. National law applied to world business inevitably leads to international controversy.

The volume concludes with an analysis of the enterprise principles evident in the substantial steps already taken by American legislatures, administrative agencies, and courts that constitute the emerging American law of corporate groups. It accompanies this review of enterprise principles with a reformulation of corporate theory and the traditional concepts of the corporation in order to deal with the jurisprudential challenges presented by corporate groups. Such a re-statement of the traditional jurisprudential views of the corporation is essential for adapting the fundamental concepts of the older legal order to accommodate appropriately the introduction of enterprise principles and the creation of a jurisprudence of relevance to the predominant enterprises of the world economy.

In sum, this volume aspires to provide the framework for future discussion of the corporate personality of the large, modern corporation. It seeks to replace outdated doctrines of corporate jurisprudence developed more than a century ago to serve the needs of a since vanished economy of small, local businesses. It asserts a newer concept of the jurisprudential nature of enterprise law that more realistically responds to the challenge to national legal systems presented by the contemporary world of multinational corporate groups.

Hartford, Connecticut P. I. B.
August 1992

Acknowledgments

This volume draws on the author's previous works considering the legal problems of corporate groups. These include the ongoing series of volumes comprising *The Law of Corporate Groups,* of which five have been published so far: *The Law of Corporate Groups: Procedural Problems in the Law of Parent and Subsidiary Corporations* (1983 and Supp. 1992); *Problems in the Bankruptcy and Reorganization of Parent and Subsidiary Corporations Including the Law of Corporate Guaranties* (1985 and Supp. 1992); *Tort, Contract, and Other Common Law Problems in the Substantive Law of Parent and Subsidiary Corporations* (1987 and Supp. 1992); *Problems of Parent and Subsidiary Corporations under Statutory Law of General Application* (1989 and Supp. 1992); *Problems of Parent and Subsidiary Corporations under Statutory Law of Specific Application* (1992).

These also include the following articles: *Amerikanisches Konzernrecht,* [3/1991] Zeitschrift fur Unternehmens-und Gesellschaftsrecht 328 (1991); *The American Law of Corporate Groups: A Summary Review,* 38 Am. J. Comp. L. 49 (Supp. 1990); *Limited Liability and Corporate Groups,* 11 J. Corp. L. 573 (1986); and *The Corporate Entity in an Era of Multinational Corporations,* 15 Del. J. Corp. L. 283 (1990).

I appreciate the gracious permission of the trustees of The Blumberg Trust, the owner of the copyright, to make extensive use of these materials and the cooperation of Little, Brown and Company and the various journals.

The preparation of this volume has been greatly facilitated by the support and cooperation of Dean Hugh C. Macgill and the law library staff of The University of Connecticut School of Law, including Professor Dennis Stone, law librarian, and Andrea Joseph. I am grateful to my colleague and collaborator, Professor Kurt A. Strasser, for his valuable criticism and suggestions. I have appreciated the helpful comments of my wife, Chief Justice Ellen Ash Peters; my colleagues, Professors Robert L. Birmingham, Mark W. Janis, Richard S. Kay, and Thomas Morawetz; and Professor John Bridge of the Faculty of Law, University of Exeter. I also wish to thank Kevin A. Hughes for assistance in checking citations. Finally, I have been assisted by comments made at seminars at which portions of the volume have been presented at The University of Connecticut School of Law, The University of Sydney Faculty of Law, the University of Warwick Faculty of Law, the Thirteenth International Congress of Comparative Law, and the Australian Society of Legal Philosophy.

Contents

II.   Entity or Enterprise in Dealing
with Corporate Groups:
The American Judicial and Statutory Response

IV.   Jurisprudential Implications

I

Historical Development

1

The Emergence of the Corporation as a Legal Unit and the Rise of Limited Liability

Centuries before there were economic or business activities conducted in corporate form, English ecclesiastical and local governmental units achieved recognition as legal units under the name of corporations.[1] These English concepts of corporations rested on medieval notions of Roman law. Although scholars vigorously disagree over the extent that Roman law accepted concepts of the corporate personality and limited liability, it is quite clear that modern corporation law has, directly or indirectly, Roman roots.[2] This accounts for the fundamental similarity between English and Continental corporation law.

The Corporation as a Legal Unit

When the Crown finally began to charter craft guilds and trading companies — the first business corporations — in the fifteenth century, an understanding of the legal nature of the corporation was already substantially in place. Indeed, it has been asserted that the fundamental legal attributes of corporate existence had been generally recognized as early as the end of the thirteenth century and gradually crystallized during the following centuries, forming the common law doctrine of corporations.[3]

With this history before them, Sir Edward Coke, writing in the beginning of the seventeenth century; the anonymous author of the extensive treatise—The Law of Corporations—published in 1702; and Blackstone and Kyd, writing in the late eighteenth century, could confidently assert what the corporation was, how it was created, and what legal attributes flowed from its organization. While they had primarily ecclesiastical and municipal corporations in mind, their commentary fully applied to business corporations as well.[4]

These jurists uniformly described the corporation as a legal unit with its own legal rights and responsibilities,[5] distinct from those of the individuals who constituted its members or shareholders from time to time. It was a creation of the law and could achieve legal status only by act of the king or Parliament. Although Coke and Blackstone also spoke of corporations created by prescription or common law, these represented ancient local or church institutions that had been long recognized as having corporate form, notwithstanding the absence of any record of royal action. Emphasizing the role of the Crown, they explained away the anomaly by implying a presumption of a "lost or destroyed" royal charter to explain their existence.

Reflecting on this concept of the corporation as a legal creation, Coke described the corporation as "invisible, immortal, and rest[ing] only in intendment and consideration of the law," while Blackstone introduced another characterization that has echoed since. He called the corporation an "artificial person."[6] Chief Justice Marshall borrowed both of these characterizations in his celebrated opinions on the status of American corporations under provisions of the Constitution.[7]

Upon creation, a corporation possessed certain inherent legal attributes. It could sue and be sued. It could contract. It could acquire and dispose of real and personal property. It had perpetual life (or later, a fixed term). Further, it had its own seal by which it could act as a corporate body distinct from its members. Until well into the nineteenth century, the grant of a seal was of paramount importance because a collective body was perceived as being unable to become bound, except by an action under its seal.[8]

There were two further attributes of great importance. Corporate shares were transferable, and corporate membership was subject to change without affecting the continuing existence of the corporation, which had a perpetual, or fixed term, of existence. This right of succession, with continuation of the corporation despite changing membership, receives especial emphasis not only in the works of Coke, Blackstone, and Kyd, but in such American commentaries as those of Story and Kent.[9]

These "core" attributes pertain to the corporation and may be exercised only by it. They are separate from the rights of shareholders and may not be exercised by them. The corporation is a separate legal institution. Although corporations had these core rights, they lacked other legal relationships with which individuals were endowed. Corporations had a somewhat restricted legal status, with a smaller aggregate complex of legal rights and duties than individuals. Coke and Blackstone assert, for example, that a corporation could not commit assault, treason, a felony, or other crime, or serve as an executor or trustee. Nor could it appear in court, except by attorney. These offenses or functions were seen as personal and, accordingly, not applicable to an "invisible" person, one who could not be excommunicated because it lacked a "soul."[10]

In the light of these limitations, nineteenth-century jurists subsequently debated whether corporations could be liable for torts or criminal offenses requiring proof of malice or intent. The courts, in the end, discarded these restrictions of corporate identity.[11] In the United States, for example, the Supreme Court did not hold until 1909 that a corporation could commit a crime of which intent was an essential element.[12] Similarly, it took special statutes to permit corporations to act as executors or trustees.

Even today, corporations may not appear in American courts without an attorney. This is so even where a corporation seeks to appear pro se in the person of its president and sole stockholder. The courts give no explanation for this result, merely describing it as long settled, as indeed it is. Whether it is still desirable in a world not as preoccupied with "invisible person[s]" and the "soul" as the worlds of Coke and Blackstone is quite another matter.

Unlike the traditional core attributes of the corporation that underlie modern corporate law, two other dimensions of the early corporation—public purposes and monopoly powers—have not survived.

Reflecting the role of incorporated boroughs and towns in the growth of the corporate concept, the early corporations were seen as a delegation by the king to accomplish public purposes. Thus, in the seventeenth century, foreign trading corporations had economic privileges because they had assumed public responsibilities in their areas of operations.[13] Of these, the extensive governmental powers over much of India that the English East India Company held for several centuries after it was chartered in 1600 provide the most well-known illustration.

In the eighteenth century, both in England and the United States, the purposes of a business corporation were still perceived as including the accomplishment of some public function. Early American corporations were typically organized to assume public functions such as the bridge, canal, turnpike, and water companies. Banks and insurance companies subsequently followed. However, manufacturing corporations, while not unknown, were very rare. The first American manufacturing corporation was not organized until 1786. By 1801, there were still only 8 manufacturing corporations in the country and only 317 corporations of all types.[14]

Early English corporations also frequently enjoyed monopoly privileges; and incorporation responding to such incentives, among others, has been described as a useful source of royal income. This early interconnection between corporations and monopolies had an adverse effect on later corporate growth, and was widely criticized both in England and the United States. As early as the start of the seventeenth century, Coke vigorously spoke out against corporate monopolies. A century and a half later, Adam Smith concluded that without monopoly advantages, business in the corporate form was inefficient and could not survive except in routine businesses, such as fire and marine insurance, canal and water companies, and banking. In fact, Smith by two centuries anticipated modern scholars in identifying management-shirking and monitoring costs as fundamental problems in the operation of corporations. These concepts apparently first made their appearance in *Wealth of Nations*.[15]

In the political debate in the United States as well, the historical associations between corporations and monopoly played an important role in fomenting suspicion and hostility toward corporations. This was apparent in the Constitutional Convention debates that resulted in defeat of a proposal to grant Congress the power of incorporation. It also appeared in the protests against grants of incorporation in various states.[16]

In time, the role of corporations changed. Professor Hovenkamp describes this evolution of corporate purpose in the United States from public purpose and monopoly to capital accumulation.[17]

Among the attributes of corporate existence, limited liability is conspicuous by its absence. At this stage of development, limited liability was a relatively unimportant concern. It did not attract particular attention until well into the eighteenth century, and it did not become law in England for another century (and only after protracted political struggle).

The concept of the corporation as a legal unit with its own core attributes thus became firmly established in England centuries before the emergence of limited liability. With the Revolution, the nascent American legal system adopted the English law of corporations without change. As Chief Justice Marshall acknowledged in the *Dartmouth College* case, "our ideas of a corporation, its privileges and disabilities, are derived entirely from the English law," and much of Justices Marshall's and Story's rhetoric in their leading corporate opinions comes straight from Coke and Blackstone.[18]

It is frequently asserted that limited liability is an essential attribute of the corporate legal identity. In fact, this very view contributed to the result reached by the House of Lords in the celebrated *International Tin Council* case, decided in 1989 after five weeks of argument.[19] Whether or not this is an accurate description of the modern English legal system, reflecting statutory developments in the nineteenth century, it is clearly not sound from an historical or jurisprudential perspective. The universal adoption of limited liability in the legal systems of the industrialized world rests on relatively modern legislative enactments reflecting politico-economic values, not on fundamental jurisprudential concepts of the nature of the corporation as a legal unit.

There is a further dimension to the problem. In the period in which limited liability became established, corporations could not acquire and hold shares of other corporations, unless expressly authorized to do so by statute or charter. Although there were some exceptions, particularly in the case of railroads, the general law was clear. As Justice Brandeis has said: "holding companies were impossible."[20] This changed a half century after limited liability had been generally adopted in the United States; New Jersey broke new ground in authorizing corporations generally to acquire shares in another corporation. In a very short time, giant corporate enterprises emerged, forming the pyramidal, multitiered corporate structures characteristic of the multinational corporations dominating today's world economy. This chronological order of events is a significant factor in any examination of the jurisprudential problems involved in the imposition of liability on parent corporations for legal transgressions of their subsidiaries.

The Emergence of Limited Liability in English Corporations

Long after the acceptance of the concept of the corporation as a separate legal unit — with its own rights and responsibilities separate from those of its shareholders — English law was equivocal on the liability of shareholders for corporate debts.[21] It was settled, of course, that corporate debts were, at least in the first instance, the debts of the corporation, not the debts of shareholders. The authority for that principle is venerable indeed, going back to Ulpian and Roman law.[22] What was not clear was whether a creditor with an unsatisfied judgment against the corporation could enforce the judgment against its shareholders and thereby impose direct liability upon them. Where the charter spoke to the problem the answer was evident, but what was the law when the charter was silent?

Direct Liability

Holdsworth asserts that as early as the fifteenth century, courts were holding that shareholders had no direct liability for corporate debts. Gower concludes that the principle of an absence of direct shareholder liability had become accepted as early as the end of the sixteenth century. Thus, the charter of the East India Company granted in 1600 provided for limited liability. On the other hand, for a number of corporations formed later, the charters either were silent or provided for unlimited shareholder liability. Thus, other scholars put direct liability later still. For example, Hobbes, writing in 1684, is still referring to unlimited liability. Further, as noted, Blackstone and Kyd, writing at the end of the eighteenth century, not only did not include limited liability among the attributes of the corporation, they deemed it not important enough to mention at all.[23]

Indicative of the uncertainty in the middle- to late-eighteenth century, the Crown, when chartering corporations, was giving some a provision for limited liability, others unlimited liability, and in still others did not refer to the matter at all. Charter applications of the time presented the same ambiguous picture.[24] However, with the passage of time, it became increasingly accepted that where the charter was silent, shareholders had the benefit of limited liability. By 1784, Attorney General (later Lord) Kenyon, in a private opinion, was advising that limited liability prevailed, and when he moved to the bench, he so ruled a few years later in a case involving a public corporation.[25]

Indirect Liability

In addition to direct liability, shareholders faced indirect liability. Where the charter so provided, or a custom of assessments existed, corporations had the power to assess or levy upon shareholders for additional capital contributions; this is the power of leviation. Although this was a power of the corporation, equity assumed jurisdiction to turn it into a source of relief for creditors. In a significant 1671 decision, *Salmon v. Hamborough Co.*, the House of Lords held that creditors could obtain equitable relief to compel a corporation to exercise its power to levy the assessments necessary to pay unsatisfied corporate obligations.[26]

The corporate power to make leviations rested on the charter or on past practice. However, where charters expressly limited the corporate power to assess, indirect liability through creditor actions in equity to compel leviations on shareholders was no longer possible. Faced with the threat of effective indirect liability, counsel accordingly responded by including clauses in the charters prohibiting assessments beyond the basic capital subscription, effectively closing the door to the imposition of indirect liability.

Such was English *corporation* law at the time of the Revolution. English *company* law, or the law applicable to joint stock companies, is a very different matter. After examination of the American experience with limited liability for corporate shareholders, the discussion will review liability of the joint stock company.

Limited Liability in the United States

At the start of the nineteenth century, limited liability was not a leading issue in the United States, and the state of the law was far from clear.[27] Although the new republic fully adopted English corporation law, the state legislatures did not share English reluctance to create new corporations. Special acts of incorporation became widespread, and by 1801 there were more than 300 American corporations. These were overwhelmingly companies undertaking to provide public services: bridges, canals, turnpikes, water supply, banks, and insurance. There were no more than eight manufacturing companies.[28]

With the onset of industrialization, this soon changed. After the introduction of the Arkwright power loom, which revolutionized mass production techniques in textiles, and the throttling of foreign imports by the embargo acts, the War of 1812–1815, and the Tariff Act of 1815, the New England textile industry grew at a truly remarkable rate. By the end of the War of 1812–1815, 128 new manufacturing corporations had been formed just in Massachusetts. As the number of textile spindles increased from some 8,000 in 1807, to 191,000 in 1820, to 1,250,000 in 1831, and as wool consumption soared from 400,000 pounds in 1810 to 15 million tons in 1830, the number of manufacturing corporations similarly grew apace, with 300 in Massachusetts alone.[29]

Assignability of shares and perpetual existence were the attributes that made the corporate form attractive to entrepreneurs forming manufacturing companies. Limited liability was of little importance. In the first thirty years of Massachusetts's existence, not a single petition for incorporation even suggested the protection, and no charter granted it. The New England manufacturing charters of the time typically expressly provided for unlimited liability of shareholders or were silent on the issue. However, this was not as clear in such states as New York and Maryland.[30]

The experience relating to charters for public- and financial-service companies was different. Public service corporation charters typically provided expressly for limited liability. Bank and insurance company charters generally provided for double liability, although isolated charters — such as the 1789 charter of The Bank of New York — provided for limited liability. Indicative of their public objectives and the scarcity of private capital in those times, the states themselves, and even cities, often invested in the shares of banks and insurance companies.[31]

In addition to direct liability of shareholders, indirect liability was also a legal reality, with charters frequently authorizing assessments. American courts were familiar with the decision of the House of Lords in the *Salmon* case. Under its influence, decisions in South Carolina, New York, and Georgia acknowledged the right of creditors in equity to enforce a corporate power to assess shareholders as required for payment of unsatisfied corporate judgments.[32]

For scholars looking at this early period of American law centuries later, it would be convenient to ascertain whether or not shareholders at the beginning of the nineteenth century were directly liable for corporate debts in the absence of any charter provision. The matter, however, was of little concern at the time, the materials are scanty or nonexistent, and no satisfying answer appears to be available.[33]

Increasing industrialization and the growth of manufacturing corporations soon brought the matter to the center of the stage, and the courts promptly settled the issue. In the absence of charter provisions, which had been common earlier, judges held that shareholders faced neither direct nor indirect liability. Thus, as early as 1816, Chief Justice Tilghman of Pennsylvania resolved the issue in conceptual terms, concluding that "personal liability of a stockholder is inconsistent with the nature of a body corporate." Justice Story similarly held in the well-known case of *Wood v. Dummer*, decided in 1824, that shareholders were not liable. By 1832, the Angell and Ames treatise took the absence of shareholder liability for granted.[34] In much the same manner, it became generally accepted that no assessment could be made on shareholders unless expressly authorized by charter, contract, or statute.[35]

The judicial recognition of limited liability of shareholders in the absence of statutory or charter provision was matched by changes in the statutory law. Early statutes, as in Massachusetts in 1809 and 1822, had expressly imposed direct liability on shareholders of manufacturing corporations. However, as the number of corporations continued to increase, the states speedily changed course. New York, which introduced pro rata double liability in 1811, New Hampshire[36] and New Jersey, which did so in 1816, Connecticut in 1818, and Maine in 1823 led the way in adopting limited liability. Massachusetts briefly persisted in its contrary policy, reaffirming statutory unlimited liability in 1825, but it soon followed the model of the other states and adopted limited liability once and for all in 1830. Rhode Island was the only New England holdout, persisting with unlimited liability as late as 1847. Thereafter, with short-lived and isolated exceptions, limited liability soon became accepted throughout the country, except in California. For more than seventy-five years after its admission to statehood in 1849, California persisted in imposing pro rata liability on the shareholders of corporations incorporated or doing business in California.

However, notwithstanding general American acceptance of the principle of limited liability, shareholder insulation from corporate debts was not complete. Until well into the twentieth century, almost all the states imposed double assessment, and in a few cases, triple assessment liability on shareholders where required for payment of unsatisfied corporate obligations. Under such provisions, shareholders could be assessed for additional amounts not to exceed the original capital subscription in the case of double assessment liability (or twice the subscription in cases of triple liability). These provisions imposing significant, albeit limited, liability survived for decades. As late as 1891, the provisions were still almost universal, but they gradually disappeared in the succeeding decades. Comparable double liability for shareholders of banks mandated by both federal and state law was more long-lived. This continued until the Depression of 1929–1933 for state banks and somewhat longer for national banks.[37]

The contrasting California history appears to be unique in the legal systems of developed countries. For decades, California continued to impose unlimited liability on shareholders in an increasingly commercial and industrial nation firmly committed to limited liability. Under the 1849 and 1879 California constitutions and implementing statutes, shareholders of all corporations incorporated or doing business in California were liable for all unpaid corporate debts incurred while they were shareholders.[38]

In an interesting departure from the earlier common law and statutory model of unlimited liability, the California law imposed pro rata, rather than joint and several, liability. Creditors could enforce their claims by direct suit against any shareholder without commencing any action against the corporation, and the shareholder was liable only for the proportion of the debt represented by his or her proportion of the stock.[39] Undoubtedly, the imposition of proportional liability, rather than full liability for all debts of the corporation, contributed to the long duration of the California doctrine.

The California statute had important constitutional implications. It applied to shareholders of out-of-state corporations doing business in California. It applied even to out-of-state corporations incorporated in states whose laws expressly insulated shareholders from any liability and to shareholders resident in such states.

After considerable litigation on the issue of the enforceability of California judgments in other states, the U.S. Supreme Court held that the Full Faith and Credit clause of the Constitution took precedence over the law of the state of incorporation. All states were constitutionally required to enforce California judgments imposing liability for unpaid corporate obligations on their residents, even though contrary to the law of the state of incorporation or the local law providing for limited liability.[40]

The California doctrine, however, was not as far-reaching as it appeared at first sight. First, the statute did not prohibit contracting around liability, and this must have occurred in significant degree. Further, the statutory liability expired within three years after the date on which an *obligation* had originally been *incurred*, not when the *default* occurred. This dramatically restricted the period of exposure. For example, the period for statutory liability could expire before the maturity date of an indebtedness.[41]

Other states also repudiated limited liability, but these departures were isolated and short-lived. Michigan in 1837, New Hampshire in 1842, Wisconsin in 1849, and Pennsylvania in 1853 all briefly reverted to unlimited liability before soon resuming the limited form.[42]

The interesting questions with respect to these fascinating survivals of shareholder liability in the United States remain unanswered. Economic historians do not tell us whether these unique legal rules of liability in isolated jurisdictions surrounded by jurisdictions with contrary rules significantly retarded economic development. During the decade prior to 1830, when Massachusetts and Rhode Island, the states with the most intense manufacturing activity, had unlimited liability while the rest of New England had moved to limited liability, there is no sign that the liability rule adversely affected development. Similarly, Rhode Island persisted with unlimited liability until 1847, or more than a decade and a half later, without losing its position as the most active industrial state in the Union, second only to Massa-chusetts. In the same manner, California, alone in imposing unlimited liability for almost a century later, grew enormously during this pe-riod.

Whether Massachusetts, Rhode Island, and California would have grown even more but for their unconventional policies is an unanswer-able question. Certainly, business forces pressing for the adoption of limited liability did complain that the unfavorable rule was driving capital to other states.[43] If this did occur, however, it would appear to have had limited effect. Thus, when Massachusetts finally abandoned unlimited liability in 1830, there was no discernible increase in the number of incorporations.[44] The issue is manifestly an attractive area for further research by economic historians.

Thus, in the United States, as in England, limited liability was not an essential attribute of corporate existence. In their enumeration of the essential attributes of the corporations, the judges of the time therefore invariably made no reference to limited liability.[45] The adop-tion of limited liability was problematic and followed political debate state by state. With the intensification of industrialization, it finally emerged as a political response to economic and political pressures, not as an inevitable consequence of the concept of the corporate entity.

English Joint Stock Companies and the Struggle over Limited Liability

The problem of the liability or nonliability of shareholders of business enterprises was originally confined to English corporation law. In the other forms of business organizations, such as the partnership or the joint stock company, the personal liability of partners or company members for debts of the firm or company was settled.

However, following the national scandal surrounding the collapse of the South Sea Bubble in 1720, corporations played a declining role in English business life. Corporate charters were difficult and expensive to obtain. During the entire eighteenth century, charters were issued for only a dozen or so corporations, of which a mere six were manufacturing companies.[46] In this legal vacuum, joint stock companies flourished.

Originally a form of partnership, joint stock companies developed into unincorporated associations organized under a deed of settlement, with trustees owning the stock and holding it for the benefit of the members, who, despite the moribund Bubble Act, held transferable shares.

With commercial enterprise increasingly turning to joint stock associations with transferable shares as a preferable alternative to pursuing the corporate form, such companies multiplied and became the predominant form for the conduct of business activity. This was paradoxical, since the Bubble Act had been enacted in 1719 to prevent the growth of just such companies. However, the Act was wretchedly drafted and almost entirely ineffective. After an abortive effort to revive it after a prolonged period of desuetude, it was ultimately repealed a century later.[47]

Modern English business law accordingly, developed as company law – or the law applicable to joint stock companies – not as corporation law, and the protracted political struggle over limited liability involved joint stock companies, not the handful of existing corporations that already had such protection.

The first efforts to limit the liability of joint stock company members arising from the partnership form of the organization were through contract. It became increasingly common for the deeds of settlement to include clauses limiting the power of the company to make calls on members and purporting to limit members' liability to the amount of their stock interest. While this disposed of direct liability as an internal matter and once and for all ended indirect member liability through assessments, it could not affect the joint and several liability of members to third parties. However, the procedural requirements involved in collection suits were so cumbersome as to provide some de facto insulation from member liability in widely held companies.[48]

Joint stock associations used a panoply of legal techniques to achieve some limited liability for members. These included such devices as inserting the term "Limited" in the joint stock company name, including an appropriate legend asserting absence of member liability on the company stationery, and inserting limitation of liability clauses in company contracts. By the mid-eighteenth century, the standard insurance policies of the English and Scottish joint stock insurance companies included clauses limiting policy liability to company capital.[49] Numerous trading companies inserted such clauses in their contracts as well. Such attempted contractual limitations became the prevalent commercial practice even though their validity as a matter of law was not settled until the middle of the nineteenth century.[50] In this manner, joint stock associations under deeds of settlement attempted to achieve the advantages of incorporation without a charter.

Notwithstanding these unresolved legal questions, joint stock associations flourished, as corporate charters continued to be difficult and expensive to obtain. Maitland observed that if the state had not finally yielded and made general incorporation available with limited liability, English commercial activity would probably have been conducted by joint stock associations contracting wherever possible for limited liability.[51]

The growth in the number of joint stock companies and the increasing pressures for new capital investment required by expanding industrialization and the growing scale of business operations inevitably made the issue of limited liability for members of associations a matter of increasing political controversy.

For three decades after the United States had generally accepted limited liability, it continued to be a highly controversial political issue in England, vigorously debated against the rising tide of industrialization. Business exerted more and more pressure for limited liability as a necessary incentive to make possible the accumulation of the substantial capital investments required by the growing industrial order. However, as in the United States, a largely agricultural society shared an underlying hostility to commercial organizations and to the large number of emerging companies. Proposals for limited liability provoked widespread opposition.[52] Limited liability was roundly criticized as inevitably leading to uneconomic, speculative, and fraudulent promotions. Thorstein Veblen suggests in addition that philosophical concerns with a policy eliminating the responsibility of individuals for the consequences of their actions also played a major role. The economists were divided.[53]

For decades, the outcome of the struggle was uncertain, with each of the contending forces temporarily achieving some success. The Joint Stock Companies Registration, Incorporation, and Regulation Act of 1844, passed under Gladstone's leadership, provided for general registration and incorporation of joint stock companies. It imposed joint and several liability on members for unsatisfied corporate obligations. However, it lasted little more than a decade. For this period, English law functioned with corporations as legal units lacking limited liability of shareholders.

Three factors contributed to the demise of the 1844 Act: It was ineffective because it did not prevent the transfers of stock as a means to avoid liability. It provided for joint and several, rather than pro rata, liability and thereby deterred investment by wealthy individuals fearing that they would be primary targets for collection. Finally, the Depression of 1845–1848 and public acceptance of limited liability for railways undermined continued opposition to limited liability.[54]

Finally, in the Limited Liability Act of 1855 and the Joint Stock Companies Act of 1856, Parliament adopted general limited liability and ended the debate once and for all.[55] It reaffirmed the provision of the 1844 Act providing for general incorporation. Thus, after decades of dispute, English law at last definitively accepted limited liability along with general incorporation. Laissez-faire had triumphed. The process had been far from inevitable, and adoption came after a long struggle.

The ultimate triumph of limited liability in England occurred centuries after the emergence of the corporation as a legal unit. It came more than a century after the onset of the Industrial Revolution and decades after limited liability had become generally accepted both on the Continent and in the United States. The English experience leaves no doubt that the extension of limited liability reflected a deliberate political decision in response to commercial pressures to achieve economic objectives. It was not an inevitable conceptual derivation from the separate jurisprudential nature of the corporate legal entity.

Limited liability was not an essential component of the English legal system under which the first hundred years of the Industrial Revolution flourished. Nor was it an inevitable component of the capitalist economic system. English industrial activity increased enormously under a legal rule imposing liability on shareholders. During this period, the investing public showed no signs of hesitating in support of enterprises conducted by unincorporated joint stock companies.[56]

A number of factors tilted the balance by mid-century toward limited liability. First was the increasing scale of capital required for exploitation of continuing progress in technological innovation. Limited liability was purportedly sought to encourage sharply increased capital investment, particularly by middle-class persons, to meet the increasing needs.

The growing distribution of share ownership and declining shareholder participation in management were still other fundamental factors contributing to the adoption of limited liability. Enterprises were becoming larger, and the number of shareholders was increasing substantially. This development had started surprisingly early. Professor Hadden reports that "By the middle of the seventeenth century the ownership of a share had clearly come to be regarded as a matter of financial rather than personal participation." By the end of the seventeenth century, there was a flourishing public market both in London and in the provinces for the shares of all the major English companies. In 1697, Parliament enacted a statute regulating stockbrokers. Stock markets had also emerged in Belgium and Holland.[57] The widening distribution of shareholdings accelerated further the separation of shareholder-investors from management participation. Under these circumstances, the lack of utility and fairness in imposing liability on investors for the acts of the managers became increasingly recognized.[58]

The pressures for limited liability had been particularly strong in the case of the English railways. Their need for heavy capital investment had led to a growing number of shareholders and widespread distribution of the shares. Their shares were traded actively in security markets throughout England. The public shareholders were investors, not owners, and their separation from participation in management was evident. Finally, railway operations involved heavy tort liability inherent in the operation of a new technology. Contractual limitations and public notice could not deal with the problem. Due to all these factors, limited liability for railways received general approval, notwithstanding some criticism that it had led to speculation in railway shares.[59] The acceptance of limited liability for the railways foreshadowed the ultimate acceptance of limited liability generally.[60]

In the years following the introduction of limited liability, there was almost a threefold increase in the number of companies registering under the company acts. Some of this may be attributed to the more prosperous times and the unhappy practices of promoters who, solely for speculative purposes, organized companies that never came into operation.[61] Some may also be attributed to changes in legal form for existing businesses. However, in view of the magnitude of the increase, it is apparent that the English adoption of limited liability had provided a significant economic incentive.

This adoption soon led to a period of speculation and security frauds that contributed to a particularly severe financial panic.[62] Although these were the very excesses of which its opponents had warned, limited liability survived. Once in place, limited liability continued as a settled principle of English company law.

Limited Liability in the Civil Law

On the Continent, limited liability surprisingly made its first appearance in Russia as early as 1805. However, the inclusion of limited liability in the Napoleonic Code de Commerce had much greater historical significance. The military might of French revolutionary armies imposed the Code by force of arms on most of Europe, and limited liability along with it. The Code proved more long-lived than Napoleon's military hegemony. While French military domination of the Continent ended with the fall of Napoleon, French cultural influence persisted. After regaining independence, the European states promptly reenacted the Code de Commerce, and limited liability continued.[63] Thus, the civil law recognized limited liability earlier than in either the United States or England.

Summary

Although limited liability could not exist without the underlying traditional legal concept of the corporation and the shareholder as separate legal units, limited liability is a different and much newer concept, emerging centuries after the mature development of the corporate concept. Prior to its acceptance corporations existed, and indeed, a growing corporate society flourished. For almost a century after its adoption in the United States, the doctrine had only spotty application, with significant areas of shareholder liability continuing.

Since the acceptance of limited liability, the form of the business enterprise has changed remarkably. Limited liability triumphed when corporations were simple, when one corporation could not acquire and own shares of another. Limited liability meant protection for the ultimate investor. Decades after corporations had become a major factor in the economy, the legislature first granted corporations the legal power to acquire and hold shares of other corporations. Major business rapidly changed form into the complex, multitiered corporate structure of the modern economy.

In the succeeding chapters, this volume examines the implications of this jurisprudential inheritance and historical development, starting with the historical emergence of corporate groups.

2

The Corporate Personality in the Courts

Jurisprudence and the Corporate Personality

The corporation is a legal unit with certain legal rights attributed to it upon its recognition by the state; these are its core rights. Questions immediately arise: How does such recognition occur? What is being recognized? What legal rights flow from recognition?

Above and beyond the essential legal attributes of corporations, there are important issues with respect to the application to corporations—as well as to individuals—of certain fundamental rights in the constitutional provisions utilizing such general terms as "person" or "citizen" or "people." Finally, there are numerous questions, of lesser importance, arising under statutory provisions and administrative regulations of general application referring generally to "person" or "whoever" or simply regulating certain conduct. When so used, are such general terms confined to human beings or are they to receive a generic construction and include corporations as well?

Over the years, the scholarly discussion of the jurisprudential nature of the corporation has been enormous. In recent years, it has been supplemented by commentaries on the nature and historical recognition of the constitutional rights of corporations.[1] Unfortunately, the commentaries, without exception, discuss the corporation in its early nineteenth-century model of a single corporation owned by shareholder-investors. None deals with the contemporary problems of the jurisprudential nature of the modern large corporation organized in the form of a group of corporations collectively conducting the enterprise. What is the corporate personality of such an enterprise?

What Is the Nature of Corporate Recognition?

Until well into the nineteenth century, recognition of a corporation for business purposes, both in England and in the United States, required a specific governmental decision to grant corporate status. In England, this took the form of a charter from the Crown or an act of Parliament. In the United States it required a legislative act. Although the issue was not as simple in the case of medieval municipal and ecclesiastical corporations, where recognition of corporate status in the early English law had also been achieved by such murky routes as prescription or common law custom, business corporations never presented this complexity.

Throughout American history, corporate recognition has required some form of state action. In the early days of the republic, and continuing for at least half of the nineteenth century, this took the form of special acts of incorporation. Perceiving special incorporation as undemocratic and corrupt, the Jacksonians made a major political objective the enactment of general incorporation statutes that would permit persons generally to utilize the corporate form. Although there had been steps toward general incorporation as early as 1811 in New York for manufacturing corporations and 1837 in Connecticut for most corporations, these were isolated occurrences.[2] General incorporation did not become fully accepted by the states until after the Civil War. Until then, special incorporation by legislative grant was the only route to incorporation in most jurisdictions.[3]

With the universal triumph of general incorporation statutes more than a century ago, corporations could be formed simply by filing certain forms and paying certain fees and taxes. The state's role has shrunken dramatically to a general specification of procedures and a ministerial administrative acknowledgment of the incorporators' compliance with the statutory formalities.

What Is Being Recognized?

Almost all general statutes of incorporation purport to grant recognition of corporate status to a group of individuals—typically three—serving as incorporators and constituting the original stockholders. Most special statutes follow the same model. Thus, one is tempted to describe the corporation simply as an organization of human beings being granted recognition as a separate legal unit with legal rights separate from those of its stockholders and members. In this sense, corporation law is simply a part of the law dealing with organizations.

While this is often true, it is not entirely correct. In many cases, the incorporators, most frequently lawyers' clerks, are acting on behalf of an existing organization desiring to continue in corporate form or for a group of persons wanting to form a new organization in corporate form. Often, however, the incorporators are acting for a single individual or an existing corporation. Thus, while some corporations are organizations of human beings, in many other cases, such as wholly owned subsidiaries or so-called one-person corporations, they are not an organized group at all. From the jurisprudential point of view, their existence makes it difficult to describe corporations generally as organizations of human beings.

A corporation more accurately is a legal unit formed by, or for, one or more other legal units. However, there is more to it. Even where the sole shareholder of the corporation is another corporation, its parent corporation, the latter in turn, has its shareholders, and, directly or indirectly, the ultimate shareholders are for practical purposes almost always human beings. To the extent that institutional investors are shareholders, as is increasingly the case, it is simply necessary to go further down the chain of ownership, but ultimately their shareholders are human beings too. Similarly, the one-person corporation by definition has a human shareholder. Thus, in the end, corporations, or almost all of them, represent the aspirations and interests of the human beings with the ultimate equity ownership.[4] This factor—reinforced by frequent references to the corporation as a "legal person"—inevitably shapes the perceptions of the nature of the corporation.

In determining the rights and duties of corporations under the various constitutional and statutory provisions drafted with reference to human beings, or using language that might support such a construction, the law finds the fact that corporations represent the economic aspirations of the human beings who are their stockholders or members a highly relevant factor.

What Basic Legal Rights Arise from Recognition?

Recognition of the corporation as a legal unit has meaning only in the context of the legal rights or attributes that arise from such recognition. As reviewed in the previous historical discussion, the core attributes of every corporation arising simply through recognition of its corporate status were clearly established early in English legal history. As reviewed in Chapter 1, corporateness automatically meant the right to sue and be sued, to contract, to hold and dispose of property, to have a perpetual (or other fixed) term of existence, and to have freely transferable shares, with its existence as a legal unit unaffected by changes in its stockholders or membership.

In the nineteenth century, jurisdictions throughout the developed world uniformly adopted the principle of limited liability, limiting the shareholders' risk of loss to the amount of their original stock subscription (or as prevailed in most American states until after World War I, to amounts double or even triple the original subscription). By virtue of such universal acceptance, limited liability has in time also come to be regarded by many as another of the core attributes of corporate existence. Some scholars go beyond the core attributes and also include in the corporate personality the constitutional rights recognized for corporations.

What Constitutional and Statutory Rights and Responsibilities Relate to Corporations?

Above and beyond the fundamental characteristics that define generally the meaning of corporateness in the legal system, there are other issues, often of great importance, with respect to the general application to corporations of the provisions of the Constitution, statutes, or administrative regulations. These questions of constitutional and statutory construction arise from the fact that the provisions in question — whether constitutional, statutory, or administrative — frequently employ terms related to human beings, but in a context that leaves open the question of whether broader application is appropriate.

When terms such as "person" or "citizen," or "people" or "whoever," are used in a constitution or statute, it is not always clear whether they are properly construed to apply to human beings in particular or whether they are more appropriately interpreted as a generic reference that includes other legal units.

The construction problem has very different dimensions in its constitutional application than in its statutory context. The constitutional provisions in question typically deal with the fundamental civil and criminal *rights* of the society and are matters of grave importance. The statutory law provisions of this nature, however, overwhelmingly impose *responsibilities* rather than grant rights. Furthermore, even in those relatively rare areas where the statutes do recognize rights, they are not fundamental ones. Instead, they tend to involve the much less significant problems of the inclusion of corporations under some advantageous statutory provision. Although jurisprudential theories of the nature of the corporation play some role in the determination of the constitutional issues, they are almost never introduced into the determination of the applicability of such statutory provisions.

Competing Theories of the Corporation

A brief review of the more prominent competing theories of the corporation in American law is the appropriate introduction to any examination of the two centuries of American judicial decisions considering the applicability of provisions of the Constitution to corporations.

The jurisprudential nature of the corporate personality for decades has attracted a remarkably wide degree of attention, and the volume of academic literature is enormous. Although it has been suggested that there are at least sixteen different theories of the corporate personality, the discussion divides essentially into three major approaches.[5]

State Action

In the early days of the American republic, prior to the adoption of general incorporation statutes, each corporation was chartered by a special act of the legislature. The American courts, led by Chief Justice Marshall, perceived the corporation as the artificial creature of the law.

In his classic formulations of what became the "artificial person" theory of the corporation, Chief Justice Marshall described the corporation in vivid terms: "A corporation is an artificial being, invisible, intangible, and existing only in contemplation of law. Being the mere creature of law, it possesses only those properties which the charter of its creation confers upon it, either expressly, or as incidental to its very existence."[6] These terms were borrowed from the English jurists, but Marshall's emphasis on the term "artificial" was his own.

The essence of this view is that the corporation is a separate juridical unit created by state action—an artificial creature of the state possessing, in addition to its essential core attributes, only such limited powers as are granted by the state. In Marshall's view, the corporation was precisely what the act of incorporation made it. Although a separate legal entity, its legal capacity beyond its core rights depended on its charter and thereby differed decisively from the fuller panoply of legal rights possessed by natural persons.

This doctrine has an ancient jurisprudential history; in one form or another it has attracted wide support over the centuries on the Continent,[7] as well as in England and the United States. It has appeared in a number of variant forms, including the artificial person, fiction, concession, or grant doctrines.[8] Notwithstanding their incidental differences and the intensity of the historic debates over these distinctions, all the forms center on the corporation as an "artificial," or "fictional," legal unit. The focus is on the state role in incorporation, not on the incorporators.

This "artificial person" theory is still widely accepted. Thus, in the recent decisions involving the application of the First Amendment to corporations, no less than four Supreme Court justices relied on Marshall's description of the "artificial person" theory in support of their conclusions, while a fifth gave it intermittent support.[9]

Private Action

At the very time that Marshall and the Court were enunciating the "artificial person" doctrine, they were simultaneously advancing a second, more complex theory of the corporate personality to supplement (but not to replace) that doctrine. In a number of important nineteenth-century Supreme Court cases considering the application of the Constitution to corporations, the Court, starting as early as 1809 and continuing until late in the century and again led initially by Chief Justice Marshall, also emphasized a very different dimension of the corporation. This was the view that the corporation, while concededly an artificial state creation with its common law core attributes, was at the same time an aggregation or association of individuals contracting with each other to accomplish their private objectives in the corporate form.[10]

This view, emphasizing private arrangements rather than state action, provided the theoretical foundation for the attribution to the corporation of constitutional rights in order to protect the interests of its human shareholders. This idea has alternatively been called the associational, aggregate, or contract theory. It also had its adherents, particularly von Jhering, in Europe, where it was also called the symbolist or bracket theory.[11]

Unlike many judges of the century, Chief Justice Taney did not accept the associational theory. Writing in *Bank of Augusta v. Earle*, decided in 1837, he criticized the associational theory as inconsistent with the concept of limited liability that had won acceptance only a few years before. He rejected the theory because he perceived that it could undermine continued acceptance of the limited liability doctrine.[12]

With the widespread enactment of general incorporation statutes making corporate status freely available and restricting state action in the formation of corporations to the determination of the formal procedures by which any group of individuals could obtain incorporation through the ministerial act of a minor official, state action became much less significant. The predominant role in corporate organization moved to the incorporators. The associational view gathered strength. Justice Field was an especially powerful adherent, incorporating the doctrine into a number of major decisions.[13] The authors of the leading corporation law treatises of the time, such as Morawetz, accepted it as the prevailing view.[14]

Although the associational theory attracted strength because it facilitated the attribution of constitutional rights to corporations, it did not reject the "artificial person" doctrine. Thus, Justice Field, a leading exponent of the associational view, was also emphasizing that corporations were "artificial persons created by the legislature and possessing only such attributes as the legislature has prescribed."[15] In no sense did the associational view imply that the corporation was not a separate legal entity of its own—separate and different from its shareholders—with the core rights traditionally recognized by the common law.

Reflecting the greatly increased prominence of the role of the incorporators and the sharply reduced role of the state, in the last fifteen years a "contractarian" or "libertarian" body of opinion has emerged that contends that corporations should primarily be recognized as private contracts between the incorporators, rather than as creations of the state. Under this view, corporations are perceived as a private contractual ordering of affairs, a simple "nexus of contracts,"[16] rather than as institutions derived from public action. Such commentators consequently argue that, as with other private contracts, the state should interfere as little as possible with the bargain reached by the contracting parties.[17]

Social Creation

Still a third theory has emerged that has also developed widespread support. This theory, resting on German sociological and philosophical roots, with von Gierke as its most prominent exponent, views the corporation as a social group with a "real" existence and a "real" will of its own, separate from the persons constituting its shareholders of the moment.[18] This has been termed the "organic," or "real entity," theory.

Looking upon the emergence of corporations (as with other groups) as a natural outcome in any society, it denies the artificial element that characterizes the state action theory. It passes over state action as merely confirming the preexisting "reality" of the organizational existence. Unlike the private action, or associational, theory, however, it joins with the state action, or "artificial person" theory, in focusing on the corporation, not on its shareholders.

Summary

It should be apparent that each of the three theories has something to contribute.[19] It is indisputable that corporations may exist only by leave of the state and that state action, even though limited to the benediction available to all through the general incorporation statutes, is an integral feature of the problem. The "artificial person" or state action doctrine provides further legitimation of a fuller application of social control through extension of the regulatory process over corporations and their economic activity.

However, it is also plain that the organization and restructuring of corporations is the result of private bargaining and private decision in which the state plays only the most formal part. It is, accordingly, appropriate to inquire as to the extent that such state restrictions of contracting by private parties of this nature are desirable. The "associational" or private action doctrine viewing the corporation as an aggregation of the shareholders has, however, conflicting implications. Insofar as corporations generally are concerned, its emphasis on the priority of shareholder interests and the negligible role of the state strengthens the argument against public control of corporate activity and affairs. On the other hand, in the case of corporate groups, this very emphasis on shareholder interests provides some support for the utilization of enterprise principles in determining the legal relationships of subsidiary corporations by reference to the interests and role of their shareholder, the parent corporation.

Finally, complex societies inevitably conduct much of their activity through organizations, many of which are long-lived—if not perpetual—have enormous resources, and, in some cases, are composed of hundreds of thousands or even millions of members. These organizations frequently continue over the years while their memberships continue to change. The suggestion that such organizations have an existence of their own distinct, in reality as well as in law, from that of their ever-changing membership is powerful. Thus, Blackstone and Kyd rewrote Heraclitus to compare the corporation and its changing membership to the River Thames that remains the same notwithstanding its ever-flowing waters.[20]

The enterprise view, bottomed on economic realities, closely resembles the real entity doctrine, which focuses on the social realities. The real entity theory thus provides some theoretical basis for a legal doctrine that seeks to concentrate on the problems presented by the economic organization and, in appropriate cases, to develop legal rights and responsibilities related to the common economic organization rather than to its formal, legal fragments arising from separate filings for incorporation of component parts of the single enterprise. The real entity view, focusing on the sociological existence of the corporate organization, strongly resembles the modern emphasis on the realities of corporate existence. In fact, enterprise law, which rests on economic realities, may be loosely viewed as a variant of the real entity doctrine—shorn of its metaphysical concept of a group will and its emphasis on the pre-juridical reality of the group—applied to corporate groups.

Although they all have something to offer, the corporate theories have limitations that should be obvious. They are all two-dimensional and do not conform to the realities of the modern world. The "artificial person" theory is undermined by the fact that the element of state creation, while still accurate, has become so substantially diluted as to resemble an "entitlement" along with the others of the era. The associational theory—resting as it does on the perception of an economic world of small corporations with relatively few shareholders contracting among themselves—hardly describes the large, modern corporation with its thousands or hundreds of thousands of shareholders barren of any connection with the original incorporators and increasingly separated from management and control. The real entity view ignores the essential role that state participation in the creation of a corporation has for its recognition as legal unit. Further, it assumes the existence of a metaphysical group will, ignoring the reality of the hierarchical and bureaucratic management and the absence of effective shareholder participation in governance of the large public corporation.

With all their limitations, the theories have some conceptual usefulness in focusing on undeniable aspects of the corporate institution. In the end, examination of the corporation in the light of the theories is useful, not only in illuminating any study of the corporate personality, but in making, as well, some contribution to consideration of enterprise law.

Constitutional Applications

The cases involving the application to the corporation of various provisions of the United States Constitution provide a particularly fertile area for examination of judicial approaches to the corporate personality. Although the concept of the separate legal personality of the corporation had been firmly embraced by the English legal system long before, and by the United States after, the American Revolution, this meant only that the corporation was a legal unit with fundamental core rights distinct from those of its shareholders. This did not provide a ready answer to the uncertainties of the application of the new Constitution to corporations. In the process of constitutional construction, theories of the corporate personality inevitably played a role in determining the extent to which corporations could invoke constitutional provisions and obtain constitutional rights in addition to their unchallenged core common law rights.

The new republic knew little about corporations. At the time of adoption of the Constitution, there were very few. As late as 1801 there were only 317 corporations in the entire country. Nevertheless, the members of the Constitutional Convention were clearly aware of the existence of corporations. James Madison, joined by Charles Pinckney, had proposed, and the Convention had overwhelmingly rejected, inclusion of an express incorporation power for the Congress.[21] Thus, the word "corporation" appears in neither the original Constitution, nor in the Bill of Rights and the later amendments. Nor do the debates or other sources throw any light on the status of corporations under the Constitution. Determining constitutional meaning and intent with respect to a class of parties with which neither the society nor the law had had much experience rendered the problem of constitutional construction even more difficult.

The language of the Constitution further complicated the problem. In provisions dealing with fundamental rights, it utilizes such general terms as "person," "citizen," and "people." Were the constitutional protections provided by provisions with such references confined to human beings or did the provisions, or some of them, protect corporations as well? Some other provisions in general terms prohibit certain acts by the federal government without referring to the classes protected. Do they apply to corporations?

In continuing litigation over the succeeding two centuries, the federal courts have struggled, and indeed, are still struggling with such questions, seeking to determine article by article and clause by clause whether corporations have the same rights as human beings. In cases arising as early as 1809 and continuing until the present time, the issue of whether corporations are protected by a constitutional provision has arisen in numerous areas, including some of the most fundamental provisions of the Constitution and the Bill of Rights.

"Citizen"
DIVERSITY-OF-CITIZENSHIP JURISDICTION:
ARTICLE III

The first corporate constitutional controversy arose in connection with diversity-of-citizenship jurisdiction. Article III, Section 2, Clause 1 provides that the federal judicial system may hear "cases" or "controversies" between "citizens" of different states. This was clear enough in the case of natural persons, but what of corporations? Was a corporation a "citizen" for purposes of this provision? If so, of what state was it a "citizen"?[22]

This question arose in 1809 in *Bank of the United States v. Deveaux,*[23] in which a corporate action on a note was brought in the federal court under diversity-of-citizenship jurisdiction. The district court dismissed for want of jurisdiction, holding that a corporation could not be a "citizen" and, accordingly, that diversity of citizenship could not arise.[24] If not reversed, this decision would have barred all litigation involving corporations — whether as plaintiff or defendant — from the federal courts insofar as common law matters or state corporation law matters were concerned.[25] Thus, the issue far transcended the impact on the immediate parties. It involved the role of the new federal judicial power over major areas of law affecting the new corporate society.

On appeal, the Supreme Court reversed. Chief Justice Marshall, writing for a unanimous court, first described the corporation as a "mere creature of the law, invisible, intangible, and incorporeal," using rhetoric borrowed almost without change from Coke and Blackstone. Marshall, however, went beyond the English jurists to give an emphasis to the term "artificial being." Thus, he agreed with the district court that a corporation — "that invisible, intangible, and artificial being, that mere legal entity . . . is certainly not a citizen." Unlike the lower court, Marshall went further and upheld the action. He disregarded the separate legal personality of the corporation and held that for purposes of determining jurisdiction the case was controlled by the citizenship of its shareholders. He stated that the "controversy is, in fact and in law, between those persons [the shareholders] suing in their corporate character, by their corporate name, for a corporate right" and the other party. The term "citizen" is only used "to describe the real persons who come into court, in this case, under their corporate name."[26]

In terms of the theory of the nature of the corporation, this rationale for the decision in *Bank of the United States v. Deveaux* represents the earliest judicial expression of the associational view of the corporation. However, the decision does not challenge the fundamental principle of entity law. Marshall made it plain that the associational view was superimposed upon, rather than replacing, entity law. Thus, he carefully referred to the corporation as a "mere creature of the law," "an artificial being," and "a mere legal entity," and emphasized that the case involved the assertion in "corporate name" of a "corporate right." The judgment was for the corporation, not its shareholders. Shareholder interests entered only to support the attribution to corporate entities of the ability to sue and be sued in federal courts under the Diversity-of-Citizenship Jurisdiction clause and thereby permitted the assertion of federal jurisdiction over litigation involving corporations in the event of diversity.

Decades later, the Court abandoned this technique of looking through corporate parties to the citizenship of their shareholders for the purpose of determining corporate citizenship for diversity jurisdiction purposes. Although recognizing that a corporation was not a "citizen" for this purpose, it nevertheless insisted on preserving the "valuable privilege" of federal jurisdiction for corporations. The Court held that irrespective of the actual citizenship of the shareholders, it would be conclusively presumed that those shareholders were citizens of the state of incorporation. Through this legal fiction the corporation received the jurisdictional opportunities open to citizens without the Court having to accord citizenship to it. Years later, however, Congress by statute confirmed corporate status as a "citizen" for jurisdictional purposes.[27]

Australian law offers an interesting contrast. The Australian Supreme Court has held that the term "resident" in the comparable provision of the Australian Constitution granting diversity-of-residence jurisdiction to the Australian federal courts does not include corporations.[28]

PRIVILEGES AND/OR IMMUNITIES:
ARTICLE IV AND THE FOURTEENTH AMENDMENT

"Citizens" is also the crucial term in Article IV, Section 2, Clause 1, which provides that "The Citizens of each State shall be entitled to all Privileges and Immunities of Citizens in the several States"; it is also crucial in the Fourteenth Amendment, Section 1, which provides that "No State shall make or enforce any law which shall abridge the privileges or [*sic*] immunities of citizens of the United States. . . ."

Bank of the United States v. Deveaux, holding that a corporation was not a "citizen" for purposes of diversity jurisdiction, cast its shadow over the construction of these references. In *Bank of Augusta v. Earle*, decided in 1839, the Court affirmed that corporations were not "citizens" and refused to apply Article IV to invalidate a state statute discriminating against foreign corporations.

Writing for the Court, Chief Justice Taney relied entirely on the artificial person theory. Pointedly refusing to apply the associational theory, he stated: "Whenever a corporation makes a contract, it is the contract of the legal entity; of the artificial being created by the charter; and not the contract of the individual members." He concluded that a corporation was "a mere creature" of local law without any "legal existence out of the boundaries of the sovereignty by which it was created."[29] Unlike *Deveaux*, the Court refused to look to the shareholders and outlaw such discrimination as a means of protecting shareholder rights.

As noted, Taney was concerned with the implications of a contrary decision resting on the associational theory for the limited liability of shareholders. Taney pointed out that if:

> Members of a corporation were to be regarded as individuals carrying on business in their corporate name, and therefore entitled to the privileges of citizens in matters of contract, it is very clear that they must at the same time take upon themselves the liabilities of citizens, and be bound by their contracts in like manner . . . [and] be liable to the whole extent of [their] property for the debts of the corporation.[30]

Taney, writing at the time of still incomplete triumph of limited liability, evidently did not want to contribute to possible reversal of this development.

However, reliance on the associational theory in other cases did not lead to any threat to the continued acceptance of limited liability.[31] Similarly, the associational theory did not lead to any challenge to the fundamental attributes flowing from recognition of the corporation as a separate juridical unit with its essential core attributes. Nor was there any movement to permit shareholders to assert directly any of the rights of the corporation.[32]

Almost thirty years later, the issue again came before the Court in *Paul v. Virginia*, decided in 1868. By this time, under *Letson* and *Marshall*, corporations were deemed citizens for purposes of the Diversity-of-Citizenship Jurisdiction clause. The Court, however, reaffirmed its conclusion in *Bank of Augusta* and again held that a corporation was not a "citizen" for purposes of the Privileges and Immunities clause of Article IV. Justice Field stated: "[T]he term citizens . . . applies only to natural persons, members of the body politic, owing allegiance to the State, not to artificial persons created by the legislature, and possessing only the attributes which the legislature has prescribed."[33]

Conceptually, the different interpretations of the two constitutional references are manifestly inconsistent. However, as a matter of constitutional development, opening the federal courts to litigation involving corporations is a very different issue than permitting states to exclude foreign corporations in matters not involving interstate commerce. The fact that the same constitutional term, "citizen," was employed did not prevent conflicting conclusions on its applicability to corporations.

The Fourteenth Amendment, adopted in 1868, also contained a Privileges or Immunities clause applicable to "citizens of the United States." Further, unlike Articles III and IV, the new amendment defined "citizens" as "persons born or naturalized in the United States," a definition difficult to apply to corporations. In *Pembina Consolidated Silver Mining and Milling Co. v. Pennsylvania*, decided in 1888 and involving the applicability of the clause to a discriminatory Pennsylvania tax on foreign corporations, Justice Field, writing for the Court and quoting from his opinion in *Paul v. Virginia* (which restricted "citizens" in Article IV to natural persons), had no difficulty in holding that the term "citizens" in the Fourteenth Amendment applied only to natural persons, not to corporations.[34]

"Person"

"Person" is the crucial term in no less than four fundamental constitutional provisions: the Equal Protection and the Due Process clauses of the Fourteenth Amendment and the Self-Incrimination and the Double Jeopardy clauses of the Fifth Amendment. The Court has held that a corporation is a protected "person" under three of these provisions—the Equal Protection, Due Process, and Double Jeopardy clauses. Nevertheless, the corporation is not a "person" protected by the Self-Incrimination clause. Although the treatment of the corporation for purposes of the Double Jeopardy and Self-Incrimination clauses has not aroused much scholarly interest, an enormous literature has appeared in recent years dealing with corporations and the Equal Protection and Due Process clauses.[35]

EQUAL PROTECTION OF THE LAW:
THE FOURTEENTH AMENDMENT

The status of the corporation under the Equal Protection clause of the Fourteenth Amendment referring to "person" first arose before the Supreme Court in *Santa Clara County v. Southern Pacific Railroad*, decided in 1886. Although the question had been argued at length in the various briefs, the Court abruptly announced: "The court does not wish to hear argument on the question whether the provision in the Fourteenth Amendment to the Constitution, which forbids a State to deny to any person within its jurisdiction the equal protection of the laws, applies to these corporations. We are all of the opinion that it does." The Court's brief announcement threw no light on the rationale for the conclusion.[36]

The *Santa Clara* decision has provoked vigorous contemporary debate. Although some scholars have looked upon *Santa Clara* as reflecting the view that the corporation was a "person" for constitutional purposes generally, with rights comparable to those of natural persons, Professor Horwitz, among others, disagrees. Setting *Santa Clara* against the legal thought of its time, Horwitz concludes that a corporation's interests for these constitutional purposes were being seen as identical to its shareholders' interests and that the Court was applying the associational theory.[37]

DUE PROCESS OF THE LAW:
THE FOURTEENTH AMENDMENT

Pembina Consolidated Silver Mining and Milling Co. v. Pennsylvania followed two years later. This involved the construction and application of two vital constitutional terms—"citizen" and "person." While, as already noted, the Court in *Pembina* refused to recognize a corporation as a "citizen" for purposes of the Privileges or Immunities clause of the Fourteenth Amendment, it simultaneously held that a corporation was a "person" within the meaning of the Due Process and Equal Protection clauses of the amendment. Justice Field, relying on the associational theory, once again stated: "Under the designation of person [in the amendment] there is no doubt that a private corporation is included. Such corporations are merely associations of individuals united for a special purpose and permitted to do business under a particular name and have a succession of members without dissolution."[38]

In *Pembina*, the Court was not apparently ready to conclude that the corporation as an "artificial person" qualified as a "person" for constitutional purposes of the Fourteenth Amendment. In order to support its result, the Court found it necessary as well to invoke the associational theory asserting that "corporations are merely associations of individuals."

The Court took the final step two decades thereafter. In *Southern Railway v. Greene*,[39] decided in 1910, the Court again flatly held "That a corporation is a person within the meaning of the Fourteenth Amendment, is no longer open to discussion." The Court went on to quote the sentence in *Pembina* referring to the corporation as a "person," while pointedly omitting from the *Pembina* quotation the very next sentence (included above) referring to corporations as "merely associations of individuals." By so doing, the Court showed that for the first time it was prepared to rely solely on an entity view, treating the corporation as a "person" without any distinction between "artificial" and natural persons. Reliance on the associational theory was no longer required for attribution of constitutional rights to the corporate entity.

The Court had at last moved beyond the artificial person theory both in its pure form and where it was supplemented by the associational theory. It had adopted a more developed concept in which the corporation was, for the first time, explicitly recognized as a "person" within the meaning of the constitutional reference. In the process, the Court emerged with a doctrine under which all forms of business organizations — whether sole proprietorship, partnership, or corporations — received very much the same constitutional protection. The development of business institutions would not be distorted by a pressure to adopt a particular form of business organization in order to claim constitutional protection.

Nevertheless, in some areas regarded as highly personal, constitutional protections for individuals and corporations may differ. Thus, several important decisions have emphasized that some constitutional rights are "purely personal," protecting only individuals depending on the "nature, history, and purpose" of the particular provision. The Self-Incrimination clause is the most prominent example. For a while, it also appeared that as the result of a dictum of the first Justice Harlan, corporate constitutional protection as a "person" was confined to "property" and did not include "liberty." Judge Learned Hand, among others, criticized this view, and it has not survived. Several recent cases upholding constitutional protection of corporate freedom of speech have properly ignored such a distinction.[40]

SELF-INCRIMINATION:
THE FIFTH AMENDMENT

Notwithstanding its earlier decisions construing "person" in the Equal Protection and Due Process clauses to include corporations, the Court in *Hale v. Henkel*, decided in 1906, held that corporations were not protected by the clause of the Fifth Amendment providing: "nor shall [any person] be compelled in any criminal case to be a witness against himself. . . ."

Justice Brown, speaking for the majority, relied on the artificial person theory and the powers of the state over corporations created by it. He stated:

> . . . the corporation is a creature of the State. It is presumed to be incorporated for the benefit of the public. . . . It would be a strange anomaly to hold that a State, having chartered a corporation to make use of certain franchises, could not in the exercise of its sovereignty inquire how these franchises had been employed, and whether they had

been abused, and demand the production of the corporate books and papers for that purpose.

He noted further that the state's "reserved power of visitation would seriously be embarrassed, if not wholly defeated in its effective exercise" by recognition of the privilege in the hands of corporations.[41]

This decision on the application of the Self-Incrimination clause is one of the most powerful examples of acceptance of the artificial person theory. However, such acceptance for this purpose did not prevent the very same justice in the very same opinion from utilizing the associational theory to include corporations under the Unreasonable Searches and Seizures clause of the Fourth Amendment, as discussed below.

Numerous American decisions have since affirmed the conclusion in *Hale v. Henkel* that corporations are not protected by the Self-Incrimination clause.[42] As Justice Murphy tried to explain in *United States v. White*, the result rests on three very different foundations. First, "the fact that the state charters corporations and has visitational powers over them provides a convenient vehicle for justification of governmental investigation." Second, "the scope and nature of the economic activities [of corporations] demand that the constitutional powers of the federal and state governments to regulate these activities be correspondingly effective." Finally,

> [t]he constitutional privilege against self-incrimination is essentially a personal one, applying only to natural individuals . . . It is designed to prevent the use of legal process to force from the lips of the accused individual the evidence necessary to convict him [and thereby avoid] [p]hysical torture and other less violent but equally reprehensible modes of compelling the production of incriminating evidence.[43]

English law is quite different. Although there is, of course, no written English constitution, there are fundamental rights, comparable to some of those in the American Bill of Rights, guaranteed by the common law. These play a quasi-constitutional role in England today, much the same as they did in Connecticut in the interval between the American Revolution and the adoption of the 1817 Connecticut Constitution.[44]

The English cases conclude that under common law the privilege against self-incrimination is a fundamental civil right of corporations as well as of human beings. The Canadian and New Zealand courts have followed the English model while Australian courts have divided.[45]

DOUBLE JEOPARDY: THE FIFTH AMENDMENT

The Fifth Amendment also provides: "nor shall any person be subject for the same offence to be twice put in jeopardy of life or limb, . . ." Notwithstanding what appears to be inescapable references to natural persons in the use of such terms as "life or limb," the Court, without expressly deciding the issue, has repeatedly assumed the applicability of the clause to corporations.[46] Relying on such sub silentio holdings, the lower federal courts have expressly held that corporations are protected by the provision.[47]

The applicability to corporations of the Fifth Amendment clauses pertaining to self-incrimination and double jeopardy are particularly interesting as a textual matter. The two clauses appear in the same sentence and share a single reference to the critical term "person" as their common subject. Nevertheless, the Court construed "person" to include corporations under the Double Jeopardy clause while excluding it from the protection of the Self-Incrimination clause. The various theories of the corporate personality cannot explain this inconsistent result. The artificial person and real entity theories appear equally applicable to the two companion clauses. Nor does the associational theory help. The loss to shareholders from the risk of trial and conviction of a corporation is very much the same under both clauses.

Similarly, the British Commonwealth experience indicates that the construction of the Self-Incrimination clause does not rest on the view that the provision is a codification of the common law. The answer, if there be one, evidently rests elsewhere.

The "People"

UNREASONABLE SEARCHES AND SEIZURES: THE FOURTH AMENDMENT

Hale v. Henkel not only involved the applicability to corporations of the constitutional protection to "person[s]" against self-incrimination in the Fifth Amendment as discussed previously. It also involved the applicability to corporations of the constitutional protection of the Fourth Amendment for "the people to be secure in their persons, houses, papers, and effects, against unreasonable searches and seizures. . . " Not without difficulty, the Court in *Hale v. Henkel*[48] held that the term "people" included corporations so as to protect them against the production of corporate records seized under circumstances, violating the provision. It did so at the same time that it was holding that the term "person" did not include corporations for purposes of the Self-Incrimination clause, as reviewed previously.

Justice Brown, who relied on the artificial person theory in deciding the self-incrimination issue, employed the associational theory to find corporations included under the Unreasonable Searches and Seizures clause. He asserted: "A corporation, is, after all, but an association of individuals under an assumed name and with a distinct legal entity. In organizing itself as a collective body, it [the association of individuals] waives no constitutional immunities appropriate to such body."[49]

Not all the justices accepted this view. Justice McKenna, although concurring in the result, was doubtful, stating: "There are certainly strong reasons for the contention that if corporations cannot plead the immunity of the Fifth Amendment [Self-Incrimination clause] they cannot plead the immunity of the Fourth Amendment." Justice Harlan, also concurring, was more positive: ". . . a corporation — 'an artificial being, invisible, intangible, and existing only in contemplation of law' — cannot claim the immunity given by the Fourth Amendment; for it is not a part of the 'People' within the meaning of that Amendment." He went further and asserted: "Nor is it embraced within the word 'Person' in the [Fifth] Amendment." In so doing, he was in conflict with the decisions assuming or holding that "person" in the Fifth Amendment did include corporations for purposes of the Double Jeopardy clause.[50]

The different results in *Hale v. Henkel* do not turn on the different terminology employed: "people" in the Fourth Amendment and "person" in the Fifth. The Court, instead, seems to have upheld the applicability of the Unreasonable Search and Seizures clause because the rights of shareholders against search and seizure could readily be attributed to the corporation under the associational theory. On the other hand, refusing to protect corporations under the Self-Incrimination clause in no way clashed with or eroded the personal claims of shareholders to be protected under the clause.

*General Constitutional Prohibitions on
Governmental Power*

The Supreme Court has considered the applicability to corporations of two constitutional provisions imposing general limitations on governmental action: the prohibitions against impairment of contracts and abridgment of freedom of speech or of the press.

IMPAIRMENT OF CONTRACTS: ARTICLE I

The celebrated *Dartmouth College* case, decided in 1819, involved a challenge to the constitutionality of a New Hampshire statute changing the governance structure of the college from that provided in the original charter. Did the statute violate Article I, Section 10, Clause 1 providing: "No State shall . . . pass any . . . Law impairing the Obligation of Contracts, . . ." The Court concluded that the corporate charter was not simply a state grant or concession; it was also a contract between the state and the incorporators. Shareholder interests were also at stake, and the amendatory statute was an unconstitutional impairment of the contract represented by the charter.

As in *Deveaux*, decided ten years earlier, Chief Justice Marshall and other justices enunciated the associational view to expand the boundaries of corporate constitutional rights, while making it plain that they simultaneously accepted the artificial person doctrine and the continued vitality of entity law in determining the fundamental nature of the corporate personality. As previously pointed out, it was in this very *Dartmouth College* opinion that Marshall expressed his classic statement of the artificial person theory, referring to the corporation as an "artificial being," and "mere creature of law."[51] The same simultaneous acceptance of both theories as complementary appears in Justice Story's concurrence: "An aggregate corporation . . . is a collection of individuals united into one collective body, under a special name, and possessing certain immunities, privileges, and capacities in its collective character, which do not belong to the natural persons composing it."[52]

FREEDOM OF SPEECH: THE FIRST AMENDMENT

The First Amendment, Clause 2 provides: "Congress shall make no law . . . abridging the freedom of speech, or of the press, . . ." This prohibition restrains such action by the states as well; after initial hesitation, the Court has held that the Due Process clause in the Fourteenth Amendment, which binds the states, also incorporates the First Amendment.[53]

In *First National Bank v. Bellotti*, decided in 1978, the Court held by a five to four vote that a Massachusetts statute restricting the use of corporate political expenditures to influence public referenda or issues, except on matters materially affecting the corporation, was unconstitutional because it violated the guaranty of free speech of the First Amendment.

Writing for the majority, Justice Powell stated that the issue was a narrow one not involving theories of corporate personality: "The proper question therefore is not whether corporations 'have' First Amendment rights, and, if so, whether they are coextensive with those of natural persons. Instead the question must be whether Section 8 (of the Massachusetts statute) abridges the expression that the First Amendment was meant to protect." Powell relied on the fundamental value of "the right of public discussion" from the societal point of view[54] and held that the corporation, as well as its officers or directors, could not be constitutionally barred from discussion of public issues.

Powell did not find it necessary to articulate his own theory of the nature of the corporation in order to dispose of the case. He merely noted the conclusion of the dissenters resting on the artificial person theory that the corporation was a creature of the state possessing only those rights granted it by the State, and characterized it as "extreme."[55]

Justices White and Rehnquist, separately dissenting, relied on the artificial person theory. Rehnquist quoted Chief Justice Marshall's well-known description of the corporation as "an artificial being" in the *Dartmouth College* case. He stated flatly that a corporation had only the constitutional rights "individual to its very existence" [again quoting from the *Dartmouth College* expression of the artificial person view] "necessary to effectuate the purposes for which states permit commercial corporations to exist." White, with whom Justices Brennan and Marshall concurred, similarly concluded: "Corporations are artificial entities created by law for the purpose of furthering certain economic goals. . . . The State need not permit its own creation to consume it." Four justices thus reaffirmed the artificial person theory.[56]

As for Powell, who viewed the dissenters' invocation of the artificial person theory as "extreme," he relied on it himself nine years later when it served his purposes in the construction of the Commerce clause.[57]

STATE GOVERNMENTAL IMMUNITY AGAINST PRIVATE SUIT

Still one further area of constitutional law has some relevance for corporate theory. As reviewed in Chapter 10, the Eleventh Amendment provides that the states are immune from suit in federal courts by private parties. In determining when a state governmental corporation has sufficient identity with the state to qualify as a governmental instrumentality immune from suit, the courts have had to resort to an analysis that is an analogue of the associational theory of the corporation. They have applied the same approach to determine whether a governmental corporation is subject to the jurisdictional limitations of the Diversity-of-Citizenship Jurisdiction clause.

Governmentally owned corporations — sewage districts, toll roads, universities, school boards, and the like — have been held constitutionally exempt in those cases where the courts have found that the governmental unit was the "arm" or an "alter ego" of the state.[58] In making this determination, the courts have evaluated a series of factors relating to the agency's existence as a juridical unit and its degree of identification with the state to bring the constitutional provision into play. However, in the end, the decision rests on the readiness of the courts to characterize, for this constitutional purpose, the governmental corporation by the identity of its shareholder. Such a characterization focusing on the nature of the shareholder has parallels to the associational view, which similarly focuses on the shareholders, not on the corporation. However, with the state as the sole shareholder, the characterization does not match other aspects of the associational view.

Summary

In the light of the Court's inconsistent applications of constitutional provisions to corporations, it should be apparent that the constitutional text plays almost no role in the decision, except in the case of the term "citizen." References to "person," even when appearing in context with such references as "life or limb," or to "people" have been construed to include corporations. Similarly, the extensive history of inconsistent utilization of conflicting theories of corporate personality indicates that the theories are employed to support results, rather than as guiding principles to help reach them. In *Bellotti*, Justice Powell echoed the concept of "purely personal" constitutional rights restricted to natural persons, which, among others, Justice Murphy had invoked in *United States v. White*, discussed previously. Powell stated "[w]hether or not a particular [constitutional] guarantee is 'purely personal' or is unavailable for corporations for some other reason depends on the nature, history, and purpose of the particular constitutional provision."[59] "[N]ature, history, and purpose," not constitutional terminology and theories of the corporate personality, control.

Statutory Construction

Many statutes—without elaboration or definition—simply refer to "person" or "inhabitant" and present a similar question of their applicability to corporations. From very early times, such terms were construed in England to include corporations where the context permitted. Thus, Coke wrote in 1626 that corporations were included under a statute providing that no "person" shall construct cottages and under another imposing on "inhabitants" the obligation of keeping bridges in repair.[60] In 1755, Lord Mansfield held similarly that a corporation was taxable under a "poor law" statute providing for the assessment of an "inhabitant or occupier."[61] The United States law followed the English model. Numerous nineteenth-century cases, including decisions by the Supreme Court, construed statutes referring to "persons" in general terms to include corporations.[62]

In more recent times, the increasing use of more sophisticated statutory draftsmanship has largely made statutory construction of this nature of historical interest. Thus, federal statutes employing the term "person" have increasingly contained a sweeping definition that includes not merely individuals and other recognized legal units, but all organized groups, whether or not otherwise recognized as a legal unit. The Securities Exchange Act of 1934, the Investment Company Act of 1940, and the National Labor Relations Act of 1935 provide typical examples.[63] Nor does the federal statutory structure rest solely on specific and widely inclusive definitions in particular statutes. The general federal statute on statutory construction provides: "In determining the meaning of any Act of Congress, unless the context indicates otherwise, the words 'person' and 'whoever' includes corporations, companies, associations, firms, partnerships, societies, joint stock companies, as well as individuals." In like manner, comparable English and Australian statutes provide that unless barred by the context, statutory or regulation references to the term "person" include corporations, among others.[64]

Although the judicial consideration of the problem on the constitutional level has relevance to the definition of the corporate personality because of the fundamental nature of the rights involved, the consideration of the same issue on the statutory level has little to contribute. Much more obviously than in the constitutional context, the decisions turn on the nature and objective of the enactment, without discussion of the theories of the corporate personality. Further, in contrast to the extension of fundamental rights under the constitutional decisions, the statutory provisions most often relate to duties, not rights. Even in those instances when they do recognize certain rights, the statutes are dealing with highly specialized problems of a minor order. Thus, the statutory experience throws little helpful light on the jurisprudential nature of the corporation beyond illustrating that "person" in most statutory usage is regularly construed to refer also to corporations.

There is one exception in which statutory construction does involve theories of the corporate personality. In a number of areas, a corporation's rights, duties, or standing to sue has been determined by reference to the character or interests of its shareholders through utilization of the associational theory. Both in the United States[65] and in England,[66] decisions have *characterized* corporations for statutory purposes as an "enemy" under wartime trade embargoes; or as "charitable" for tax and other purposes; or as "governmental," because of the identity of their shareholder or shareholders.

Summary

Debate over the competing theories of the nature of the corporate personality flourished for decades and produced an enormous literature. It was set in perspective by Professor John Dewey in 1926 and for almost four or five decades was largely put to rest. Dewey dismissed the debate as an academic exercise without larger reality. He emphasized that corporate rights and liabilities were the product of the law and that the legal implications or meaning of "the corporation" was "whatever the law makes it mean."[67] Thereafter, until the rise of the Libertarians a half-century later, discussion of the nature of the corporate personality languished. However, it has again begun to attract considerable scholarly attention.

Dewey's view does not do full justice to all aspects of the problem. First, in the law, concepts have a life of their own because of their influence over the thinking of judges and their usefulness in justifying conclusions. These dual aspects of judicial decision-making have clearly been evident in this review of the judicial treatment of corporate personality in constitutional cases. Second, the use of particular language has a cultural force of its own. Identification of the corporation as a "person" may start as a metaphor, but its usage gives rise to an association between the attributes of a person and those of the corporation. Indeed, the application of the term to corporations arises because of the plausibility of such an association.[68]

Finally, in neither the cases nor the discussion has there been any attempt to look upon the corporation as anything other than a separate legal unit: separate from its shareholders and possessing the traditional core attributes recognized long ago. Each of the theories on the nature of the corporation that has been advanced in the United States has accepted entity law without challenge. In the areas where debate about these various theories has played a lively role, it has centered on the constitutional rights to be accorded to the corporation in addition to the core common law rights. Whatever theory is used to support the outcome—the constitutional rights attributed to the corporation or the shareholder interests recognized in such an attribution—the traditional concept of entity law has remained unimpaired. The debate has related only to the details of the superstructure erected on a universally accepted foundation.

Corporate theory plays an uneven role in the construction of the constitutional provisions and in determining their applicability to corporations. In most cases, it is a factor of at least surface significance. In others, it is not even mentioned. However, its prominence in so many cases of importance makes a review of corporate theory in the constitutional context imperative in any examination of the problem.

The judicial evaluations of the relationship of the corporation to the state and a determination of the constitutional claims of the corporation by reference to the interests and claims of its stockholders make the decisions of keen interest. Although the nature of the corporation's existence as a legal unit remains fundamentally unchanged, notwithstanding the affirmative or negative conclusions of the courts on the applicability of certain constitutional provisions, the corporate theories playing some role in the decision are of importance.

It is possible, of course, to define the corporate personality solely in terms of the fundamental core attributes of the corporation as a legal unit. In such a case, the constitutional decisions must then become consigned to some other body of inquiry that might be called corporate theory. Although this strips the discussion of the constitution-based legal features of the modern corporation, it is a fair question whether any constitutional protection, whatever its importance, relates to the essential nature of the corporation. Thus, one can hardly contend that the corporation is a fundamentally different legal institution because the courts do, or do not, construe the Constitution to extend a privilege against self-incrimination or protection against double jeopardy or some other constitutional protection.

When one, however, considers limited liability involving statutory, rather than constitutional, determination, the argument cuts closer to the bone. Has some fundamental change in the corporation as a legal unit occurred when in a particular jurisdiction a particular legislature enacts a statute changing the prior legal rule either to provide for limited liability or to impose unlimited liability? Although the corporation's traditional core attributes have remained unchanged, the nature of the shareholders' relationship to the corporation and to its creditors has changed fundamentally. With the shareholder liability rule so firmly and universally fixed in all developed nations, limitation of liability has thus become widely accepted as one of the modern core attributes of the corporation and as a part of the corporate personality.

Thus, in the decision of the House of Lords in the *International Tin Council* case, Lord Oliver concluded that Parliament's creation of the International Tin Council with "legal personality" necessarily meant corporate status and limited liability.[69]

This integration of limited liability into the core attributes illustrates that the corporate personality is not frozen in time and that the traditional attributes of corporate existence do not fix the boundaries of the corporate identity.

In the end, the issue does not seem momentous. Restriction of the content of the corporate personality to the core attributes arising from recognition of the corporation as a legal unit simply means that the jurisprudential nature of the corporation as illuminated by its judicial treatment for various constitutional purposes must then be discussed under the separate heading of corporate theory. Whether included under corporate personality or segregated under corporate theory, the constitutional experience is a vital and inseparable part of any jurisprudential view of the corporation in the American system. However, the picture changes when one moves to the judicial systems of other nations. In any attempt to define the jurisprudential nature of corporations under legal systems generally, national variations, such as the American constitutional experiences, become essentially irrelevant.

Above and beyond the foregoing, there is one major deficiency in the debate over corporate constitutional rights and corporate personality. It has entirely ignored two fundamental developments of recent decades: one economic and one political. These developments are the dramatic shift from concern with corporate *rights* to concentration on the increasingly important question of corporate *responsibilities*, and the emergence of corporate groups as the predominant economic institution of our times.

Profound changes have taken place in the American economic structure since the introduction of the Arkwright loom in 1809 led to the astonishing growth of the textile industry and the industrialization of New England. The world of the early nineteenth-century manufacturing economy — small enterprises conducting limited local business — has disappeared. The corporate form has increasingly replaced proprietorships and partnerships, and business enterprises have vastly increased their scope of operations, the amounts of their capital investment, and the extent of their markets.

The emergence of corporate groups following New Jersey's fundamental change in the traditional corporation law saw an almost immediate acceleration of industrial concentration and the speedy growth of businesses of much greater complexity and scale. World business replaced national business, as national business had earlier replaced regional and local business. The modern multinational corporations of enormous size and complexity dominate the economies of the world. Corporate groups with parent corporations, subholding companies, and scores, if not hundreds, of subsidiaries have replaced the smaller, more simple corporate enterprises with their shareholder-investors. Corporate law and theories of the corporate personality shaped long before to serve the needs of a much different world have become antiquated. New corporate law and new corporate theory are required to respond to the challenge presented by corporate groups to the legal systems of the world.

With the laissez-faire priorities of the past, legal developments were concerned with further definition and extension of the legal *rights* of corporations. Today, the challenge ahead is very different. It is concerned with the increasing concentration of industrial organization, with corporate power and abuse, with the unresolved dilemma of corporate governance, and the increasing necessity of more comprehensive regulatory controls over the economy and the conduct of business. These elements have become widely accepted features of the political environment in all developed countries. In the United States, regulatory programs dealing with such developments are common. Thus, in areas such as transportation, securities, tax, labor relations, pension, discrimination, environment, energy, foreign trade and investment, and restrictive trade practices, among others, comprehensive regulation controls economic activity. The point of such social controls is not to extend corporate *rights* but to impose *statutory duties* on the business enterprise. The thrust of legal developments has changed directions.

This political transformation is matched by a revolution of the economic structure, with major business enterprises generally consisting of affiliated corporations collectively conducting their businesses as corporate groups. Recognizing this changed economic reality, Congress for decades has recognized that effective regulation required the abandonment of nineteenth-century law focusing on the traditional concepts of the corporate entity. Effective regulation has required a more extensive scope, going beyond the particular entity directly subject to regulation to include the parent corporation controlling it, its own subsidiaries controlled by it, and its sister subsidiaries under common control. Effective regulation of corporate groups has required a new perception of corporate law, and enterprise principles utilizing such standards as "control" have been widely accepted, particularly in complex, statutory regulation. In consequence, traditional concepts of the separate corporate entity are becoming increasingly outmoded and are being replaced by a new law of corporate groups.

Accordingly, it is appropriate at this point to examine the emergence of corporate groups since the "turning point in American business history"[70] when, one hundred years ago, New Jersey amended its corporation laws and for the first time permitted corporations generally to acquire and hold stock of other corporations and thus to organize corporate groups. The discussion will then turn to the greatly strengthened panoply of governmental regulatory controls over economic activity in general and over corporate groups in particular. These fundamental aspects of modern society have presented a massive challenge to the legal system and have led to the increasingly comprehensive legal developments that comprise the emerging American law of corporate groups.

3

The Emergence of Corporate Groups

Limited liability triumphed in the United States at a time when corporations lacked the power to acquire and hold shares of other corporations unless expressly granted by special statute or charter provision. Corporate groups were virtually unknown. It was not until 1889–1893, about sixty years after Massachusetts had provided the climax to American acceptance of limited liability, when states, starting with New Jersey, began enacting statutes granting such powers to corporations generally. Thereafter, corporate groups of great size speedily emerged. The holding company and the corporate group replaced trusts as the favored structure for the expanding industrial concentration characterizing this rampant period of American capitalism. This chronology had great implications for the development of American corporation law.

Corporate Power to Acquire and Hold Stock of Another Corporation

In the nineteenth century, American law was settled that in the absence of an express grant in the statute or its charter a corporation had no power to purchase the stock of another corporation.[1] Such acquisition of stock of another corporation was prohibited without regard to whether the other company was conducting a similar business or was in an entirely different one.[2]

This was common law doctrine reflecting several powerful pressures. First, courts stubbornly resisted any extension of corporate powers beyond the express provisions of the legislative grant in the charter. This was the age of strict construction. Where the legislature had not granted a corporation the power to acquire shares, the courts would not infer one.[3]

The doctrine was also seen as a necessary barrier to the ready evasion of the restricted business purposes specified in a corporation's charter. Such an action as purchasing stock of another corporation was seen as an improper expansion of the restricted corporate purpose. The courts reasoned that a failure to include the power to purchase shares in the enumeration of corporate powers indicated an intention to exclude it and that such an acquisition was therefore ultra vires. As the Supreme Court said in *De La Vergne Refrigerating Machine Co. v. German Savings Institution*, decided in 1899:

> But as the powers of corporations, created by legislative act, are limited to such as the act expressly confers, and the enumeration of these implies the exclusion of all others, it follows that, unless express permission is given to do so, it is not within the general powers of a corporation to purchase the stock of other corporations for the purpose of controlling their management.[4]

Although the doctrine of ultra vires was frequently advanced as the rationale for the result, the lack of authority rested on a more formidable basis. Thus, in several cases, the corporate charter did expressly include the power, making it impossible to contend that exercise of the power was ultra vires. Nevertheless, courts invalidated stock purchases, reasoning that the inclusion of the power in the *charter* was unlawful where the corporation *statute* did not contain such an authorization.[5]

Second, there was deep suspicion and hostility of corporations generally, particularly among Jacksonians.[6] Finally, these concerns of strict constructionism and general anticorporate feeling were reinforced by deep antagonism to monopolies, particularly where a court concluded that a purchase of stock represented not merely an investment, but an attempt to gain control of the other corporation and perhaps monopoly power over the market as well.[7]

As stated by a Georgia court of the time in holding invalid a corporation's acquisition of stock of another corporation:

> a corporation is a mere creature of the law, and only exists at all, for the purposes declared in its charter, and has absolutely no powers but

those which the law confers upon it. . . . It has ever been considered
the very highest public policy to keep a strict watch upon corporations,
to confine them within their appointed bounds and especially to guard
against the accumulation of large interests under their control.[8]

Although the early common law rule barred acquisitions of stock
generally, even for investment, courts increasingly focused on the link
between the purchase of stock and the acquisition of control over
the corporation whose shares were being acquired.[9] The nineteenth-
century judges had a firm understanding of the significance of stock
ownership and its relationship to direction of the corporation's business and affairs. Thus, the use of the term "control" in this context
was early known to the law. Corporate cases of the period contain
numerous references to "control," leaving no doubt that the concept
assumed a prominent role in lawyers' understanding and usage from
the early days of the American republic.

This major restriction on corporate power — the lack of authority
to acquire stock — was firmly established at common law. Some states,
of which New York and Illinois are examples, went further and
enacted statutes as well, expressly prohibiting corporations from acquiring and holding stock in other corporations.[10] While there were
limited exceptions to the doctrine, they did not undermine the fundamental doctrine. Thus, the general prohibition did not bar a corporation's acquisition of stock in the ordinary course of business, in payment of a debt, or in liquidation.[11]

This general prohibition was essentially unchallenged in American
law for almost the entire nineteenth century, except in isolated aber-
rant jurisdictions.[12] There were also some statutory departures. New
York permitted manufacturing corporations to acquire stock of other
corporations serving as a source of supply.[13] On infrequent occasions,
in special acts of incorporation, the legislature did include the power
to acquire stock in a corporation's charter. These departures were
typically confined to three areas. First, banks and insurance companies, important sources of capital in a capital-poor country, were
authorized to buy shares for investment.[14] Second, water and gaslight
companies were authorized to finance their growth by sale of stock to
neighboring manufacturing companies, whose holdings were often
restricted to a maximum of ten percent.[15] The third, and most important group, were the railroads. A number of states granted charters
or enacted special statutes authorizing railroads to purchase shares of

other railroads to facilitate the acquisition of interconnecting lines and thereby contribute to the expansion of regional transportation. Such statutes were enacted for the Baltimore & Ohio Railroad as early as 1832, and again in 1846; for the Pennsylvania Railroad in 1855; and for railroads generally in New Jersey in 1849.[16] Railroads thus comprised the first corporate groups in the country.

Insofar as manufacturing corporations were concerned, most state legislatures consistently refused to include the power to purchase shares in corporate charters, both during the period of special incorporation statutes and in the later general incorporation laws that replaced special incorporation acts as the nineteenth century proceeded.[17] Although there were some departures from the well-established general rule, these were not historically significant.[18]

When charters contained no express grant of authority, as was overwhelmingly the case, the common law prohibition prevailed, and corporations, even railroads and gas utility companies, were barred from acquiring or holding stock of other companies. With the acquisition of stock as a possible technique to accomplish corporate combination and industrial concentration unavailable, the efforts of bankers and industrialists in the last quarter of the nineteenth century to organize the large producers in a particular industry into a dominating group led to the development of the trust device.[19] Rockefeller in oil and the Havemeyers in sugar refining are leading examples of this development. In this form of corporate control, trustees held the shares of formerly competing companies in trust for the beneficial owners. While the trust certificate owners continued to receive the economic benefits of ownership, the trustees had the power to vote and controlled the companies in question, permitting domination of the relevant markets.

In fact, market domination was frankly held forth as the "real intent" of large-scale corporate existence and bluntly defended as "part of the best growth and sound expansion of the American nation. It is essentially a part of the successful, aggressive American policy of commercial supremacy [needed] to compete with other nations."[20]

As is well known, trusts became a leading political issue of the late-nineteenth and early-twentieth centuries. Popular hostility to the trusts grew apace, and antitrust legislation and trust-busting litigation followed. In 1890, the New York courts held the Sugar Trust to be unlawful, and in 1892, the Ohio courts outlawed the Oil Trust.[21] The Sherman Antitrust Act was adopted in 1890. It became plain that trusts could no longer serve as the machinery for industrial combination. Driven to new legal devices, beleaguered corporate counsel recognized that the power to acquire shares of competitive corporations, if available, would serve as an alternative route to gain centralized control of competing firms and achieve market concentration, perhaps even avoiding the Sherman Act.[22]

The Emergence of Corporate Groups

As the trust device came under increasing attack, New Jersey — "eager to enrich its treasury with license fees from corporate promoters"[23] — enacted its ground-breaking statutes in 1888, 1889, and 1893.[24] The 1888 statute was narrowly circumscribed. It made no dramatic change, merely following the model of an older New York statute. It authorized only acquisition of stock of a company "manufacturing and producing materials necessary for [the purchaser's] business," thereby permitting some vertical integration.

Reversing a century of common law development, the later acts, drafted under the leadership of James B. Dill, accomplished dramatic change. They dropped all restrictions and expressly authorized businesses incorporated in New Jersey to acquire the stock of "any other company which the directors might deem necessary." This sweeping authorization opened the door to the formation of every type of holding company and corporate group.

These new statutes — without previous parallel in the United States — provided an alternative route to industrial combination, replacing the trust device that was then being outlawed. The sponsors of the legislation justified the change politically as a lucrative source of state revenue to enable New Jersey to deal with its tax problems. It also created for Dill and his associates, including the governor and other political leaders, the opportunity to profit handsomely themselves by organizing the Corporation Trust Company to serve as the New Jersey representative of out-of-state firms incorporating or reincorporating in the state.[25]

In 1896, the New Jersey statutes were further revised in a comprehensive statute drafted by Dill. These revisions relaxed in still other areas long-standing statutory restrictions on corporate power and conduct that had been part of the prior New Jersey law and statutes of other states as well.[26] Corporate response to the new statutes was not long in coming. Although it started slowly, it soon developed into a full flood as lawyers throughout the country came to understand the opportunities presented. Corporations rushed to reincorporate in New Jersey. These included such giants as Standard Oil, United States Steel and American Sugar.[27] It was estimated that by 1900, ninety-five percent of major American corporations were incorporated in New Jersey.[28] The anticipated tax revenues poured in. By 1902, New Jersey had paid its entire public debt, and corporation fees and taxes just on the New York firms incorporated in New Jersey paid for virtually the entire current budget.[29]

In this manner, corporate groups replaced trusts as the preferred technique for achieving corporate concentration and emerged as an increasingly powerful force in the economy. New Jersey had opened the door, and other states followed suit. New York was the first. Faced by a flight of its corporations to New Jersey, New York moved promptly to stave off the loss of franchise tax and filing fee revenues and amended its statutes to provide similar authority. Other leading corporate states, including Delaware and Maine, followed in permitting corporations generally to acquire stock.[30] As a contemporary observer pointed out, "New Jersey [had] destroyed the effect of the drastic measures taken elsewhere to stop the growth of great combinations of capital."[31] The prominent journalist Lincoln Steffens excoriated New Jersey in an article entitled "New Jersey: A Traitor State. How She Sold Out the United States."

While the statutory law was giving way on this point, judicial resistance to the breach in traditional doctrine continued. Thus, some early decisions under the new dispensation restricted exercise of the new power to stock purchases incidental to the charter purposes of the acquiring corporation.[32] Other courts were hostile to corporate reorganizations leading to the creation of holding companies controlling previously independent businesses. These courts perceived that corporate restructuring was serving as a device to achieve monopoly or to accomplish restrictive trade practices. This was particularly evident in jurisdictions that still did not permit corporate acquisitions of stock where cases occurred involving reorganizations in which local corporations were being acquired or consolidated to form holding companies under the expanded New Jersey or similar statutes. Such acquisitions were frequently held to be unlawful because they were against public policy or prohibited by the Sherman Act.[33]

For a while, public support grew for federal incorporation to deal with the inability of states to regulate corporations. In 1910, President Taft so recommended to Congress, including a prohibition against intercorporate ownership of stock among the features of a proposed statute. However, this effort was unsuccessful and faded away.[34]

The new device increasingly received legal acceptance,[35] particularly as more and more state legislatures followed the New Jersey model and changed their corporation laws to match. In New Jersey itself there were second thoughts for a brief period. Woodrow Wilson succeeded in achieving repeal of the offending provision in 1913, but in the face of declining charter fees, the reform lasted only four years.[36]

With the states competing for charter and franchise fees and the ability of corporations to reincorporate wherever the local law was most appealing, the ability of any particular state to resist the development was enfeebled. This was plain in the pressures that led to the New York experience in the 1890s and New Jersey's return to the new dispensation in 1917. Gresham's law prevailed, and eventually, all states changed their statutes. The general corporate authority to acquire stock of other corporations became an accepted aspect of American corporation law. With the availability of the new corporate device, well described as a major "turning point" in the history of American business,[37] the concentration of American industry in the hands of fewer and fewer producers commenced by the trust movement intensified. This development speedily led to a profound change in industrial structure.[38] Corporate groups soon grew to occupy a commanding role in American industry and eventually in the world economy as well.

Corporate Groups and Limited Liability

Limited liability had won political acceptance when corporate groups were unknown. Limited liability for shareholders presupposed a world in which the corporation constituted the enterprise and the shareholders were investors in the enterprise. The doctrine protected the investors from the risks of the business.

When, more than a half-century later, corporations were for the first time generally empowered to acquire stock of other corporations and corporate groups emerged, the reality abruptly changed. The affiliated companies comprising the group—the subservient subsidiary corporations and their dominant parent shareholder—collectively conducted the enterprise. Did the older doctrine of limited liability of shareholders now protect the component companies of the new corporate groups in addition to the ultimate investors in the enterprise (the shareholders of the parent)?

As subsequent developments have made so clear, this was a question of major importance confronting the courts for the first time. It is striking that no court apparently even recognized the existence of the issue. Certainly, no court ever discussed the problem. Limited liability of corporate groups, although one of the most important legal rules in modern economic society, appears to have emerged as a historical accident.

This surprising development largely arose as a result of the formalistic jurisprudence of the times. Legal conclusions were deduced logically in syllogistic fashion.

- Limited liability protected shareholders.
- A parent corporation was a shareholder of the subsidiary.
- Ergo, limited liability protected parent corporations.

Such logic ignored economic realities and made a mockery of the underlying objective of the doctrine. It overlooked the fact that the parent corporation and its subsidiaries were collectively conducting a common enterprise, that the business had been fragmented among the component companies of the group, and that limited liability—a doctrine designed to protect investors in an enterprise, not the enterprise itself—would be extended to protect each fragment of the business from liability for the obligations of all the other fragments.

Modern law has faced the challenge of responding to the consequences of this unwitting choice ever since. Thus, in the multitiered corporate group, with its first-tier, second-tier, and even third-tier subsidiaries,[39] traditional entity law provides multiple layers of limited liability, with each upper-tier company insulated from liability for its lower-tier subsidiaries. Four, or even five, layers of limited liability in complex multinational groups are not uncommon.

As corporate groups assumed an increasingly predominant position in the national and international economy, this doctrinal development has produced in time the serious jurisprudential challenge that today faces the legal systems of the Western world.

A central feature of the complex business organization, whether termed the holding company, the corporate group, the enterprise, or "the firm," is the concept of "control." This is the power to direct the affairs of the component or subsidiary corporations and therefore achieve a coordinated central direction of the activities of the enterprise.[40]

As explored in the next section, "control" (in some statutes broadened to "controlling influence") has been the standard utilized by American statutory and administrative law, almost to the total exclusion of other tests, for the imposition of enterprise principles both in regulatory and revenue statutes. European jurisdictions employ similar terms as the standard for determining the outer boundaries of regulatory statutes.

Corporate Groups and the Regulation of Business Activity

As corporate groups became increasingly prominent in American economic affairs, the implications for federal and state regulatory programs became evident. In time, corporate groups and holding companies were perceived as leading to a very serious breakdown of federal and state regulatory programs in such widely diverse areas as railroads, public utilities, retail chain stores, and branch and interstate banking. After elaborate and well-publicized federal and state legislative investigations, public pressures ultimately led to a great wave of reform statutes, notably during the New Deal. The new statutes extensively introduced enterprise principles into the statutory regulatory system, thereby bringing the holding company and its affiliated companies under effective public control.[41]

When twentieth-century statutory law gradually began to deal expressly with the problems presented by statutory groups, the concept of "control," long established in the corporation law, was utilized from the start as the principal foundation in the selective application of enterprise law. After being used in the Internal Revenue Code commencing in 1917, the term became the fulcrum for enterprise law in the wave of the New Deal statutes in the 1930s. Commencing with the Securities Act of 1933, the Emergency Transportation Act of 1933, the Securities Exchange Act of 1934, and the Federal Communications Act of 1934, the new regulatory statutes used the concept of "control" (sometimes supplemented by "controlling influence") as the standard for imposing statutory obligations. The statutes applied not merely to the company conducting the activity being regulated but also to other companies or parties not otherwise subject to the statute that "controlled" the regulated company. Frequently, the statutory program was extended beyond the "controlling" company to affiliated companies "controlled" by or under "common control with" the regulated companies as well.

II

Entity or Enterprise in Dealing with Corporate Groups: The American Judicial and Statutory Response

4

Early Judicial Attempts to Adapt Entity Law to the New Economy of Corporate Groups

The doctrine of entity law, regarding the corporation as a separate juridical person with its own rights and obligations distinct from those of its shareholders, presents obvious opportunities for manipulation, particularly where the corporation is owned and controlled by a single shareholder. Accordingly, it was inevitable that, notwithstanding the development of entity law and its reinforcement by the adoption of the policy of limited liability, the courts would develop an accompanying corrective doctrine to avoid the grotesque consequences that would otherwise result from unyielding application of the doctrine.

In cases mainly involving individual shareholders manipulating a controlled corporation, the courts gradually developed a supplemental doctrine providing an escape from entity law. In "exceptional" circumstances involving "abuse" of the corporate form, courts would disregard the corporate entity and its accompanying feature of limited liability and impose liability on the controlling shareholder. This eventually came to be known as "piercing the corporate veil," after the vivid image employed by the courts.

Disregard of the Corporate Entity

As it became apparent that the traditional legal doctrine of entity law and limited liability lent themselves, in unscrupulous hands, to fraudulent practices, courts of equity began to formulate a corollary to permit equitable relief from the harsh consequences of the legal rule. As a nineteenth-century writer put it: "a corporation is often organized to act as a 'cloak' for frauds. Such cases are becoming common, and the courts are becoming more and more inclined to ignore the corporate existence, when necessary, to circumvent the fraud."[1] Thus, in language similar to the metaphors of "piercing the veil jurisprudence" that subsequently emerged, one court stated in a related context that courts can "strip off disguises"; corporations "can readily be disrobed" where they are used to serve an unlawful purpose.[2]

Utilizing traditional equity powers, courts would disregard a party's attempt to interpose a corporate form in order to accomplish fraud or illegality. As the Minnesota Supreme Court put it: "Where the corporate form is used by individuals for the purpose of evading the law, or for perpetration of fraud, the court will not permit the legal entity to be interposed so as to defeat justice."[3]

Cases considering disregard of the corporate entity (frequently described as the corporate fiction) began to arise in some numbers, even in the nineteenth century. Because corporations generally lacked the authority to acquire stock in other corporations, a state of affairs that persisted until almost the end of the century, these cases overwhelmingly involved corporations with individual controlling shareholders. Problems involving corporate groups necessarily came later, except for isolated cases involving railroads.

Some of the early cases involved corporations with little, if any, existence in reality; corporations lacking assets, employees, or even business. This kind of entity was disregarded as a "paper" or "sham" corporation or as a "mere instrument."[4] Others involved transfers of individual assets without consideration to controlled or related corporations in order to avoid creditors. Courts granting recovery of the transfers as fraudulent conveyances disregarded the formal existence of the corporation as a separate entity and emphasized the underlying interest of the controlling shareholder.[5] Still other cases involved the use of corporations in an attempt to bypass the individual shareholder's personal obligations or otherwise accomplish a fraudulent or illegal objective.[6] In such egregious cases, the courts also invoked equitable principles to surmount legal forms. Finally, there were a number of cases involving parent corporations that undertook construction programs, particularly railroad extension lines, by utilizing newly organized subsidiaries lacking capital or equipment. Where such a parent sought to avoid liability when a program was unsuccessful and abandoned, the courts had little difficulty imposing liability, viewing the conduct as essentially fraudulent.[7]

The doctrine had severe limitations. In its early state, it was tightly restricted to cases of fraud or illegality, the traditional factors generally calling for the intervention of courts of equity. Application of the doctrine of entity law was rigid. In the statutory area, for example, it facilitated ready evasion of statutes through the device of controlled corporations. In their rhetoric, the courts professed a theoretical readiness to disregard entity law, "where the corporate form [was] used . . . for evading the law." In practice, however, they frequently refused to depart from entity law and effectively undermined the regulatory policy.

Thus, reflecting the dominance of the traditional doctrine, courts would rigidly apply entity law even where it created serious obstacles to the enforcement of statutes and led to ready evasion of a statute merely by organization of a controlled corporation to conduct the prohibited activity. For example, courts held that:

- ownership by a parent railroad corporation of a subsidiary coal mining corporation did not violate the Pennsylvania constitutional prohibition against common carriers from engaging in mining or manufacturing articles for transportation over their lines;[8]
- the ownership of real estate by a domestic corporation whose shareholders were aliens did not violate a constitutional prohibition against aliens owning real estate;[9] and
- acquisition of a parcel of real property by a corporation with black shareholders did not violate a restrictive land covenant prohibiting ownership by negroes.[10]

Entity law was briefly challenged in one fundamental respect that was of relevance to corporate groups. Thus, in some early decisions in cases involving individual shareholders, courts concluded that the concept of the separate corporate personality distinct from that of its shareholders did not apply when there was only one shareholder; corporate existence, while continuing, was viewed as "suspended."[11] Under this view, wholly owned subsidiaries, accordingly, would lack separate existence, and intragroup limited liability would not be available, at least for such subsidiaries.[12] This departure from the traditional doctrine was short-lived and soon repudiated,[13] even in the case of subsidiary corporations in which the parent was the sole shareholder.[14] However, as late as 1931, one treatise writer, while recognizing a conflict in the cases, was contending that the better view "suspended" corporate existence so long as the corporation had only one shareholder.[15]

There is an interesting English parallel to this abortive development. In its decision in the celebrated *Salomon* litigation, the Court of Appeal refused to recognize the debenture claim of Salomon, the principal shareholder, against his insolvent corporation, contending that the other purported shareholders were his dummies and that the company lacked separate legal existence with only one shareholder.[16] The House of Lords reversed, upholding the separate existence of even such a corporation. This decision, much criticized over the years, is the foundation of entity law in England and the Commonwealth countries.

Corporate Groups in the Courts

So long as corporations were generally barred from acquiring stock of other corporations, corporate groups — except for railroad and telegraph systems — were virtually unknown. Consequently, prior to the turn of the century, legal controversies involving corporate groups were rare. When they did arise, they almost invariably involved railroads, and the judicial response to the problem was strongly influenced by the railroad context in which they arose.[17] The early railroad cases aside, American law dealing with the problems presented by parent and subsidiary corporations is exclusively twentieth-century law.

In 1854, the Supreme Court for the first time faced the issue of intragroup liability. *York & Maryland Line Railroad v. Winans* involved the alleged patent infringement liability of a Pennsylvania subsidiary for patented railway cars. The cars operated on the subsidiary's line from York, Pennsylvania, to the Maryland boundary, where they continued on to Baltimore on the line of its parent, the Baltimore & Susquehanna Railroad, a Maryland corporation.

The subsidiary defended, contending that it was only a nominal organization to satisfy the formal requirements of Pennsylvania law requiring local incorporation of railroads operating in the state. The parent furnished the cars and managed and operated the subsidiary's line. However, in its reports to the Commonwealth, the subsidiary listed "a president and directors, . . . conductors, engineers, and agents." Further, book entries credited the subsidiary with one third of the net profits of its line.

The trial court charged the jury that the plaintiff was entitled to recover on such facts, whether "they [the subsidiary] are to be regarded as partners, or as principal, or agent" of the parent. The Supreme Court affirmed, concluding that the subsidiary was a principal, relying both on its reports to the Commonwealth, which the Court held the subsidiary was estopped from denying, and also on the sharing of profits.[18]

In the twentieth century, this would be a routine case involving "reverse piercing the veil" in which courts routinely refuse to allow a corporate component to deny its independent existence in an effort to defeat liability for its obligations. However, 140 years ago, this was an entirely novel problem for which the courts had fashioned no jurisprudence. This appears not only to be the first decision of the Supreme Court but the first appellate decision in the country to consider the legal interrelationships of parent and subsidiary corporations.

The rationale of the Supreme Court and the trial court's charge illustrate the conceptual difficulties that the courts of the time had in dealing with the new legal problems arising from intragroup integration of operations. In attempting to conceptualize the imposition of intragroup liability, the courts, as in *York & Maryland Line R.R.*, were forced to rely on analogies from partnership and agency law.

Forty years later, in 1895, the Supreme Court again was called upon to consider intragroup relationships in *Lehigh Mining and Manufacturing Co. v. Kelly*.[19] A Pennsylvania corporation instituted an action in the federal district court in Virginia against a Virginia corporation to settle title to Virginia land. The Pennsylvania corporation relied on diversity-of-citizenship for federal jurisdiction. The Pennsylvania corporation had been recently organized by the shareholders of a Virginia corporation that had been claiming title for the prior ten years. Further, the Virginia corporation had conveyed its title to the land to its sister Pennsylvania company without any consideration only one month before the institution of the action. The Court dismissed the case. It held that jurisdiction was lacking because the transfer was a collusive attempt to utilize "the mask" of the newly incorporated Pennsylvania sister company to achieve the necessary diversity of citizenship. By characterizing the corporate restructuring as fraudulent, the Court escaped from the confines of entity law under which diversity existed as a matter of form between the Pennsylvania plaintiff[20] and the Virginia defendant.

Indicating the strength of entity law, three justices dissented, unwilling to disregard the legal title of the Pennsylvania company, even on these facts. They contended that because the transaction had not been concealed, it could not be regarded as fraudulent; in their view, legal forms were controlling, except where fraud was involved.

Railroad Litigation and the Beginnings of Enterprise Law

Railroads, representing one of the most dynamic areas of the expanding industrial age, formed the earliest corporate groups, and nineteenth-century litigation about legal issues involving corporate groups involved railroads in all but a few cases.[21] The development of the law was inevitably influenced by the fact that the cases presenting these issues involved railroad empires of great size and importance that were operating integrated rail systems under strongly centralized management. The interconnected rail lines of the component companies were held out to the public as a single system, or "road," with a system timetable of available trains. The system name was prominently displayed on the equipment, timetable, and tickets, and the engines and cars of one subsidiary, bearing the system name and often staffed by employees of that or another subsidiary, ran regularly over the tracks of the system, even where owned by another subsidiary.

The economic reality that the railroads of the country were increasingly being organized into a series of great systems that operated through trains over the interconnected tracks of the various component subsidiary and lessee corporations played an important role in the development of the law for decades. As cases — both contract and tort — involving component companies of railroad groups began to come before the courts in increasing numbers, the Supreme Court and other courts were ready for a while to depart from traditional corporate law concepts, to examine the legal issues in the light of the reality of system operation and control, and in some cases to fashion new law to apply enterprise principles. This development, although short-lived, represents the beginnings of the American law of corporate groups.

All courts accepted the traditional corporation law doctrine that the corporation and its shareholders were separate legal units. Shareholders could not sue on corporate claims, did not own corporate assets, and were not liable for corporate debts. Some courts simply stopped there, preventing the imposition of group liability for acts of a particular subsidiary. The significant thing is that for a while some courts, including the Supreme Court, in some but not all decisions, and certain other courts, including the Court of Appeals for the Second Circuit, were not ready to close the discussion at this point. They sought to go further and to develop new theories of what is now called enterprise law, under which the legal interrelationships of parent and subsidiary corporations could be determined on a group or system basis.

The jurisprudence of corporate groups developed on separate fronts in the Supreme Court of the United States: different chains of decisions considered the legal interrelationships of the component companies of corporate groups for purposes of contract law, tort liability, statutory law, and procedure, including service and jurisdiction. Interestingly enough, the decisions in many of these areas only referred infrequently to the decisions in the others.

Contract

The decision of the Supreme Court in a case involving the Rock Island and the Union Pacific lines provides a useful illustration of how the integration of the tracks of component companies of a group to form a group system exerted powerful influence over the thinking of the court. *Union Pacific Ry. v. Chicago, Rock Island & Pacific Ry.* involved the validity of a 999-year contract between the Rock Island line and a Union Pacific subsidiary. This contract provided Rock Island with equal trackage rights over a bridge line of the subsidiary, thereby opening a shorter route for Rock Island between Chicago and Denver.

Union Pacific later sought to repudiate the contract on the ground, among others, that its subsidiary received no consideration for the use of its property because the rental was to be paid directly to Union Pacific. In the circuit court, Justice Brewer, sitting as a circuit justice, rejected the contention. He first referred to the "extensive railway system" of each party characterized by "unity of interest and a unity of control" on each side. He went on to state: "The Union Pacific Company owns substantially all the stock of the [subsidiary] and a contract by a company that the rental for the partial use of its property shall be paid directly to the stockholders, instead of to the company, surely cannot be declared beyond the power of the corporations. This is all that need be said."

The Supreme Court reached the same conclusion and in the same terms. Chief Justice Fuller spoke of the five thousand miles of railroad operated by the Union Pacific and the three thousand miles by Rock Island. He upheld Brewer's decision, noting that its stockholders had also entered into the contract, that each of the subsidiary's incorporators was a Union Pacific officer or employee, that its road was built with Union Pacific funds, that its stock was held by Union Pacific officers or employees in trust for Union Pacific, that the two roads had common officers, and that "in their operation no distinction had ever been made between the two roads; and their earnings had gone into and their expenditures been paid from a common treasury."[22]

The striking thing about the opinions is not the conclusion, but the reasoning, with its emphasis on the integration of the constituent lines into a common system. Courts are, not surprisingly, hostile to parties seeking to repudiate an obligation by challenging a feature on their own side of affairs.

Phinizy v. Augusta & K.R. Co. involved the Central Railroad of Georgia. The court described the line as a "great system," and "a large and powerful combination of railroads, forming a complete system, under one controlling management, all of which were made contributory to the Central Railroad of Georgia. . . . This great combination had obtained and exercised complete control over [the subsidiary] and had made it an integral part of the system—one of the feeders on the system."

The case related to the claim of the receiver of the parent railroad against the receiver of the subsidiary for operating expenses of the latter, which were advanced by the parent. The court rejected the claim, stating:

> This subordinate road was conducted as a part of a great system, — a system conceived and created by the Central [the parent] for its benefit solely. Every part of the system contributed to the good of its creator, and to this end the interest of the Central, and not of the feeders, was the dominating idea. The advantages derived by the Central from the operations of the other parts of the system were vastly disproportionate to those derived by the contributing roads. . . . In short, under the complete domination of this majority vote, the subordinate road was conducted, not with a view to the interest of its stockholders and creditors, but for the benefit of the central figure of the system. No implied contract, therefore, could arise.[23]

Tort

The tort decisions involving railroad groups are of particular interest because they gave rise to "system" analysis, which applied enterprise principles to intragroup tort liability. The 1894 and 1900 decisions of the Supreme Court in *Pennsylvania Railroad v. Jones* and *Chesapeake & Ohio Railway v. Howard* reached mixed results in dealing with the liability of railroad groups.[24]

Relying on integrated operations and system analysis, the *Pennsylvania R.R.* decision upheld the imposition of passenger liability upon three operating subsidiaries, while rejecting liability against their parent corporation. The Court's distinction rested on the nature of the evidence of the parent's actual involvement in the operations of the train in question.

In *Chesapeake & Ohio Ry.*, the Supreme Court held that it was not an error to permit the case to go to the jury where the Chesapeake & Ohio operated and controlled the train as well as holding itself out as a continuous system. Although these decisions upholding imposition of intragroup liability may be explained in terms of the extent of the parents' participation in the operation of the trains in question, they also gave some support for looking at the integrated nature of railroad operations and for system analysis as a basis for liability. The ultimate standard remained open.

Then, an impressive number of courts, led by the Court of Appeals for the Eighth Circuit in 1901 and the Second Circuit in 1904 and 1906, rejected entity principles in considering the tort liability of the affiliated companies of a railroad "system" to passengers, shippers, and employees. In *Lehigh Valley Railroad Co. v. DuPont*, for example, the Court of Appeals for the Second Circuit, invoking the partnership analogy, upheld liability "where the lines of several railroad corporations are conducted as a single system for the purposes of the traffic between different points originating upon either . . . although the general management of each road is retained by the railroad owning it." Subsequently, in *Lehigh Valley Railroad Co. v. Delachesa*, the same court decried the time spent on determining the details of the relationship between the parent and its subordinated companies in the system, noting that it was not of practical significance "but merely whether it [the parent] should be called upon to pay out of one or another of its several purses."[25]

Other courts followed this lead, and system jurisprudence became prominent. Railroad parent and affiliate corporations were often held liable for negligence of subsidiaries and affiliates with which they conducted an integrated system. However, the doctrine was not universally accepted. System analysis for railroads clashed with traditional entity law and "piercing the veil jurisprudence," which had become firmly established by this time in areas other than railroads. Notwithstanding the numerous cases applying system analysis to impose intragroup liability in tort, other federal courts and many state courts firmly adhered to entity law and rejected such an enterprise approach. The decisions were irreconcilable.[26]

With the decision of the Supreme Court in *Davis v. Alexander*[27] in 1925, the system concept for application of enterprise principles in litigation involving railroad groups appeared to have triumphed. Relying upon the *Lehigh Valley* cases that had first introduced system analysis, and borrowing their metaphor, Justice Brandeis, speaking for the Court, said: "where one railroad company actually controls another and operates both as a single system, the dominant company will be liable for injuries due to the negligence of the subsidiary company."[28] Most interestingly, Brandeis made no reference to his striking reaffirmation of entity law in *Cannon Manufacturing Corp. v. Cudahy Packing Co.*, decided only eight months earlier. (This decision in the area of jurisdiction is discussed in the section on "Service of Process and Jurisdiction.")

Although *Davis v. Alexander* appeared to be a landmark, it proved to be short-lived. In the very next year, Judge Cardozo and the New York Court of Appeals in the celebrated *Berkey v. Third Avenue Railway* case flatly rejected system law. Explaining away *Davis v. Alexander* as resting on its facts (which Brandeis had not discussed in his opinion) Cardozo firmly applied traditional entity law in an opinion "characterized more by its felicity than by its lucidity."[29]

The decision in the *Berkey* case for practical purposes ended the matter. Although isolated subsequent decisions involving railroads relied on *Davis v. Alexander*,[30] system analysis has become a dead letter. Since the *Berkey* decision, entity law and "piercing the veil jurisprudence" has become firmly established as fundamental American tort law, even in the case of railroad systems. This early attempt to develop enterprise principles for determination of torts of the country's then most prominent integrated enterprises proved abortive.

However, system, or enterprise, liability did survive in another integrated transportation industry. In the New York taxi industry, in cases where the business was operated through fleets of taxicabs owned by a number of affiliated companies under common ownership and control and utilizing integrated facilities, liability was imposed on the operating companies conducting the business. Limited liability for the controlling shareholder survived, however, when it was not participating in carrying on the business and was solely an investor.[31]

Statutory Law

In the Commodities clause of the Hepburn Act of 1906, Congress attempted to respond to widespread shipper complaints of discriminatory rates in the case of railroads acting both as common carriers and private shippers. The Commodities clause made it unlawful for any railroad to haul any article in which "it may own . . . or have any interest, direct or indirect."[32]

Four major cases before the Supreme Court between 1909 and 1920 involved the application of the Commodities clause to railroad parent corporations and their coal-mining subsidiaries. Did a railroad have "any interest, direct or indirect," in the coal of its subsidiary and did it violate the clause when it transported the coal?

In its initial decision in 1909 under the act, *United States v. Delaware & Hudson Co.*, the Court gave the act a restrictive construction, with a rigid application of entity law as the controlling standard for determining the outer limits of application of the act. The Court held that "mere ownership" of all the stock of a "bona fide" corporation was insufficient to give the parent railroad "an interest, direct or indirect," in the coal being shipped. With the interposition of a subsidiary or affiliate, the statute became inapplicable as long as the controlled company was "bona fide."[33]

In *United States v. Lehigh Valley Railroad*, decided in 1911, the Court again recognized that the shipments of commodities of "bona fide" companies were not precluded by the statute, despite corporate affiliation, as in cases where "the fact that the two corporations were separate and distinct legal entities [had] been regarded in the administration of the affairs of the coal company." The Court, nevertheless, upheld the complaint and held that the statute applied because the "power [of the parent's control] was exerted in such a manner as to so commingle the affairs of both as . . . to make such affairs practically indistinguishable and therefore to cause both corporations to be one for all purposes."[34]

In *United States v. Delaware, Lackawanna & Western Railroad*, the Court again held the act applicable to railroad and coal-mining companies owned and controlled by substantially the same shareholders. Although the Court appeared ready to accept that common officers, common directors, common stock ownership, and the fact that the railroad had organized the coal company were not necessarily fatal to bona fide status, it held that such facts required that a contract between companies so interrelated receive "close scrutiny" because of the "unity of management" and because the companies were "clear[ly] not dealing at arm's length." The contract obligated the coal company to sell only to the railroad, required it to fulfill orders of railroad customers, even if unprofitable, and permitted the railroad to reduce the amount of its orders, thereby affecting the base market price. The Court, thereupon, held that the coal company was an "agent or instrumentality" of the railroad and that the contract was invalid under the Commodities clause.[35]

In *United States v. Reading Co.*, the Court reached substantially the same result in a case involving a holding company owning and controlling railroad and coal-mining subsidiaries. The district court had relied on the fact that the railroad company was not a stockholder of the coal company and that the operating companies had a separate accounting system and separate operations, stressing "the importance of maintaining the theory of separate corporate entity." The Court reversed, describing the subsidiary as "the coal mining department" of the group, and holding that there had been an "abdication of all independent corporate action" by the operating companies to the holding company and "a surrender . . . of the entire conduct of their affairs." It stated:

> [Stock] ownership . . . does not necessarily create an identity of corporate interest . . . such as to render it unlawful under the commodities clause . . . yet, if where such ownership is . . . not . . . in a manner normal and usual with stockholders, but for the purpose of making it a mere agent or instrumentality or department of another company, the courts will look through the forms to the realities of the relation between the companies as if the corporate agency did not exist and will deal with them as the justice of the case may require.[36]

In large measure, the Commodities clause decisions, resting on such metaphorical guidelines as "agent," "instrumentality," or "department," gave rise to the "instrumentality doctrine" variety of "piercing the veil jurisprudence" that thereafter dominated American corporate law. This doctrine rested on the firm recognition of entity law and of the separate existence of the subsidiary or controlled corporation, from which exceptions were possible only under a loosely defined metaphorical standard that defied precise analysis.

The Interstate Commerce Commission was not ready to allow the forms of corporate structure to defeat effective implementation of the national railroad regulatory program, and it continued to litigate. In subsequent decisions in 1936 and 1948, the government twice failed in its effort to reverse the previous holdings of the Court. In *United States v. Elgin J. & E. Railway*, with Justices Stone, Brandeis, and Cardozo dissenting,[37] the Court flatly reaffirmed its earlier restrictive construction of the act.

In a stinging dissent, Justice Stone lamented that the decision reduced the Commodities clause to a "cipher." He argued that the steel company's "domination in fact" was all that was necessary for violation of the Act, and that "scrupulous recognition of the separate entities" should not permit avoidance. Commentators deplored the reliance on formal criteria, the disregard of the purposes of the legislation, and the resulting easy avoidance of the statute.[38]

In 1948, the issue came for a final time before the Court in *United States v. South Buffalo Railway*, which involved a rail subsidiary of Bethlehem Steel. The composition of the Court had completely changed, with only Roosevelt appointees sitting. The government invited the Court to overrule *Elgin*. By a vote of five to four, the Court declined. It did not defend *Elgin*, but it held that the Court should respect the refusal of Congress to respond to the appeal of the commission after the earlier decisions that the statute be changed. It then applied the *Elgin* doctrine, stating:

> Bethlehem, as a stockholder, of course controlled South Buffalo. It did not, however, disregard in either the legal or economic sense the separate entity of its subsidiary or treat it as its own alter ego. On the contrary, it rather ostentatiously maintained the formalities of separate existence. . . . Its identity has been preserved in form and in substance — *the substance of separate corporate existence being itself largely a matter of form.* Under the *Elgin* case, and until Congress shall otherwise decide, this is sufficient.[39] [Emphasis added.]

Where the affairs of the railroad and the shipper had been kept distinct as a matter of form, the Court held that the statute was inapplicable, whatever the economic realities. This brought the dispute over construction to an end. Entity law and formalism had triumphed, and evasion of public regulation through formal corporate restructuring was readily available.

Service of Process and Jurisdiction

In like manner, in *Peterson v. Chicago, Rock Island & Pacific Railway*, decided in 1907, and in *Cannon Mfg. Co.*, decided in 1925, the Court strongly upheld entity law concepts for purposes of such procedural matters as service of process for the institution of a law suit and jurisdiction of the courts.

The *Peterson* case involved two of the operating subsidiaries in the Rock Island system, using the integrated Rock Island system timetable, with employees serving both companies and wearing Rock Island uniforms. Nevertheless, the Court disallowed service on personnel of one as constituting valid service of process for the other. Although it recognized the existence of common control and integrated operations, it sought to distinguish between control over the election of management and control over the corporate property and business, harkening back to the decision in *Pullman's Palace Car Co. v. Missouri Pacific Railroad* two decades earlier.[40]

In the *Cannon* case,[41] the only one of these decisions not involving railroads, the Court considered the question of whether North Carolina had jurisdiction over a Maine parent corporation by reason of the in-state nexus of its North Carolina subsidiary. Justice Brandeis, who was to write the opinion upholding "system" analysis and enterprise principles in dealing with railroad tort liability in *Davis v. Alexander* only eight months later, was the author of the opinion in *Cannon*, which rested on entity law in all its formalistic rigor. Although he acknowledged that the parent dominated the subsidiary "immediately and completely" and exerted its control substantially in the same way as it did over its unincorporated divisions or branches, he held that the "corporate separation, though perhaps merely formal, was real," and that jurisdiction was lacking. Where, as a matter of form, the subsidiary was a separate and distinct corporate entity, its in-state activities would not support the assertion of jurisdiction over its out-of-state parent. Brandeis took pains to acknowledge, however, that cases involving substantive rights were without application for this procedural question.[42] In fact, the experience in substantive areas including both statutory law and tort liability was quite different.

With this review of the rise and ultimate decease of system analysis for railroad intragroup tort liability and the movement of the Supreme Court towards entity law and "piercing the veil jurisprudence" in other areas, the discussion now turns to review of the development of "piercing the veil jurisprudence" as applied to corporate groups in the American law generally.

Conceptual Problems in the Disregard of the Corporate Entity

In dealing with the novel problem of corporate groups and the liability of one group component for the obligations of another, the courts had great difficulty in developing a satisfactory conceptual framework for analysis. In the early stages of the development of the law, some courts, as in *York & Maryland Line R.R.*, seized on the concepts of partnership and agency as the basis for intragroup liability in cases of economic integration of the operations of the affiliated companies.

The partnership analogy did not long survive. Although for a while isolated references to the partnership concept continued to appear,[43] the inherent difficulties of squeezing the distinctive economic organization represented by the corporate group into the requirements of the partnership law[44] apparently soon became generally recognized.[45] By the end of the century, use of the partnership concept as a rationale disappeared.

While equally flawed, the agency analogy has had a longer life and is still occasionally invoked. For a while, nineteenth-century courts seized upon the concept of agency law and sought to treat the parent's control over the subsidiary as the equivalent of the principal's power to direct the activities of the agent.

Scholars, however, agree that "agency" in its common law sense clearly does not describe the parent-subsidiary relationship. Fundamentally incompatible with a principal-agency relationship, the subsidiary is acting in its own name and on its own behalf. Although the economic results ultimately inure to the benefit of the parent through dividend or liquidation distribution, the subsidiary's acts are reflected in its operating statement and balance sheet, not in its parent's. Second, agency is a consensual relationship, and the relationship must rest on an understanding, not simply on the interrelation of the companies. In these cases, the subsidiary has not been authorized to bind the parent corporation and has not purported to do so. Further, as Judge Learned Hand and many others have pointed out, such an expanded concept of agency that derives the relationship solely from the parent's "control" would prove too much. Because control exists in virtually every such case, the expanded doctrine would make every parent liable for every act of a subsidiary.[46]

"Agency" is also been used in a very different sense. With the emergence of "piercing the veil jurisprudence" and judicial decision-making resting on metaphors, "agency" also emerged as a conclusory metaphor utilized "to explain" the application of "piercing the veil jurisprudence," along with such other metaphors as "instrumentality," "alter ego," "department," "conduit," "puppet," and the like.

Notwithstanding scholarly criticism, isolated survivals persist until this day, with courts on occasion continuing to justify the imposition of intragroup liability in a particular case by loose references to agency. Usually, such usage is little more than an appeal to metaphor-dominated "piercing the veil jurisprudence." On occasion, it rests on a failure to understand the requirements of common law agency. At still other times, courts, unready to analyze the problem further, simply throw up their hands and uphold the existence of agency for purposes of attributing parent-subsidiary liability or amenability to jurisdiction or other legal consequences, while acknowledging that their use of the agency doctrine cannot rest on the traditional common law standards for determining the existence of an agency relationship. However, these courts do not then explain how it is different and why it is the proper solution for the problem.

Other than the abortive references to partnership and the flawed references to agency, the older cases provided little guidance, relying on a hopelessly vague reaffirmation of equitable principles. The following pronouncement in *Whittle v. Vanderbilt Mining & Milling Co.* provides a typical example: "The doctrine [of corporate entity] is technical, and a court of equity will disregard it, and treat the corporation, not as an entity, but an association of persons, *whenever justice between the parties so requires* [emphasis added]."[47] So general a standard as "whenever justice between the parties so requires" obviously provided little guidance for application in cases not involving the use of the corporate form for "fraud or illegality," the traditional factors leading to the utilization generally of equitable principles to override legal forms.

A few years later, this standard was expanded in a formulation that, although hardly any more helpful, has become widely quoted. In *United States v. Milwaukee Refrigerating Transit Co.*, the court stated that it would disregard the corporate entity whenever it was utilized to "defeat the public convenience, justify wrong, protect fraud, or defend crime."[48] This not-particularly-useful standard has been faithfully recited by literally scores of courts down to the present day, even though it manifestly provides no real standard for decision.

Adaptation of the "Alter Ego" Concept

As early as 1898, the courts were reviewing the relations between parent and subsidiary by invoking the "alter ego" concept in terms hardly distinguishable from contemporary usage. Thus, Justice Taft's opinion in the Circuit Court of Appeals in *Harris v. Youngstown*

Bridge Co., involving the relative priority of a parent company's mortgage and a mechanic's lien on its subsidiary's property, discloses that the circuit judge had disregarded the entity of one of two affiliated corporations because he had:

> found that the contract company was nothing but an alter ego of the bridge company, with no real, independent existence, and with no capital or means of carrying out the contract except what the bridge company furnished it [and that it was a] case of a nominal and subsidiary corporation of the bridge company, acting really as its agent. . . .[49]

This is one of the earliest references to "alter ego" as the metaphor for an impermissibly close relationship between parent and subsidiary corporation that gives rise to a disregard of the separate corporate identity of the controlled company. During this period of American law, "alter ego" was a term that had become increasingly prominent in corporate law in an entirely different context, not involving parent and subsidiary corporations at all. "Alter ego" had become a familiar concept to lawyers of the time in cases involving corporate torts; the decisions fell into two classes of cases. Numerous decisions involved a plaintiff-employee injured through the fault of a fellow-employee trying to escape the strictures of the fellow servant rule that normally absolved the employer from liability. In these cases, courts found corporate or employer liability on finding that the negligent employee, typically a foreman or supervisor, was acting as the "alter ego" of his principal or employer, and therefore could not be viewed as a fellow servant. Accordingly, the acts of the individual were the acts of the employer for this purpose, and the fellow servant rule did not apply.[50]

Other decisions imposed liability on an employer because of the attribution to the employer of the fraudulent representation, the knowledge, or the action as a "nominee" of a servant or agent, who was similarly characterized as the employer's or principal's "alter ego."[51]

Unlike later developments in corporate law,[52] there was no suggestion in these invocations of the alter ego concept that the agent or employee ceased to be a separate entity to accomplish the result. The attribution of liability flowed from the nature of the interrelationship between the parties, not from the nonexistence of a separate entity; this was thus closer in concept to common law agency than to later "piercing the veil jurisprudence."

This doctrine, with which all courts were familiar, was borrowed to provide the rationale when courts thereafter sought to impose liability on a parent corporation or controlling shareholder for the acts of a subsidiary or controlled corporation. Only a number of these early cases involved sham corporations without assets. Others involved subsidiaries — with substantial assets — that were actively conducting business.[53]

The twentieth century unfolded with development of the "alter ego" theory as a convenient route to disregarding the corporate entity. The courts seized on the concept of the alter ego as a description of that type of subsidiary whose acts gave rise to the imposition of liability upon its parent corporation or controlling shareholder(s). However, in such cases the courts initially reached their legal result by asserting that by reason of the "rare" or "exceptional" features of the relationship, the subsidiary lacked separate legal existence. In such event, there was only the single entity of the parent corporation (or controlling shareholder) that was consequently liable. It was only after considerable maturation of the doctrine that courts were ready to recognize that the subsidiary ceased to be a single entity only for purposes of the case at bar and the issue presented and that it retained its separate identity for other purposes.[54] Even today, however, some courts applying the "alter ego" doctrine still assert that the subsidiary's separate corporate existence is being disregarded and that liability is being imposed because the parent and subsidiary (or controlling shareholder(s) and controlled corporation) represent only a single legal entity. Thus, even today, the modern theory goes well beyond the theoretical framework of its nineteenth-century origins in fellow servant law.

Eventually, the original doctrine, which required a showing of actual fraud or illegality for the invocation of equitable intervention to disregard the legal entity, gradually developed into a broader doctrine under which "wrongful," inequitable, "morally culpable," or "fundamentally unfair" conduct is sufficient for equitable intervention, even though actual fraud or illegality is not involved.[55] Even today, however, some courts still ponder over whether or not actual fraud is a necessary element for "piercing the veil," although only rare decisions seem to continue to hold that it is essential.[56]

By World War I, the volume of litigation involving alleged abuse of the corporate form and an attempt to disregard the corporate entity had attracted scholarly attention, began to produce an extensive literature, and ultimately produced a jurisprudence of its own: the jurisprudence of "piercing the corporate veil."

"Piercing the Veil Jurisprudence"

By the 1920s, "piercing the corporate veil" became a prominent doctrine, and a substantial legal literature emerged that analyzed the numerous reported cases and attempted to formulate the legal principles on which they were based.[57]

Under traditional "piercing the veil jurisprudence," which has largely persisted in the United States until the present, courts in "rare" or "exceptional" cases impose liability upon a shareholder for obligations of a corporation under one or another of the three variants of the doctrine: "instrumentality," "alter ego," and "identity." The widely invoked "instrumentality" doctrine, first formulated in Frederick Powell's 1931 volume, has three factors:

> (a) the "control" by the shareholder was so intrusively exercised as to show that the corporation had no separate existence of its own;
> (b) the corporation had been utilized to commit some fraudulent, or wrongful, or inequitable, or "morally culpable" or "fundamentally unfair" act to the detriment of creditors; and
> (c) the conduct had resulted in loss to creditors.[58]

The "alter ego" variant of "piercing the veil," while employing the very same elements, is expressed somewhat differently. Under the "alter ego" doctrine, "piercing the veil" is said to be appropriate when:

> (1) such unity of ownership and control exists that the two affiliated corporations have ceased to be separate and the subsidiary has been relegated to the status of the "alter ego" of the parent; and
> (2) where recognition of the two companies as separate entities would sanction fraud or otherwise lead to an inequitable result.[59]

The "identity" doctrine is much the same. Notwithstanding the somewhat different formulations of the three variants, their substance is the same; courts and commentators generally treat them as equivalent in all respects.

The foregoing standards are hopelessly general. Accordingly, the courts have recognized that application of traditional "piercing the veil jurisprudence" is fact-specific, depending on the "totality" of all the circumstances. This further underscores the lack of usefulness of the standard as a guide to decision.

There have been, however, some departures from the doctrine, as well as efforts at a more detailed definition. Thus, in cases where the subsidiary or controlled corporation was simply a sham lacking assets, employees, or a realistic existence, many cases have applied the doctrine without regard to the further requirement of a showing of wrongful or inequitable conduct. Similarly, in at least two other areas—jurisdiction and torts—a number of courts have pierced the veil on a showing of what the court regarded as excessive control by the parent corporation, again without regard to any factor of wrongful or inequitable conduct.

In *Castleberry v. Branscum*, the Supreme Court of Texas, apparently recognizing these variations, attempted to reformulate "piercing the veil" or disregard of corporate entity. Reproving the lower Texas courts for assuming that "alter ego" was "a synonym for the entire doctrine of disregarding the corporate fiction," the Texas Supreme Court restricted the "alter ego" doctrine to cases where the separateness of the corporate entity had ceased and restricting liability to the entity would result in injustice. It noted that there were numerous other circumstances for "piercing the veil" where the "alter ego" doctrine would not apply. The court stated:

> We disregard the corporate fiction, even though corporate formalities have been observed and corporate and individual property have been kept separately, when the corporate form has been used as part of basically unfair device to achieve an inequitable result. . . . Specifically . . .
>
> (1) when the fiction is used as a means of perpetuating fraud;
>
> (2) where a corporation is organized and operated as a mere tool or business conduit of another corporation;
>
> (3) where the corporate fiction is resorted to as a means of evading an existing legal obligation;
>
> (4) where the corporate fiction is employed to achieve or perpetuate monopoly;
>
> (5) where the corporate fiction is used to circumvent a statute; and
>
> (6) where the corporate fiction is relied on as protection of crime or to justify wrong. [footnotes omitted.]

The court added inadequate capitalization as still another basis for disregard of entity.[60]

Almost all courts treat the foregoing situations as wrongful or unfair conduct satisfying the second element in the "alter ego" or "instrumentality" doctrines. If this analysis in *Castleberry* is to be taken at face value, the Texas Supreme Court has in effect eliminated the first element of the "alter ego" doctrine, and wrongful or unfair conduct alone will establish an independent basis for imposition of liability. If later cases sustain such a liberalized construction, this will mark a significant milestone in the decline of entity law. However, its impact in Texas will be restricted to fields of the law other than contract. Promptly after the decision, the Texas legislature basically overruled the decision insofar as contract liability was concerned.[61]

Finally, it is noteworthy that although Texas has recently been a leading jurisdiction in distinguishing disregard of entity in contract from disregard in tort, the court did not discuss this element of the problem at all.

In summary, "piercing the veil jurisprudence" is first concerned with a determination of the extent to which the corporate forms have been respected or corporate formalities observed, particularly with respect to the extent and manner in which the controlling shareholder exercised "control." If such has not been the case, these courts conclude that the business and affairs of the corporation and its controlling shareholder have become so intertwined that the corporation and shareholder constitute only a single legal entity. The subsidiary or controlled corporation is then characterized by reference to one or more of a formidable galaxy of colorful metaphors as no more than the "adjunct," "agent," "alter ego," "conduit," "department," "instrumentality," "puppet," or "tool" of the shareholder, and liability imposed on the parent or controlling shareholder upon proof of some form of inequitable conduct detrimental to creditors.

This is jurisprudence by metaphor or epithet. It does not contribute to legal understanding because it is an intellectual construct, divorced from business realities. The metaphors are no more than conclusory terms, affording little understanding of the considerations and policies underlying the court's action and little help in predicting results in future cases. The courts express their results in very broad terms that provide little general guidance. As a result, American lawyers are faced with hundreds of decisions that are irreconcilable and not entirely comprehensible. Further, the doctrines are rigidly and indiscriminately applied across the full spectrum of the law as a transcendental conceptual standard without regard to the very differing objectives and policies involved. "Piercing the veil" contract decisions are applied to decisions involving cases in tort, cases in substantive law to matters involving procedure, and common law cases used to decide cases of statutory application. Few areas of American law have been so sharply criticized by commentators.

There have been isolated dissenting views.[62] Not all courts have been ready to follow the rigid concepts of entity law and the disregard of entity according to the foregoing principles. Thus, in *Farmers' Loan & Trust Co. v. Pierson*, decided by a lower New York court, Justice Bijur long ago stated:

> . . . a corporation is more nearly a method than a thing, and that the law in dealing with a corporation has no need of defining it as a person or an entity, or even an embodiment of functions, rights, and duties, but may treat it as a name for a useful and usual collection of jural relations each one of which must in every instance be ascertained, analyzed, and assigned to its appropriate place according to the circumstances of the particular case, having due regard to the purposes to be achieved. . . .
>
> The rights and obligations that are comprised within the compass of the word change not only with time but with locality. Limited liability of the shareholders is a comparatively recent invention. Limited and unlimited liability existed side by side, even within this state, under the Laws of 1875. The extent of limited liability varies under different statutes.[63]

This was wisdom, indeed, but the eloquent statement was largely ignored at the time, and is still largely ignored by most courts. Entity law, and "piercing the corporate veil" as its safety valve in rare or exceptional cases, became firmly established as the governing law, and it is still dominant today. Although—as shown in the volumes comprising *The Law of Corporate Groups*—the doctrine is beginning to erode, the process is still in its early stages. Whereas such erosion may clearly be seen in such private litigation as torts and in certain procedural questions, including jurisdiction, venue, and service, it is even more evident in judicial decisions construing statutes of general application in which Congress has not addressed the question of entity or enterprise. Finally, in statutes of specific application to controlled corporations, since 1933 Congress has increasingly adopted enterprise principles and abandoned traditional entity law in considerable measure in enacting major regulatory programs. The next chapter reviews these important developments.

5

The Increasing Acceptance
of Enterprise Principles

Development of Enterprise Law: General

"Piercing the veil jurisprudence," however clumsy and unsatisfactory, has become an established feature of American law. It provides a minimum safety valve for the legal system, providing an escape from the rigid confines of entity law. Developed by an extension of established principles of equity jurisprudence in cases involving corporations controlled by individual shareholders, over the years it has been applied to corporate groups as well. The decisions provide a rich source of enterprise law. Such decisions have been joined by an impressive number of statutes, administrative regulations, and judicial decisions in allied areas, which provide a demonstration of the surprisingly wide dimensions that the growing application of enterprise principles is assuming in American law. This experience is occurring across a wide spectrum of American law, reaching far beyond the narrow limitations of traditional "piercing the veil jurisprudence." It may well be termed the American law of corporate groups, consisting of the following:

1. *Liberalized "Piercing the Veil Jurisprudence"*—judicial doctrines, particularly liberalized applications of traditional piercing the veil jurisprudence, in matters involving corporate groups in private controversies at common law, particularly in tort.
2. *"Unitary Business"* doctrine—judicial development of the uni-

tary business theory for determining the constitutionality of "unitary tax" apportionment.

3. *Statutes of General Application* — judicial and administrative developments in the construction of and application to corporate groups of general statutes that make no specific reference to corporate groups or enterprise principles.

4. *Statutes of Specific Application to Corporate Groups* — legislative and administrative developments in the enactment of statutes and regulations that expressly adopt enterprise principles and apply to corporate groups, sometimes for pervasive, industry-wide regulation of corporate groups, but most frequently for selected purposes in statutes otherwise resting on entity law.

5. *Judicial Procedure* — judicial developments in the law of judicial procedure, often codified as judicial rules of civil procedure. This is particularly evident in such areas as res judicata and collateral estoppel, statutes of limitations, discovery, and the scope of injunctions.

6. *Bankruptcy* — legislative and judicial developments in particular areas of the law of bankruptcy, particularly equitable subordination, substantive consolidation, and voidable preferences.

This wide-ranging development of enterprise principles in American law reflects the increasing recognition by legislatures, administrative agencies, and courts that principles of entity law developed in the very different economic world of centuries ago ignore contemporary economic realities and constitute serious obstacles impeding effective social ordering of corporate group activities. In order to permit effective implementation of legal objectives, whether statutory or common law, in matters involving corporate groups, the increasingly anachronistic principles of entity law are beginning to yield in many areas to those of enterprise law. This is particularly true in the statutory area, but as will be seen in the following summary review, is evident elsewhere as well.

Liberalized "Piercing the Veil Jurisprudence"

Everywhere in the United States, state corporation law follows traditional entity law. Although there are isolated references to parent or subsidiary corporations in state corporation statutes, these are restricted to ancillary matters. Many states, for example, prohibit voting by a subsidiary of any shares of its parent that it owns, or prohibit a subsidiary from purchasing shares of its parent when the parent is barred from doing so.[1] California provides for the use of consolidated group accounts for purposes of determining the legality of dividends.[2]

Many state corporation statutes expressly provide for the limited liability of shareholders; many others are silent. This makes little difference in the end. In no American jurisdiction does the presence or absence of such a statutory provision for limited liability play a significant role in determining whether corporate existence in the particular case is to be respected or disregarded. The issue and imposition of liability upon shareholders remain questions for judicial decision according to common law rules. In state jurisprudence, common law controversies decided in the courts, not state statutory corporation law, are the battlegrounds for the choice between entity law and enterprise principles.

The traditional barriers of entity law, with its concept of the independent legal existence of the corporation separate from its shareholders, stand in the way of any attempt to attribute to shareholders (even to parent companies of subsidiaries) any legal consequences for actions of a subsidiary or controlled corporation. As noted, under the traditional view such attribution or imposition is possible only in equity, where courts in rare and exceptional cases may intervene according to the principles of "piercing the veil jurisprudence."

The traditional view is still the fundamental doctrine governing the legal relations between American corporations and their shareholders. For decades, "piercing the veil jurisprudence" has been applied as a transcendental doctrine throughout the law, irrespective of the nature of the particular problem or area of the law in issue. Although in recent years some courts have been using "piercing the veil" more selectively, others still continue to utilize the doctrine as formulated in contract cases to decide cases in tort, or in substantive matters to decide problems in procedure, or in private law controversies to decide questions of public law. They do so even though the underlying objectives and policies of the law in the various areas differ profoundly, and even though the clashing values and interests are fundamentally different.

The law, however, appears to be in a process of accelerating change. With the decline of formalism as the controlling force in American jurisprudence, the hold of traditional entity law on American courts in cases involving corporate groups is visibly, albeit slowly, weakening. In the place of the rigid standards traditionally applied as a conceptual matter indiscriminately throughout the law, modern courts have become increasingly concerned with implementation of the underlying objectives of the law in the area involved in the case at hand.[3]

The jurisprudential change has contributed substantially to the growing development of enterprise law. In a number of areas – of which tort law, some parts of bankruptcy law and of procedure, and judicial construction of statutes of general application are the leading examples – enterprise principles are beginning to achieve recognition. Although traditional entity law continues to predominate in the legal system generally, courts are turning to enterprise principles in re-solving legal problems involving constituent companies of corporate groups.

The courts applying enterprise principles agree that the mere exis-tence of "control," while an essential element required for application of enterprise principles, is, in and of itself, insufficient for the imposi-tion of common law intragroup liability. Application of enterprise principles requires two additional fundamental factors. One relates to the economic unity of the group; the other is concerned with imple-mentation of the objectives of the law in the area in question.

First, the application of enterprise principles requires highly inter-twined operational and economic relationships between parent and subsidiary corporations.

Second, enterprise law must better implement and prevent frustra-tion of the underlying purposes and objectives of the law in the area in question than utilization of traditional entity law would. Unless such objectives are served, economic unity of the group is unlikely to be sufficient for application of enterprise principles.

Where the foregoing factors can be shown, the increasing number of common law courts applying enterprise law will do so, notwith-standing the absence of other factors essential for application of tradi-tional "piercing the veil jurisprudence." Such elements, unnecessary for enterprise law, are the lack of indicia of the separate existence of the subsidiary, including lack of respect for corporate formalities or lack of offices, equipment, employees, and so on; and the presence of inequitable or wrongful conduct detrimental to creditors.

In selected areas, the courts have increasingly been fashioning new doctrines of enterprise law and have taken a radically different approach to the attribution of legal consequences from one constituent company to another. These courts are attributing legal consequences to one legal unit by reason of its special relationship to another one. Most often, they are concerned with the imposition of liability; on occasion, they are dealing only with the recognition of rights. In procedure, they sometimes may be doing neither, only shaping rules for the conduct of judicial business.

In this attribution of legal consequences, the courts may be perceived as fashioning a new concept of judicial identity in which the decision is supported by deeming the constituent corporations of a corporate group, notwithstanding their separate corporate forms, to comprise but a single legal unit for the purposes at hand.

American courts have made considerable progress in the difficult case-by-case evolution of a doctrinal standard for application of enterprise principles. In the more forward-looking decisions, both in common law controversies and in construction of statutes of general application,[4] the courts have moved well beyond emphasis on the formalistic factors that had constituted previously the core of traditional "piercing the veil jurisprudence." This may be termed "liberalized piercing the veil jurisprudence." The courts are concerned instead with the economic realities. Do the separate corporations actually function as integral parts of the group or do they operate as independent businesses? If the former is true, will application of enterprise principles better implement the underlying policies of the law in the area?

In this formulation of enterprise principles, the courts have the burden of determining two fundamental issues. First, they must decide whether the adoption of enterprise principles or the retention of traditional concepts of entity law will best serve the underlying purposes and objectives of the particular area of the law under consideration. Second, they must also determine whether, in the case before them, the relationship between the affiliated corporations is so intertwined as an economic reality that the application of enterprise principles is appropriate. Although such an undertaking could be avoided by providing for the application of enterprise law in every parent-subsidiary relationship, this presents many problems. In any event, such a far-reaching step, even if deemed desirable, is clearly not feasible at the present stage of American law. The modern American experience is beginning to provide an answer to this definitional problem.

The factors that define the economic contours and the decision-making structure of the group and that are becoming recognized as the central points for inquiry in determining the nature of the interrelationship between a parent corporation and its subsidiaries are the following:

Control. In all cases in the area it has been accepted that the existence of the parent corporation's "control" over the decision-making of the subsidiary, even when combined with the presence of common officers and directors, is not decisive in and of itself. These cases go further and inquire into the extent that such control has been exercised. They are particularly concerned as to whether there has been an excessively intrusive intervention by the parent and its personnel into the decision-making of the subsidiary when compared to "normal" management patterns in the contemporary business world. The parent's exercise of control over day-to-day decision-making, for example, is already widely recognized as one form of unacceptable exercise of control that will lead to imposition of liability (or other legal consequences) on the parent.

Control by the group over such matters as determination of general policy; planning; budgets and capital expenditures; executive salaries and bonuses; and group use of manuals and guidelines setting forth group policies with respect to such matters as personnel, safety, purchasing, labor relations, public relations and affairs, accounting, finance, ethical standards, and the like have received differing receptions by different courts. As should be evident, the realities of the extent of exercise of "control" in the particular case present a difficult issue of considerable subtlety and complexity. That extent, while not decisive, occupies a central role among the factors considered by the courts.

Economic Integration. A second factor of major importance is the extent of economic integration of the business conducted by the parent and subsidiary corporations of the group, particularly where the companies collectively conduct complementary fragments of a common business. This includes such matters as the extent of intragroup purchases and sales reflecting integration of various stages of the production and distribution processes, group warranties, group purchasing, warehousing, and marketing, group credit, and group property and casualty insurance.

Financial Interdependence. The extent of the financial interdependence of the group and its constituent companies is an additional factor of significance. In this supporting area, do the separate corporations function as an integral part of the group, rather than operate independently? Does the subsidiary have adequate capital of its own comparable to that of its independent competitors? Does it finance itself independently or does it meet its financing needs through loans or advances from the group or by borrowing from banks or other lenders on the basis of guaranties by the parent corporation or sister subsidiaries in the group? Financing by group affiliates using intragroup guaranties, for example, has become so common in the United States that it has generated a special law and literature of its own.[5]

Administrative Interdependence. Corporate groups increasingly seek to achieve economies of scale by centralizing administrative support services for the constituent companies of the group, either in the parent or in service subsidiaries organized for that purpose. These centralized supporting services include legal, tax, accounting, finance, insurance, engineering, research and development, public relations and public affairs, employee education and training programs, safety, and similar functions.

Overlapping Employment Structure. This factor includes such matters as group personnel career patterns involving movement of employees from one group company to another, intragroup exchange of employees, group employee training programs, group insurance, benefit plans such as option, pension and profit-sharing, and the like.

Common Group Persona. A final factor is the use of a common group persona in the conduct of the group business. In this area of integrated operations, the constituent companies of the group utilize the same group trade name, trademarks, logo, and in some cases even color schemes and style of uniforms around the world.

These factors provide the most promising building blocks available at the present time for the construction of an American doctrine of enterprise law.

An increasing number of courts, although still in the minority, have used these factors to identify whether a subsidiary is so integrally intertwined with its parent corporation and its group that enterprise treatment is deemed necessary to accomplish the underlying policies and objectives of the law in the particular matter at hand. This standard reflects an economic pattern of integrated or unitary group functioning and goes well beyond the elements of "control" and overlapping proprietary interest inherent in every parent-subsidiary relationship. American courts require such a demonstration before they will utilize enterprise principles in a legal order still wedded generally to entity law.

American law has thus seen the beginning of new judicial attitudes toward the application of "piercing the veil jurisprudence" to corporate groups. The rigid traditional doctrine is increasingly being modified to serve the needs of modern economic society. This process is still in the early stages, but it is already having its impact on the American legal system. In order to implement more effectively the objectives of the law in the particular area involved in an individual case, courts are sloughing off numerous elements of the traditional, rigid standards of conventional "piercing the veil jurisprudence." Thus, compliance by a subsidiary corporation with the customary formalities for the conduct of corporate business, such as separate records, stationery, bank accounts, offices, and the like, and similar indicia of its "real" existence as a separate corporation may not be deemed particularly important. Nor does adequacy of initial capitalization play a decisive role.

In traditional "piercing the veil jurisprudence," the existence of some fraudulent, inequitable, or other "morally culpable" or "fundamentally unfair" conduct detrimental to creditors has been typically viewed as essential for application of the doctrine. Modern cases, even in common law areas, are departing from this requirement in an impressive number of decisions, dramatically expanding the capacity of the legal system to disregard the confining limitations of entity law. In the construction and use of statutes of general application, this development is particularly prominent.

The Supreme Court and Enterprise Principles

The Unitary Tax Cases

One of the outstanding formulations of enterprise principles in American judge-made law is the "unitary business" doctrine developed by the Supreme Court in five decisions from 1980 to 1983.[6] These decisions upheld the constitutionality, under the Due Process and Equal Protection clauses, of state taxation of local components of multinational groups, computed by unitary tax apportionment formulae taking into account the worldwide activities of the group of which the local activities were a constituent part.

The decisions require that the in-state unit and the out-of-state-or-country affiliates included in the apportionment formula base be collectively engaged in the conduct of an integrated "unitary business" and do not represent "discrete" business enterprises. Emphasizing "the underlying economic realities" and the "unity or diversity of the business" as an economic matter, and its operation as "a functionally integrated enterprise," the Court has stressed group involvement in the business of its components. It has required proof of "substantial mutual interdependence" of the components and of the "contributions to income resulting from functional integration, centralization of management and economies of scale."[7]

The formal segregation of functional departments as independent profit centers is irrelevant where the departments are parts of a "highly integrated business which benefits from an umbrella of centralized management and controlled interaction." Such an interrelationship is demonstrated by such features as the availability of "essential corporate services for the entire company, including the coordination of . . . operational functions," the use of "centralized purchasing," or a centralized marketing system involving "[a] uniform credit card system, uniform packaging, brand names and promotional displays." The test of economic integration of the business supersedes the technical legal forms of separate organization or functional administrative divisions.[8]

The doctrine has its restrictions. Thus, in *F.W. Woolworth*, the Court refused to find that the group constituted a unitary business where the foreign subsidiaries autonomously performed such major functions as selection of merchandise, store site selection, advertising, and accounting without any "centralized purchasing, manufacturing, or warehousing" or "central personnel training"; where financing was independent of the parent; where there was no exchange of personnel; and where these subsidiaries had their own accounting, financial staff, and outside counsel. Further, in *ASARCO* the Court held that mere existence of control by the parent is not sufficient; it must be exercised.[9]

Other Leading Decisions Applying Enterprise Principles

In a number of other decisions, the Supreme Court has similarly adopted enterprise principles in dealing with the legal interrelationships of parent and subsidiary corporations. These decisions, rejecting "piercing the veil jurisprudence" and resting squarely on enterprise principles, include such celebrated cases as *Taylor v. Standard Gas & Electric Co.* and *Anderson v. Abbott*, decided in the New Deal Era, and the *Cuban Foreign Trade Bank* case and *Copperweld Corp. v. Independence Tube Co.*, decided recently. All are discussed in the following sections.

TAYLOR V. STANDARD GAS & ELECTRIC CO.

Taylor v. Standard Gas & Electric Co., known also as the *Deep Rock* case, involved the treatment in bankruptcy of the claim of a solvent parent corporation (Standard) in the reorganization proceedings of its subsidiary, Deep Rock Oil. Public preferred stockholders of Deep Rock resisted the Standard claim. They alleged financial and management abuse of the subsidiary to the parent's advantage and relied on "piercing the veil jurisprudence." The lower courts rejected their contentions, holding that the rigorous requirements of the "instrumentality" rule and "piercing the veil jurisprudence" had not been satisfied.

The Supreme Court reversed, holding that reliance on "piercing the veil jurisprudence" was unnecessary. The general equitable principles governing bankruptcy cases controlled. In light of the subsidiary's inadequate capitalization and financial dependence upon the parent, the parent's excessive participation in management, and the parent's utilization of control to manipulate intragroup transactions to its own benefit, the parent's claim was subordinated to the claims of public investors; in the end, the parent received nothing for its claim.[10] Thus, the Court superseded entity law to reach an enterprise result.

ANDERSON V. ABBOTT

Anderson v. Abbott involved the application of the double-assessment shareholder liability provisions of the National Banking Act to the shareholders of a bank holding company owning all the stock of an insolvent national bank. The holding company had been originally organized as part of a recapitalization in which bank shareholders exchanged their bank shares for holding company shares. The lower courts found that the holding company had been organized in good faith, was not a sham, and had not been formed as a means for avoiding statutory liability.

The Court, by a five to four vote, held, nevertheless, that the statutory assessment applied to the holding company shareholders. The Court emphasized that "realities not forms" should control and that failing to hold the provision applicable would defeat the statutory objectives, putting "the policy of double liability at the mercy of corporation finance."[11]

THE *CUBAN FOREIGN TRADE BANK* CASE

The *Cuban Bank* case, *First National City Bank v. Banco Para El Comercio Exterior de Cuba*, involved the legal interrelationship of the government of Cuba and its wholly owned credit bank. First National City Bank, sued by the Cuban bank on a letter of credit, asserted by way of counterclaim its claim against Cuba for expropriation of all its Cuban assets.

Applying American law, Justice O'Connor, speaking for the Court, upheld the counterclaim. She rejected counsel's reliance on entity law and "piercing the veil jurisprudence," warning "against permitting worn epithets to substitute for rigorous analysis." On broad consideration of "equitable policies" similar to disregard of entity where it would "defeat legislative policies," she concluded that the American bank's claim against Cuba, the controlling shareholder, could be offset against the claim of the Cuban Bank. She thus treated the controlled corporation and its controlling shareholder as one for the purpose of the case.[12]

The opinion is an outstanding demonstration of the overriding principle that application of enterprise theory and rejection of entity law should be determined according to the particular considerations presented by the case at bar in the light of the underlying policies and objectives of the law in the area in question. The Court rejected application of the formal conceptualism of "piercing the veil jurisprudence."

COPPERWELD CORP. V. INDEPENDENCE TUBE CO.

In the *Copperweld* case, decided in 1988, the Court was faced with the issue of whether a parent corporation and a wholly owned subsidiary could conspire with respect to anticompetitive practices in violation of Section 1 of the Sherman Antitrust Act. The Court adopted enterprise principles to decide the matter, rejecting the "piercing the veil" analysis that it had employed in earlier decisions when considering aspects of the issue. The Court held that the "coordinated activity of a parent and its wholly owned subsidiary must be viewed as that of a single enterprise." Accordingly, an intragroup conspiracy was impossible because the parent and subsidiary "always have a unity of purpose or common design." The group components were not a joining of different economic interests, and there was "nothing inherently anticompetitive" in their common action. Lower courts have applied the decision also to partly owned subsidiaries when the parent corporation held eighty percent or more of the stock, but have divided where lesser stock ownership was involved.[13]

Statutory Law

As noted, the American legal system, like those of the Western world generally, is grounded on entity law — the view that each corporation is a separate juridical person, even when owned and controlled by another corporation with which it conducts a common business enterprise. However, in an era of multinational corporations, where the economies of the world are closely interlocked and major economic activity is overwhelmingly conducted by centrally controlled corporate groups consisting of scores or even hundreds of affiliated corporations functioning in many different countries, entity law — however accurately it reflected the economic society of the early nineteenth century when it developed — has become hopelessly anachronistic. The entity law concept of the corporate juridical personality no longer matches the economic reality. Legal systems the world over are accordingly struggling with the development of new concepts of corporate personality to deal with this urgent problem. Although this evolution is apparent in all areas of American law, it is most evident in statutory law, where legislatures, courts, and administrative agencies are attempting to transcend the limitations of the corporate entity doctrine in order to achieve effective implementation of regulatory and revenue-raising statutes.

The application of American statutory law to corporate groups provides an even greater demonstration of the acceptance of enterprise principles than the developments in various areas in American common law, procedure, and bankruptcy law. This development in statutory law arises in two quite different contexts.

First, there are the statutes of general application, which prohibit or regulate specified behavior without any particular reference to corporate groups. In cases involving the application of such statutes to corporate groups, the courts (and administrative agencies subject to review by the courts) have the burden of construing and applying the statutes to determine the circumstances under which they should be given an enterprise, rather than an entity, construction. Examples include laws in the areas of antitrust and trade regulation, labor, employment discrimination, employee retirement, the environment, and patent, copyright, and trademark, among others.

Second, there are the statutes of specific application, in which Congress has expressly referred to corporate groups and has itself employed enterprise principles in the formulation of the regulatory program or the tax laws. These include the Bank, Savings and Loan, and Public Utility Holding Company Acts, which rely on enterprise principles to accomplish pervasive, industry-wide regulation. They also include statutory programs that introduce enterprise principles in selected areas while continuing to use entity law in others. These include securities, transportation, communication, foreign economic affairs, foreign investment in the United States, and the Internal Revenue Code.

In the statutes of specific application to corporate groups, Congress has expressly adopted enterprise law, and the burden upon the courts is sharply reduced. These statutory provisions have provided the richest reservoir of utilization of enterprise principles in American law.

Corporate Groups under Statutes of General Application

In the area of statutes of general application, Congress has not expressly addressed the issue of the application of the statute to constituent companies of corporate groups. The text of the statute provides no unmistakable guide, and the courts have the burden of making the fundamental choice between enterprise or entity law in determining the appropriate construction and application. In approaching this task, the American courts have a degree of freedom that is markedly lacking in other countries with different judicial traditions, such as Great Britain.[14]

In dealing with the important responsibility of statutory construction, American courts have used at least three different analytical frameworks. Many courts continue to look at such issues through application of traditional "piercing the veil jurisprudence" as a transcendental doctrine underlying the legal structure as a whole. In so doing, these courts disregard the fact that vital issues of public policy, not private controversies at common law, are concerned. Other courts are increasingly turning from the rigid formalistic analysis of traditional "piercing the veil jurisprudence" and are focusing on the concerns of public policy involved in statutory construction and implementation. They proceed by reliance both on a statutory variant of liberalized piercing the veil and on doctrines of liberal statutory construction. They emphasize the different nature of the responsibility before the court in cases involving corporate groups and controlling shareholders under statutory law.

The courts that abandon the rigid formalistic analysis of traditional "piercing the veil jurisprudence" focus on the concerns of public policy involved in statutory construction and implementation. Courts are increasingly recognizing that the construction of public policy statutes should not be governed by principles of entity law developed for the solution of private-law controversies involving such issues as contracts, torts, or property. The construction of federal statutes is a federal question for which state doctrines of entity law and "piercing the veil jurisprudence" are providing less and less guidance. Instead, federal courts increasingly construe the text of the statute in the light of the history and experience of the statutory program and the underlying objectives and policies of the law. Even where the court utilizes "piercing the veil jurisprudence," the doctrine is reformulated into a different and less demanding standard than that for private law purposes. An overriding concern with implementing the statutory program, preventing its frustration, and barring evasion and avoidance by corporate restructuring plays a decisive role. In consequence, the cardinal element of "piercing the veil jurisprudence" in private matters requiring proof of wrongful or inequitable conduct is brushed aside as irrelevant in cases of public law.[15]

In order better to pursue such matters, courts that are refusing to be bound by the rigid limits of traditional "piercing the veil jurisprudence" also are typically evaluating factors relative to the economic realities of the enterprise involved in the litigation. This includes the already noted supplemental factors such as the extent of exercise of "control" by the parent corporation or group; economic integration;

financial and administrative interdependence; overlapping group employment structure; and use of a common group public persona. In such an evaluation, the theoretical desirability of application of enterprise principles or retention of entity law and limited liability for group component companies will necessarily differ from statutory area to statutory area, as the underlying legal objectives and policies vary.

The unsuitability of traditional "piercing the veil jurisprudence" for statutory problems should be evident. Determination of the scope and application of general-application statutory law manifestly involves very different values, interests, and policies. The courts should be concerned with matters of public policy and interest far removed from the values and interests involved in common law controversies between private parties. Jurisprudential doctrines developed in litigation at common law between private individuals, which rely on matters of corporate form and such considerations as the existence of conduct unfair to creditors, should not constitute a barrier to reliance on enterprise principles in construing the scope of statutes.

Entity law that insulates a parent corporation from the regulatory obligations imposed on its subsidiaries and that permits parent corporations to sidestep regulatory obligations through the device of organizing subsidiary corporations presents serious dangers for the effective implementation of the statutory program, manifestly creates a high risk of frustration of the statutory objectives, and opens avenues for evasion and avoidance. Since the 1930s, American courts and administrative agencies have, accordingly, struggled to formulate new legal concepts to overcome such limitations of entity law. They have done so through the utilization of enterprise principles, notwithstanding the lack of any express reference in the statute. In this way, they apply the statutory regulatory program not only to the subsidiary corporation directly conducting the activity covered by the statute, but also to its parent corporation (or controlling shareholders), and in some cases, to its affiliated corporations as well. They have done so notwithstanding the rigid limitations of traditional "piercing the veil jurisprudence."[16]

In some cases, liberalized "piercing the veil jurisprudence" serves as the basis for an enterprise application of a statutory program to the corporate group involved in the case at hand. In others, it co-exists with, or merges almost imperceptibly into, a "liberal" or "broad" construction of the statutory provision, utilizing normal principles of statutory construction to apply to the parent and sometimes also to the other group components, as well as to the particular subsidiary involved.

Such liberal statutory construction reflects an increasing recognition of the economic reality that regulatory statutes concerned with business activity will often require application in major respects to corporations that are members of a corporate group engaged in the common conduct of fragments of an integrated business under central coordinated direction. In the light of such recognition, courts are led to delineate the outer reach of statutes in the light of the purposes and policies of the act. They also must explore the nature of the legislative response to the social or economic problems at which the statute is directed. The text is to be read in the context of the full historical background. In recent decades, American courts have so construed statutes in a manner that will best implement the statutory objectives, avoid frustration of the statutory program, and prevent evasion or avoidance. However, very recent Supreme Court decisions in other contexts indicate that the Court in the future may revert to more literal applications of the statutory text.[17]

Corporate Groups under Statutes of Specific Application

In other regulatory statutes, Congress has responded in a more sophisticated manner to the limitations of entity law and has specifically attempted to transcend its limitations. Such statutes are expressly made applicable not only to corporations conducting the activity being regulated, but also to other corporations in the groups of which the corporations in question are components. These statutes may be termed statutes of specific application.

The specific-application statutes fall into two groups. The first group (the pervasive statutes) includes regulatory statutes that use enterprise principles as the technique for the pervasive regulation of a few key industries. These include such statutes as the Bank Holding Company Act, the Savings and Loan Holding Company Act, and the Public Utility Holding Company Act. In these statutes, the statutory focus is on the group. Among other aspects of the pervasive nature of these regulatory programs, the statutes regulate entry into the market and the scope of the enterprise. To accomplish such objectives, these statutes inevitably are concerned with the group as a whole. Enterprise law underlies the entire statute.

Statutes of specific application include a second group as well. This group (the selective statutes) expressly uses enterprise principles for selected areas of a regulatory or revenue program, while relying on entity law in most other respects. Examples include statutes regulating railroads and trucking, air transportation, shipping, communications, and securities. None of these statutes deals with such matters as the scope of the enterprise. Aside from the transportation industries, these programs similarly do not restrict entry into the market. Unlike the pervasive statutes, the selective statutes focus on the regulated company rather than on any group of which it is a part. They are not concerned with group affairs, except in a number of selected areas in which regulation of the activities of the regulated company are expressly made applicable to other companies within the group as well.

Although most of the selective specific-application statutes are regulatory statutes, the class also includes the Internal Revenue Code, which is primarily concerned with raising revenue and not with regulation. With very different objectives than the regulatory statutes, the provisions of the Code deal directly with the problems presented by the component companies of corporate groups (along with other related taxpayers), in the implementation, and prevention of evasion, of the tax laws.

All the specific-application statutes attempt to supersede the entity law concept of the separate juridical personality of each corporation by introducing—in one form or another—enterprise principles to expand the statutory coverage. They include interrelated corporations in the areas where such inclusion is deemed essential for effective implementation of the statutory program. This presents the fundamental problem of definition: How is the corporate group or enterprise to be defined in order to include the component corporations of the group under the statute in issue?

It should be evident that any such definition of the corporate group or enterprise must be carefully tailored to the particular objectives of the statute in question in order to serve those objectives most effectively. In the tax laws, for example, statutory provisions extending tax benefits to a selected class of taxpayers must be drafted very restrictively to confine the benefits to the interests intended. By contrast, those provisions in the tax laws intended to impose tax obligations or to prevent evasion of tax obligations must be drafted very expansively to achieve the impact desired. To ignore the implications of different statutory objectives in order to develop a transcendental concept of enterprise law or universal definition of the corporate group to be applied throughout the legal system would be an error of the first magnitude.[18]

Definitional standards must not only be realistic in terms of the activity or industry being regulated; they must effectively implement the particular objectives of the statutory program in question. Regulatory programs differ manifestly from each other. They differ in the underlying problems with which they contend and in the statutory objectives. This reflects such factors, among others, as the nature of the industries being regulated, their characteristic structural and operational features, their impact on the economy and the society, and the perceived abuses of unregulated activity.

With differing underlying problems and differing statutory objectives, the scope of the regulatory program and the standard for definition of the group will also differ. As a result, with the uniform application of a transcendental concept of enterprise patently unworkable, the American statutory experience reflecting such considerations has produced a rich variety of alternative definitional standards developed to serve varying statutory objectives.

Save in isolated cases,[19] American law employs the concept of "control" as the decisive unifying factor for defining the "enterprise" or the group for the purpose of determining the scope of American specific-application statutes. As reviewed in Chapter 7, European statutes of specific application do the same. However, while "control" is the near universal standard for defining "enterprise," the formulation of the term differs to a surprising degree in the various specific-application statutes. These differences in part reflect the basic variations in the statutes, but they would also appear to reflect less than meticulous drafting. Such dramatic differences in formulation present an important problem in comparative law, which thus far has been almost entirely neglected in the literature.

The concept of "control," which is the essential feature of the corporate group, has deep historical roots in American corporate law. From the early nineteenth century, courts and the profession have utilized the term to refer to the power of the majority at the annual shareholder meeting to elect the board of directors and direct the affairs of the corporation. Originally employed with respect to corporations controlled by individual shareholders, it was immediately applied to corporate groups when they emerged.[20]

As explored in the following section, "control" (in some cases broadened by a supplementary reference to "controlling influence") has been the standard used by American statutory and administrative law, almost to the exclusion of other standards, for the imposition of enterprise principles both in regulatory and revenue statutes. European jurisdictions similarly employ the term "control" or variants such as "controlling influence," "dominant influence," or "decisive influence," as the linchpins of enterprise regulation, to the virtual exclusion of other standards.

Whatever problems with respect to the application of the concept of "control" in other contexts,[21] questions as to the existence of "control" within the corporate groups almost never arise. Most subsidiary corporations in corporate groups are wholly owned. Even where they are not, their identification with the group and the conduct of their operations under its central direction leaves little doubt as to the existence of control.

What, then, are the various definitions of "control" in the specific-application statutes and what factors appear to lead to the selection of one formulation over another?

THE CONCEPT OF "CONTROL"

In approaching the crucial problem of defining the enterprise subject to the regulatory program through the concept of "control," two guiding rules would appear appropriate. First, the statutory formulation should effectively implement the objectives of the particular governmental regulatory program under consideration. Second, the formulation should adequately respond to the special features of the economic and corporate organization of the industry being regulated.

By reason of these fundamental factors, at least in part, the definitions of "control" used in the statutes present clearly discernable patterns. The regulatory statutes and the revenue statutes adopt very different approaches. Similarly, the pervasive regulatory statutes and the selective regulatory statutes, although much more closely allied in their approach, also adopt somewhat different definitional patterns.

Pervasive Statutes Focusing on the Group. In the specific-application statutes undertaking pervasive industry-wide regulation, the statutory focus is on the group. The pervasive statutes—the Bank Holding Company, Savings and Loan Holding Company, and Public Utility Holding Company Acts—employ two unique factors that distinguish their definitional approach from those of the selective statutes:

1. They supplement the standard of "control," which is defined in much the same manner as in many selective statutes, with an alternative, less demanding standard of "controlling influence"; and
2. They include a statutory presumption of "control" arising from ownership or control of a specified percentage of the voting securities. The Bank Holding Company Act, the Savings and Loan Holding Company Act, and the Investment Company Act of 1940 employ a presumption arising from twenty-five percent stock ownership or control. The Public Utility Holding Company Act is unique in utilizing ten percent as the standard. Illustrative of the drafting pattern of these statutes is the relevant provision from Section 2(a)(7) of the Public Utility Holding Company Act. It generally defines a holding company to include "any company which directly or indirectly owns, controls, or holds with power to vote 10 percentum or more of the outstanding voting securities" as well as any person able "directly or indirectly to exercise (either alone or pursuant to an arrangement or understanding with one or more other persons) . . . a controlling influence over . . . management or policies."[22]

In addition, the pervasive statutes, like many of the selective statutes, supplement their definition of "control" to sweep under their regulatory programs not simply the parent or subsidiaries of the regulated company, but their sister subsidiaries in the group as well. The pervasive and many selective statutes expand the scope of coverage of the statutory program to include not only the company being regulated, but every other company "controlling, controlled by, or under common control with" the regulated company—in short, the entire group.

The common features evidenced by the three holding company statutes reflect a statutory focus on the totality of operations of the group.[23] This reflects statutory objectives of high priority. One such priority is concern about the scope of the *permissible* activities of the group, that is, the permissible scope of the business enterprise which it conducts. Such an emphasis may arise from quite different causes. In the case of the Bank Holding Company and Savings and Loan Holding Company Acts, which deal with depository institutions, it reflects a concern that the lack of stability and financial soundness of one subsidiary depository institution may affect the stability and soundness of others. In the Public Utility Holding Company Act, it stems from a legislative objective to simplify the corporate structure of the industry and to achieve geographically integrated utility systems.

Whatever the particular concern, each leads to the same pressure to focus on the industry structure and on the groups that conduct it rather than simply on the regulated company and its activities. This common focal point explains the common definitional standards of the statutes and the elements distinguishing them from the definitional standards in the selective statutes.

Selective Statutes Focusing on the Regulated Company. Other industry-wide statutory programs, notably those regulating railroads and trucking, air transportation, shipping, communications, and securities, focus on the regulated company or activity, not on the group. Although dealing in a far-reaching manner with the problems of a particular industry, these statutes are typically not concerned with the scope of the enterprises of which the regulated companies are part, but deal primarily with the particular regulated company. They are more concerned with important public issues as access to the market and the prices and operations of the regulated company as they affect consumers, employees, and the communities in which they operate.

Although the selective statutes do not focus on groups, the fact that large American corporations typically operate as members of corporate groups requires the statutes, nevertheless, to regulate selected areas involving the relationship of the regulated company to its affiliated corporations and its group. Thus, the selective statutes typically deal with such matters as the acquisition of "control" of a company, in order to regulate access to the market; intragroup transactions to which the regulated company is a party, in order adequately to regulate pricing and return; and the establishment of accounting and reporting controls over the group as a whole, so as to obtain full disclosure of intragroup relationships. However, none of these statutes is concerned with the scope of the enterprise.

Accordingly, although selective statutes also utilize the concept of "control" to deal with these matters, the statutory formulation of the term takes a different form. They do not refer to a specified percentage of stock ownership as giving rise to a presumption of the existence of "control," as in the pervasive statutes, or (except in some statutes restricting foreign ownership of American enterprise) to a specified percentage of stock ownership as an absolute objective standard, as in the revenue statutes. Instead, these statutes in some cases rely on a general functional definition relating to control over corporate decision-making; in other cases they merely specify the term, "control" without further amplification, delegating detailed formulation to administrative determination on a case-by-case basis. They do so to avoid having a fixed definition serve as a blueprint for avoidance of the statutory program.

Unlike the pervasive statutes, the selective acts do not contain or use the term "controlling influence." However, the omission has not narrowed the scope of the statutory application to corporate groups.

In determining the existence of "control," administrative agencies play a role of major importance. In *Rochester Telephone Corp. v. United States*, the Supreme Court long ago gave "control" an expansive meaning, holding that "control" was a "practical concept . . . to be determined by a regard for the actualities of intercorporate relationships" and "to encompass every type of control in fact." In applying this conception, the Court firmly recognized the primary role of the administrative agencies. It held that an agency's determination of the existence of "control" was a determination of fact and was conclusive, if supported by the record.[24]

As in the case of the pervasive statutes, the selective statutes typically, but not universally, use "control" to extend the scope of their regulatory programs not merely to the parent or other party in control of the regulated company, but to the constituent corporations of the group as a whole. American law accomplishes this through use of the familiar formulation imposing the program, not merely on the regulated company, but on all companies "controlling, controlled by, or under common control with" the regulated company. However, unlike the pervasive statutes, the selective statutes apply to the group as a whole only for limited purposes in carefully delineated areas.

Revenue Statutes. The revenue statutes differ sharply from regulatory statutes in their approach. Whatever the objective underlying a particular provision, the Internal Revenue Code (the Code) is, with unimportant exceptions, concerned only with revenue matters: the imposition of tax, the creation of exemptions or other special treatment with respect to taxes, and the prevention of evasion and avoidance of taxes. Effective implementation of these objectives in a world of corporate groups necessarily requires numerous provisions dealing with the many problems presented by the economic interrelationship of corporate groups and their components, and of other related parties.

In a revenue-raising system resting on returns filed by taxpayers, it is essential that the tax statute be, to the extent possible, comprehensible and capable of ready application. Although in many respects, as every American taxpayer knows, the Code utterly fails to achieve this objective, nevertheless, this aspiration has apparently been one of the factors shaping the drafting of the provisions dealing with corporate groups. The definitions utilized thus clearly reflect a perceived need for clarity and ease of application.

Although the details of formulations differ sharply, the various statutory definitions employed by the Code, like those of the regulatory statutes, overwhelmingly utilize the language of "control." However, the Code has a very different definition of the term from that found in the regulatory statutes. Instead of the general, functional definitions of "control" typically used by the specific-application regulatory statutes, or the presumptions utilized by the pervasive-application statutes, the tax provisions, with isolated exceptions, rely solely on numerical benchmarks of stock ownership, which serve as absolute objective standards.

In fact, although the Code consistently uses the term "control," this use in many cases is a misnomer. In the regulatory area, "control" is in all cases a term of art referring to the capacity to determine, or in some cases influence, the decision-making of another company. In the tax laws, it is never more than a term of drafting convenience, without intrinsic meaning of its own. It is a merely a statutory drafting device incorporating by reference an absolute, objective standard consisting of the particular numerical benchmark of stock ownership specified in the section. In many cases, this benchmark includes ownership of stock without voting rights and is, therefore, unmistakably not primarily concerned with "control" over the decision-making.

The various sections of the Code use many different numerical benchmarks of "control." In fact, the Code contains no less than nine major definitional models. As if this bewildering multiplicity was not confusing enough, each of those models includes variations in its application, thereby creating additional subvariations as well.

The statutory benchmarks of "control" in the Code range from "at least 50 percent" or "50 percent or more" to "more than 50 percent" and "at least 80 percent." Sometimes, the benchmarks are applied to "voting stock." In other instances, they go beyond voting shares and refer to the "total value of all the stock" or "the total number" of shares.[25]

Accordingly, the revenue statutes present a sharp contrast to the regulatory statutes in this respect. The striking aspect of the Code is that it relies almost exclusively on absolute, objective numerical benchmarks. Only in a few isolated sections does the Code use a general functional test of the broad, expansive nature comparable to the standards customarily employed in the specific-application regulatory statutes. The principal section of the Code proceeding in this manner, Section 482, is one of the major weapons the Internal Revenue Service uses in dealing with tax manipulation in transactions between parties under common control, and it is highly appropriate for the Code to depart from reliance on numerical benchmarks in such a provision.[26] The other two instances are relatively unimportant.

It is quite clear that the statutory drafting reflects an overriding priority for clarity in order to facilitate business planning and tax reporting. Where there are exceptions, as in the area of tax manipulation attacked by Section 482, the parties seeking to evade tax liabilities are hardly in a position to complain of any lack of clarity in the application of the broadly worded provision.

In summary, the utilization of "control" for tax purposes is a very different matter from the use of the concept in the specific-application regulatory statutes. Although its inclusion in this review is essential for a complete understanding of the American statutory scheme, it provides few lessons when considering the problems in the definition of "control" for purposes of imposing enterprise principles in other areas of the law.

Standards Other than "Control." In addition to definitions resting on "control," the statutory law experience offers isolated examples of other techniques for defining the corporate group for the purposes of applying enterprise principles. Such alternative approaches are provided by the handful of doctrines turning not simply on "control," but on the integration of operations of the affiliated corporations.

The most innovative development is the "integrated enterprise" standard for imposition of liability on parent corporations or controlling shareholders for statutory violations of their subsidiaries or of controlled corporations under the Age Discrimination Amendments Act of 1984. This standard consists of four factors: (a) interrelation of operations; (b) centralized control of labor relations; (c) common management; and (d) common ownership or financial control.

The statute codifies the long-established standard of the National Labor Relations Board (NLRB) for determination of a "single employer" for resolution of certain labor relations matters under the National Labor Relations Act (a general-application statute).[27] The courts have also applied the standard in numerous decisions in related areas, such as wage and hours laws and antidiscrimination in employment.

Isolated provisions of the regulations under the Internal Revenue Code provide the other example of the utilization of "integrated enterprise" under American statutory law.[28] Both standards resemble in some respects the "unitary business" doctrine developed by the Supreme Court in testing the constitutionality of state taxation, which was discussed previously.

Although the two "integrated enterprise" standards in the statutory law are of considerable conceptual interest as much more sophisticated standards than "control," they have limited significance outside of the immediate areas in which they have been employed. The "integrated enterprise" standard in the labor, employment, and antidiscrimination laws has no application outside the labor area. Further, it has limited usefulness as a theoretical model of enterprise law because it is primarily concerned with the labor operations of the group and ignores all other dimensions of the enterprise. Similarly, the "integrated enterprise" standard under the Internal Revenue Code is used only in obscure sections for very restricted purposes and is manifestly unsuitable for wider application. However, although these alternative approaches are not particularly helpful, their identification of integration of operations as the decisive factor for imposition of group liability in the areas to which they do apply is a helpful analogue, supporting the judicial decisions employing this consideration as one of the key elements making for judicial utilization of enterprise principles in other areas.

Summary. The specific-application regulatory statutes provide extensive guidance on the nature of "control" over corporate decision-making through their examples of alternative models of defining "control." Although they offer a surprising number of different formulations of "control," the fact of the matter is that the formulations strongly resemble each other, and these differences would appear to relate only to relatively infrequent, marginal cases.

In evaluating the numerous, not dissimilar statutory model provisions available, American scholars are fortunate that the very same ground has already been explored in the preparation of the Federal Securities Code by a distinguished group of judges, scholars, and practitioners led by the nation's senior scholar in the area, Professor Louis Loss.[29] Section 202(29) of the Securities Code defines "control" as follows:

> (a) "Control" means the power, directly or indirectly, to exercise a controlling influence over the management and policies of a company . . . (either alone or pursuant to an arrangement or understanding with one or more other persons), whether through the ownership of voting securities, through one or more intermediary persons, by contract, or otherwise.
>
> (b) (1) A person who (either alone or pursuant to an arrangement or understanding with one or more other persons) owns or has the power to vote more than 25 percent of the outstanding voting securities . . . is presumed to control.
>
> . . .
>
> (4) Any such presumption may be rebutted by evidence.[30]

This definition, including use of the more expansive term "controlling influence" and a presumption arising from ownership of twenty-five percent of voting securities, substantially follows the model provided by the pervasive statutes. In the light of the decades of judicial and administrative experience in applying these terms, the tautological nature of the definition does not, in fact, impair its usefulness. "Control" and "controlling influence" may present some ambiguities in some contexts, but not in the case of corporate groups where the very existence of the group testifies to the reality of "control."

The utilization of a twenty-five percent benchmark as a rebuttable presumption of control accurately reflects the reality of the American corporate world. In the large public corporation, with its stock widely distributed among tens, hundreds, or tens of thousands of shareholders,[31] stock ownership in an amount much less than the mathematical certainty of a majority of the voting shares will suffice for "working control." Where there is no other block of shares of comparable size, holdings of even less than twenty-five percent will normally mean working control.[32] The Code reflects this reality, thereby simplifying problems of proof while preserving, on the one hand, the opportunity to rebut the presumption in those exceptional cases where this might be possible, and, on the other hand, the opportunity to establish the existence of control resting on ownership of even less than twenty-five percent stock ownership.

The American statutory experience further underscores the usefulness of supplementing such a definition of "control" — including its supporting elements, "controlling influence" and a presumption resting on a numerical benchmark of stock ownership — with the familiar formulation in American specific-application statutory law under which the scope of the statutory regulatory program is expanded to include not only the group component conducting the regulated activity in question, but also any person "directly or indirectly controlling, or controlled by, or under direct or indirect common control with" the group component in question.[33]

When, however, one turns from specific-application regulatory statutes to other areas of the law where Congress or a legislature has not provided the definitional answer, the problem of the application of enterprise law is very different indeed. It becomes a judicial, rather than a legislative, question. The problem is no longer the relatively simple issue of draftsmanship of the appropriate statutory provision; it is the much more complex one of the development of standards to guide courts in the determination of the application of enterprise principles to the decision of a case at hand in the light of the objectives of the law in the area in question.

As noted, the courts must then determine two fundamental issues. First, they must decide whether the adoption of enterprise principles or the retention of traditional concepts of entity law best serves the underlying purposes and objectives of the particular legal area under consideration. Second, if they determine that enterprise principles should prevail at least in some cases, they must then deal with the fundamental problem of deciding when the relationship between affiliated corporations is so intertwined that the application of those principles is appropriate. They must define the standard for application of enterprise law. Although such an undertaking could be avoided by providing for the application of enterprise law in every parent-subsidiary relationship, such a far-reaching step, even if deemed desirable, is clearly not feasible at the present stage of American law.

The modern American experience in the formulation of concepts of enterprise for purposes of construing and applying general-application statutes and in common law areas, particularly torts, is beginning to provide an answer to this definitional problem. As noted, this development focuses not merely on "control," but on such aspects of the economic contours of the group as its extent of economic integration, financial and administrative interdependence, overlapping employee policies, and use of a common public persona.

Closely related to all three of the preceding categories of enterprise law — common law controversies, statutes of general application, and statutes of specific application — are the legal problems of parent and subsidiary corporations in the fields of judicial procedure and bankruptcy. In these areas, the problem represents an amalgam of judicial doctrines and statutes that introduces varying elements of the foregoing categories.

Judicial Procedure

Enterprise concepts have made considerable inroads in American judicial procedure, although as elsewhere, entity law generally prevails. In some areas, such as the assertion of jurisdiction and the accompanying problems of service and venue, the contest between the conflicting doctrines is at its most controversial. In this area, the law had been dominated for decades by the 1925 Supreme Court decision in *Cannon Mfg. Co.* enshrining entity law and formalistic analysis as the governing standards.[34] However, the *Cannon* doctrine is undergoing continuing erosion. Even those courts prepared to follow *Cannon* generally will apply enterprise standards in jurisdictional matters where the parent exercises day-to-day control over the subsidiary. Other courts have gone further and have held *Cannon* obsolete in light of the Court's subsequent decision in *International Shoe Co. v.*

Washington,[35] which established "minimum contacts" with the forum as a constitutional standard for assertion of jurisdiction. In antitrust litigation, in particular, enterprise concepts have found their widest acceptance in expanding jurisdictional concepts. In the special area of products liability, the "stream of commerce" doctrine has provided an independent route for assertion of jurisdiction and has made the debate over enterprise and entity essentially irrelevant. Jurisdiction continues to be one of the most litigated areas involving the clash of enterprise and entity.

In a number of other procedural areas, "control" is the decisive consideration, and this has led to full acceptance of enterprise principles. This is evident in res judicata and collateral estoppel, statute of limitations, and discovery. Other procedural areas in which enterprise notions have been accepted include the scope of injunctions. In a number of these areas, including statute of limitations, discovery, and injunctions, the Federal Rules of Civil Procedure have codified prior judicial decisions adopting enterprise approaches.[36] In all these areas, "control" is the decisive factor in the attribution of legal responsibilities (and in the cases of res judicata and collateral estoppel, the attribution of legal rights as well) from one group constituent to another.

Entity law, however, generally still prevails in such other areas as counterclaim, set-off, and joinder.

Bankruptcy

American bankruptcy law, too, has moved to increasing acceptance of enterprise law in a number of areas. These include equitable subordination, voidable preferences, and, to some degree, substantive consolidation. Although entity continues to prevail elsewhere in bankruptcy law, there are signs of change, particularly in such areas as fraudulent transfers and jurisdiction. In significant measure, these developments reflect the increasing role of financial interdependence in affiliated companies with group financing and group cross-guaranties. Doctrines in different areas of bankruptcy law have been evolving to deal with the special problems presented by intertwined financial interests. Although these developments fundamentally rest on enterprise principles, the courts, thus far, have not recognized their common conceptual foundation.

Equitable subordination of the claims of a parent corporation or sister subsidiary to the claims of general unsecured creditors in the bankruptcy of a subsidiary corporation provides an outstanding example of the movement of the law. In four landmark decisions, the Supreme Court rejected the standards of traditional "piercing the veil jurisprudence" and enunciated new standards for evaluating intragroup claims and those of other corporate insiders. In place of entity law and "piercing the veil" as the governing standards, intragroup claims now are subject to special scrutiny and are evaluated according to equitable principles governing conduct by fiduciaries. The parent corporation or other insider must demonstrate not only the fairness of the intercompany transaction giving rise to the claim, but the fairness of its other interrelationships with the subsidiary (or controlled corporation) as well. This was no less than a conceptional revolution.[37]

Section 547 of the Bankruptcy Code fully employs enterprise principles in dealing with voidable preferences. Under that section, subject to certain limitations, any transfer of property by an insolvent debtor to or for the benefit of a creditor that is an "insider" is voidable if the transfer is made within one year of bankruptcy. The statute defines "insider" to include any "person in control" or an "affiliate." It defines "affiliate" to include persons owning or controlling twenty percent or more of the voting securities of the debtor (that is, a parent); or any corporation with twenty percent or more of its voting securities directly or indirectly owned or controlled either by the debtor (that is, a subsidiary) or by an entity that directly or indirectly owns or controls twenty percent of the voting securities of the debtor (sister subsidiary).[38]

Substantive consolidation, a judicial doctrine with no counterpart in the Bankruptcy Code, is still another area receiving considerable development of enterprise principles. In substantive consolidation, the bankruptcy proceedings of interrelated companies are consolidated and administered jointly, with assets and liabilities of the affiliated debtors pooled and all intercompany claims and guaranties eliminated, insofar as unsecured creditors are concerned. It is comparable to the Continental concept of extension of bankruptcy. A number of courts have noted that the development of the substantive consolidation doctrine is a response to the "prevalence" of parent and subsidiary corporations and the rise of multitiered corporate enterprises.[39]

Among the factors leading to such consolidation are the nature of creditor expectations; significant economic integration; intragroup financing and guaranties; difficulty in segregating and ascertaining individual assets and liabilities; commingling of assets and intercompany transfers; and implementation of the administration, and increasing the feasibility of reorganization, of the debtors. Although injury to individual creditors from consolidation is recognized, it is, nevertheless, proper if creditors as a whole are benefited.

The Different Faces of Enterprise Law

Enterprise law, thus, consists of four quite different classes of situations:

1. Common law jurisprudence involving private controversies, where enterprise law rests on two factors. First is the nature of the group interrelationship, consisting of the intertwined structure and operations — including the significant exercise of control — together with economic integration, administrative and financial interdependence, intertwined personnel policies, and group persona. The other is an evaluation of the significance of the adoption of enterprise principles for implementation of the objectives of the law in the legal area involved;

2. Judicial construction of statutes of general application, where enterprise law rests on a somewhat lesser showing of such group interrelationship and on an evaluation of the significance of the adoption of enterprise principles for implementation and prevention of frustration of the objectives of the statute.

3. Statutes of specific application to corporate groups, where "control," and "control" alone, is almost invariably the crucial statutory standard.

4. Judicial decisions in the fields of judicial procedure and bankruptcy. These areas are amalgams of judicial doctrines and statutory codifications. In procedure, the standards employed reflect the particular procedural doctrine at issue, ranging from primary emphasis on "control" in res judicata, collateral estoppel, discovery, and scope of injunctions to much more complex standards in such areas as jurisdiction. In certain areas of bankruptcy, the courts are reaching enterprise results through application of the historic standards of equity jurisprudence in the

light of the economic realities of the group debtors before the court.

Enterprise law thus reflects very different considerations as the nature of the fundamental jurisprudential problem before the court changes. In the statutes of specific application, the basic decision with respect to the application of enterprise law has been made by Congress or a legislature; the courts have only the lesser role of determining its precise application. In common law controversies between private parties and in the construction of statutes of general application, the courts have the basic decision of choosing between entity and enterprise law. In discharging this demanding responsibility, their decisions are strongly influenced by the differing policies and objectives of the law in the common law area and the interrelationship between the outcome of the decision and statutory implementation, or frustration or evasion of the statute, in the case of statutes of general application. In consequence, enterprise principles take on different content in the various areas, and it is foolish to expect that any consistent or transcendental body of jurisprudence will emerge. The choice between enterprise principles and entity law will reflect the values and interests at stake and the fundamental nature of the choice to be made by the court in the case at hand. Decisions applying enterprise principles will vary as the nature of the problem and local perceptions of the jurisprudential problem changes. Enterprise law will necessarily be untidy and inconsistent.

Although entity law and its corollaries — limited liability and "piercing the veil jurisprudence" — are unquestionably still the foundation of American corporate law, the challenge presented by corporate groups to the legal system has resulted in the widespread adoption of principles of enterprise law in many disparate areas. Where implementation of the underlying legal policies and objectives in the particular area so requires, legislatures, administrative agencies, and the courts are increasingly ready to depart from entity law and apply enterprise principles in cases involving component companies of corporate groups. These developments over the past sixty years have reached the stage where they must be recognized as having created a new jurisprudence of their own: the American law of corporate groups.

6

Economic Dimensions:
The Role of Limited Liability

Under traditional doctrines of entity law, the concept of the separate personality of the corporation insulates the legal consequences of the actions of one related party, such as a subsidiary corporation (or controlled corporation) from being attributed to its parent corporation (or controlling shareholders). In a significant number of cases, these legal consequences relate to matters of procedure, nonmonetary duties, or restrictions on behavior under statutory law. In these areas, consideration of the application of enterprise principles to supersede traditional entity law does not involve the determination of liability, and the doctrine of limited liability plays no role in the choice between enterprise and entity law. Utilization of entity law in such cases rests solely on the traditional concept of the separate corporate personality.

In many other areas, however, the legal consequences of enterprise principles do directly involve the imposition of liability upon one or more constituent corporations of a group for the obligations of another constituent corporation. In those cases, the use of enterprise principles involves not only the abandonment of traditional principles of entity law but also the repudiation of limited liability. The focus is no longer purely conceptual; it involves issues of profound economic importance.

Although there is no sign of political interest in reconsidering the principle of limited liability as the governing general rule, the doctrine has attracted considerable academic attention. In the last two decades, a virtual flood of scholarly inquiries has examined the economics of limited liability and its role in modern finance capitalism.[1] Accordingly, any review of enterprise principles and the jurisprudential nature of the corporate group would be less than complete without at least a summary discussion of the relationship of such commentary to the doctrine of limited liability.

The earlier chapters of this volume have traced the early development of the doctrine of the separate personality of the corporation and the much later acceptance of the doctrine of limited liability. Historically, it is clear that commercial and manufacturing corporations and entity law co-existed and flourished in many jurisdictions for decades before the acceptance of limited liability. These jurisdictions included Massachusetts until 1830, Rhode Island until 1847, California until 1931, and England until 1855.

As limited liability began to be accepted, the United States presented a striking phenomenon: some states continued to function with unlimited shareholder liability, while adjoining states were operating simultaneously under systems of limited liability. However, it does not appear that the level of economic development in the jurisdictions with unlimited liability was significantly affected by the co-existence of vitally different legal rules in adjoining jurisdictions. Although the specter of capital fleeing the jurisdiction was held out during the political struggle over the adoption of limited liability, there is no indication that it had in fact happened.[2]

Thus, although Rhode Island for seventeen years, from 1830 to 1847, was the *only* state in New England with unlimited liability, it continued as a center of manufacturing activity, second only to Massachusetts. Further, with the example of Rhode Island before it, New Hampshire, after adopting de facto limited liability in 1816, reversed course and reverted to unlimited liability in 1842 for several years. Similarly, California persisted in pro rata shareholder liability until well into the twentieth century, long after every other state had adopted limited liability.

Along with these illustrations, history provides still another example that has been largely ignored in the current discussions of limited liability: the predominance for many decades of double or triple shareholder liability in the great majority of the states throughout the nineteenth, and well into the twentieth, centuries, before finally disappearing after World War I. Thus, it may fairly be said that the

U.S. economy did not fully operate under limited liability until well into the twentieth century.

Along with entity law, the doctrine of limited liability of shareholders characterizes the corporation law of all Western nations. Limited liability very strongly reinforces the concepts of the separate corporate personality and entity law. Although it is not a necessary theoretical consequence of the entity doctrine, it is manifestly an important factor to be taken into account in weighing the desirability of using principles of enterprise law.

Limited Liability for Whom: Public Shareholders or Constituent Companies of the Group?

The application of enterprise principles rests on two major factors. One is the "control" of the parent corporation over the constituent companies of the group and the collective conduct of a common enterprise under its central direction. The second is the economic integration of the business of the group. Shareholders of the parent who are not part of the control group present neither of these two factors. As previously noted, except for *Anderson* applying a federal double assessment statute dealing with national banks, there does not appear to be any case in American or English law that has used enterprise principles to impose liability on the *public* shareholders of a group's parent corporation. Similarly, when courts impose liability under enterprise principles on the parent corporation (or controlling shareholder) of *partly owned* subsidiaries (or controlled corporations), they impose *one hundred percent* of the liability on the controlling shareholder, notwithstanding its lesser share of the stock of the subsidiary.

Thus, at the outset, it should be understood that utilization of enterprise law relates solely to the elimination of limited liability *within* the group. Enterprise law does not affect—directly or indirectly—the existing protection of limited liability that insulates the public shareholders of the parent company or minority-owned subsidiaries from group liabilities. This volume, focusing on the role of enterprise principles in the law of corporate groups, is concerned with limited liability only to the extent that the commentary throws some light on the relationship of the doctrine to the consideration of the imposition of intragroup liability. It assumes a continuation, without change, of the general doctrine for shareholders generally.

The surprisingly extensive economic literature on limited liability that has emerged in recent decades has two major limitations. First, in a world in which major economic activity is conducted by corporate groups, the discussion is overwhelmingly concerned with limited liability for shareholders generally, ignoring the very different problems presented by corporate groups. Only a few of the contributions recognize the crucial distinction between the public shareholders of the parent corporation and the parent and subholding companies of a corporate group in their role as shareholders of the lower-tier group companies.

Because the parent has "control" and typically conducts an economically integrated common business collectively with its subsidiaries, many of the contentions advanced by the economists with respect to the efficiency of limited liability for public shareholders do not apply within the corporate group. As a result, much, in fact the greater part, of the theoretical commentary is irrelevant.

Second, with isolated exceptions, the discussion typically ignores the extensive historical data available from the operation of corporations in jurisdictions prior to the adoption of limited liability. Thus, in several jurisdictions, of which California until 1930 is the leading example, unlimited liability meant pro rata liability for shareholders. Much of the theoretical discussion has erroneously assumed that unlimited liability necessarily means joint and several liability, as was the rule in England until 1855. This is unfortunate, because joint and several liability presents difficulties that simply do not arise under a pro rata system of liability. These theoretical discussions that dwell on the inherent weaknesses of joint and several liability are, accordingly, not only incomplete but also misleading.[3]

Furthermore, much of the discussion seeks to justify limited liability by adverting to the assumed collection costs of any legal regime providing for shareholder liability. This is done apparently without any recognition of the increasingly sophisticated techniques of the much improved equity creditors' bill procedures for prosecuting shareholder liability that had developed by the close of the nineteenth century. Nor does it take into account the potentialities, largely unexplored though they may be, of modern procedural developments such as class actions. Finally, the issue of collection costs becomes unimportant in cases of intragroup liability asserted against one or more affiliated corporations rather than against many thousand shareholders.

The Perceived Advantages of Limited Liability

The literature suggests a significant number of important economic advantages flowing from a system of limited liability. In essence, these relate to four major factors: (a) encouraging investment without participation in control (or absentee ownership), thereby promoting large-scale investment and corporate activity; (b) promoting the efficiency of the capital markets; (c) avoiding the allegedly intolerable inefficiencies of a liability system; and (d) stimulating entrepreneurial risk-taking and risk diversification.

Of these four advantages, only one—encouraging risk-taking and diversification—is at all relevant to corporate groups. The others, which pertain to public shareholders, simply become inapplicable when a parent corporation is substituted as shareholder in the place of tens of thousands of public investors.

Encourages Investment by Absentee Investors

Scholarly commentators suggest that the imposition of corporate liability upon investors for debts arising from management decisions would tend to confine investors to placing their monies in the relatively few corporations in which they could either participate in management or could monitor management decision-making closely. Thus, limited liability is seen as vital to making possible the widespread distribution of corporate shares among millions of Americans, thereby contributing to substantially increased capital investment. In brief, limited liability is held to permit the separation of ownership and control that underlies modern finance capitalism.

Even in the case of public shareholders, this argument is flawed because it assumes that limited liability must take the form of joint and several unlimited liability. In light of the enormous risks attendant upon activities of large-scale enterprises relative to shareholder wealth, the liability of a shareholder for *all* the obligations of the corporation would tend to deter investment and inhibit the widespread distribution of shares, which are two factors contributing to the generation of the enormous amounts of capital required by a large firm.

Pro rata liability, however, as employed for seventy-five years in California, does not present the specter of the individual shareholder overwhelmed by responsibility for the grand total of corporate liabilities. Instead, pro rata liability inherently distributes the corporate debts among all shareholders. This reduces exposure sharply, particularly in the very large corporations with huge capitalizations and high distribution of shares. Thus, a substantial shareholder of Exxon Corporation holding one thousand shares (with a present market value of about $62,000) of the 1,813 million shares outstanding would have an exposure limited to 0.00003034 percent of any unsatisfied liabilities. As should be apparent, pro rata liability dramatically transforms the problem.

In the case of corporate groups, there can be no concern over the liability exposure of absentee owners. Far from being an absentee owner, the parent corporation has "control." It directs and in varying degrees participates in the management of the subservient companies. It intensively monitors their performance. The public investment market is not involved at all, and there is no need to retain limited liability as essential for encouraging widespread public distribution of the subsidiary's shares.

Nor does application of enterprise law to the group have any impact on the investment decisions of shareholders of the *parent*. As noted, enterprise law involves no change of the liability rule for public investors in the parent company. Thus, a legal rule imposing unlimited liability on a parent corporation for the debts of its subsidiaries under particular circumstances should not discourage nor interfere with the widespread distribution of share ownership among the public shareholders of the parent in any way.

Promotes Capital Market Efficiency

Under joint and several unlimited liability, shareholders paying corporate debts are entitled to contributions from other shareholders. Accordingly, wealthy shareholders concerned with the possibility of such liability would be under pressure to monitor the wealth of fellow stockholders as well as the financial condition of the enterprise. Such additional monitoring would cause increased information costs for corporate shareholders relative to corporate lenders. This would impair the efficiency of capital markets as well as skew investments. Commentators have accordingly asserted that limited liability is essential for well-developed securities markets.

This contention also has serious deficiencies. It ignores economic history. It has no application to a system of pro rata liability. Finally, it, too, is irrelevant in the case of corporate groups.

For more than a century and a half before the introduction of limited liability in England in 1855, there were well-developed markets in the securities of joint stock companies operating under joint and several liability. Historians report that by the end of the seventeenth century, securities markets for shares of the major English companies flourished both in London and the provinces. By 1697, Parliament had found it necessary to enact a statute regulating stockbrokers. Nor was England unique. By this time, The Netherlands and Belgium also had security markets.[4] Joint and several liability of shareholders was clearly not the barrier suggested in the theoretical discussion.

Moreover, concern over the costs of monitoring the wealth of fellow shareholders rests entirely on the right of shareholders subjected to liability for corporate obligations under a regime of joint and several liability to contribution from their fellow shareholders.

This right of contribution arises because liability is unlimited. Under a system of pro rata limited liability, however, shareholder liability is limited to their proportionate share of corporate debts, and no right to contribution arises. Accordingly, questions with respect to the wealth of fellow shareholders and the ensuing extent of collectability of a claim for contribution against them are irrelevant.

Finally, insofar as corporate groups are concerned, the parent corporation is typically the sole shareholder, and concern with the wealth of fellow shareholders would not arise, even under a joint and several liability regime.

Avoids Alleged Inefficiencies of Unlimited Liability

Commentators have contended that unlimited liability involves a number of costly inefficiencies. These pertain to increased monitoring costs, costly and ineffective collection procedures, and the expense of contracting around liability. These contentions have some weaknesses in the case of public shareholders and are quite irrelevant in the case of corporate groups.

MONITORING AND INFORMATION COSTS

Agency costs of information and of shareholder monitoring of management performance arise whenever shareholders do not participate in management. Such costs are a feature of corporate existence, except in the case of very small enterprises. They arise whatever the liability rule. However, as the scale of exposure would dramatically increase under any unlimited liability regime, the costs would be intensified. Shareholders liable for corporate risks would have a substantially increased incentive to supervise management decisions affecting their liability.

The change in the liability rule for corporate groups would make no difference in the case of agency monitoring and information costs for the group. Within the group, the parent is already engaged in management of group affairs and plays a dominant role in the affairs of the subsidiary. Elaborate reporting procedures and information flows are already available, and unlimited liability would lead to no additional procedures and costs to achieve such results. The group's monitoring and information objectives do not take on new dimensions depending on whether a particular activity is conducted by a branch, division, or subsidiary. Further, as noted, enterprise liability relates only to the parent. A change in the liability rule would not affect public shareholders and their existing monitoring and information costs.

COLLECTION COSTS FOR CREDITORS

Unlimited liability is portrayed as contributing to the threat of suits against thousands of shareholders, presenting severe problems of collection. It said to be hopelessly inefficient.[5] History does not support this contention. As noted, although most jurisdictions in the United States had accepted the general principle of limited liability by 1830, shareholder liability still continued, to a substantial degree, for about a century thereafter in the form of the double and triple shareholder assessment statutes and constitutional provisions. This form of shareholder liability persisted in most jurisdictions until well after World War I.

Faced with collection suits against shareholders arising from the widespread existence of shareholder double or triple assessment liability, American law and equity jurisprudence responded with the development of more flexible and effective collection procedures. The much improved creditors' bill in equity that had evolved by the last quarter of the nineteenth century dealt effectively with many of the procedural difficulties. Similarly, the English statutory law dealing with shareholder liability in the period before the final approval of limited liability progressively improved the efficiency of collection. Although some procedural problems, of course, did exist in both countries, they do not appear to be as intractable as assumed.

The claim of creditors against shareholders generally in any particular corporation under the laws of a jurisdiction could be established in a single lawsuit, with the court's judgment entitled to full faith and credit in all other jurisdictions, even in those with different liability rules.[6] In any suit against a particular creditor, the only issue to be determined was the number of shares held by the particular shareholder.

In addition, the concern with the inefficiencies of collection procedures ignores the modern context in at least two important respects. First, developments in recent decades with respect to improved class actions permit the prosecution of action against *classes* of defendants, enabling creditors to simplify collection litigation. While such class action procedures against defendants are still rare and their limitations uncertain, intensified development of the remedy would undoubtedly accompany any relaxation of limited liability.[7]

Finally, the crucial problem of shareholder liability arises in the case of the insolvent corporation. The bankruptcy court with jurisdiction over the debtor corporation would provide a centralized forum for the determination and collection of shareholder liability. In brief, the problems of multiplicity of collection suits against thousands of public shareholders in the event of abandonment of limited liability appear to have been exaggerated.

In any event, concern over the availability and efficiency of remedies for collection against a large number of public shareholders does not arise where liability is being imposed upon a corporate group. Creditors proceed directly against the parent corporation and sister subsidiaries. Public shareholders are not involved at all.

CONTRACTING AROUND LIABILITY

One of the advantages attributed to limited liability is the insulation of shareholders from liability without the necessity of negotiating contractual agreement to achieve the same result. Under a role imposing shareholder liability, parties desiring to avoid liability would have to insist on inclusion of an appropriate no-liability or nonrecourse clause in the underlying agreement. However, such contracting around the rule would not be burdensome in many situations. It would be particularly easy to accomplish in the many transactions that are already normally conducted through use of a standard form contract. All that is required is to change the form.

In fact as reviewed in Chapter 1, just such contracting around the prevailing legal rule was a normal feature in English and Scottish insurance policies in the period before the adoption of limited liability. The English and Scottish insurers were joint stock insurance companies with members subject to joint and several liability. Their standard insurance policies expressly restricted liability to the insuring company's own assets, thereby effecting limited liability long before the enactment of the 1862 statute extending limited liability to such companies.[8]

Where standard contracts could not be used, however, the need for contracting around to limit liability becomes a more serious matter and would represent an additional cost. In some cases, such as obligations to involuntary creditors, contracting around liability would be impossible, and parties would have to look to insurance, where available, to protect themselves.

The need to contract around the general doctrine to achieve a contrary outcome is a consequence of any legal rule. Under limited liability, parties bargaining for shareholder liability are currently obliged to contract around the law and expressly so provide, or alternatively to insist on guaranties or similar assurances from shareholders or others. Thus, whatever the rule, transaction costs for contracting around inevitably arise. It is not clear that such contracting is significantly more burdensome under unlimited liability than under limited liability. On the contrary, requiring business corporations to include such provisions in their forms to restrict exposure may be less onerous than imposing this burden on the other contracting parties. It remains to be seen under which alternative contracting around would in fact be more difficult and costly. To the extent that this factor has merit, however, it applies, unlike some of the other contentions, both to parent and subholding companies in corporate groups and to other shareholders.

ENCOURAGES ENTREPRENEURIAL RISK-TAKING

Limited liability accomplishes risk-shifting not created in the marketplace and thereby encourages investors to incur risks they would otherwise not undertake. This makes for an increased level of economic activity, encourages increased diversification, and contributes to a more favorable overall investment outcome. The elimination of unlimited liability for shareholders generally seems to have played a significant role in capital accumulation and the growth of large-scale industry. Although early nineteenth-century corporate business had grown enormously under the older unlimited liability rule, it is far from clear that the complex economies of the developed nations of the world, with their need for much greater amounts of capital, would have evolved as fully without limited liability. The disincentives arising from a change in the rule have to be taken into account.

Corporate groups considering new investment are subject to this factor along with corporations generally; this cost, where it in fact arises, must be taken into consideration in their case as well. However, in the case of corporate groups, the seriousness of the problem arising from a change in the liability rule is sharply less than in the case of investors generally.

The basic question is, What constitutes new investment? Where a corporation conducting an existing business fragments that business among a number of companies or spins off a particular activity to a newly organized subsidiary, it is only engaging in corporate restructuring on the legal level. The "firm" remains unchanged. Further, new investment, from an economic view, is not involved at all. Even where the restructuring relates to the conduct of economic activity unrelated to the existing line of business in areas of special risk, deterrence of the investment must be balanced against the economic costs arising from the externalization of the liabilities arising from the risky activities. One of the primary purposes of societal rules of liability pertaining to risky activity is to encourage producers to reduce or avoid the risks, not to externalize them. In this area, enterprise law furthers, not impedes, economic objectives.

Similarly, in broadening the reach of statutory law, enterprise law fulfills the objectives of overriding importance. In enacting the statutes, the legislature has made a decision on socio-political policy that is its to make. Enterprise principles seeking to implement the underlying policies and objectives of the statute and to prevent ready evasion serve important systemic needs.

Conglomerate enterprises present the same problem in different form. A change in the liability rule would play a role in the decision-making process. When a group considers the desirability of diversifying its risks by investment in an entirely new industry, as in the reported cases of United States Steel acquiring Marathon Oil, R.J. Reynolds (tobacco) acquiring Nabisco (biscuits), or Mobil Oil acquiring Montgomery Ward (merchandising), the prospect of enterprise liability could well deter the acquisition.

However, the acquisition of an existing business, whether for cash or issuance of securities, is not a new investment as a matter of economics; although form has changed and greater diversification of risk is available, the underlying economic activity is unaltered. The problem of deterring new investment arises only if, subsequent to acquisition, the parent is deterred from making additional group funds available to the newly acquired activity. This, however, presents very much the same theoretical problem as new investment in the existing business. The group, notwithstanding its new conglomerate dimension, continues to constitute a single "firm," linked by control, financial, and administrative interdependence.

Multinational groups face an allied problem as well. The application of enterprise principles by host countries may create significant disincentives to multinational local investment and a consequent risk of subjecting the worldwide group as a whole to the local policies. Chapter 7 reviews the problems that may arise in the event of acceptance of enterprise principles at different times by countries around the world. It also reviews the ensuing difficulties for developing, and other, countries when other, more attractive features of local markets are not perceived as fully offsetting this factor.

However, the political dimensions of the problem tend to dwarf its economic implications. Where, as in Argentina in the *Deltec* episode reviewed in Chapter 8, the application of enterprise principles represents a highly politicized response to what is perceived as foreign exploitation, the economic consequences may not receive a high priority.

Summary

Whatever the theoretical conclusion with respect to the desirability of retaining limited liability in the case of public investors, an issue irrelevant to enterprise law, it should be clear that most of the asserted advantages of a limited liability regime are simply inapplicable in the case of corporate groups. The only economic factors supporting continuance of a limited liability rule for the subsidiary corporations of corporate groups appear to be the possibility of increased costs of contracting around the liability rule and a negative pressure against entrepreneurial risk-taking.

However, as noted, the contracting around problem is a consequence of any legal rule, and it has not been demonstrated that the problem is significantly more costly in having the group contract around liability than it is by imposing this burden on the public generally. Moreover, this concern relates only to contractual liability arising from genuine bargains and has no relevance to involuntary conduct, such as other forms of contract liability, or to tort or statutory law at all.

As for deterring new investment, the argument similarly has sharply reduced application. In tort, it is offset by the concern against creating externalities and in statutory law, by the need to implement the statutory objectives. Whatever its validity in other areas, the argument has less significance than first appears. So much for the advantages of limited liability. What of its disadvantages?

Undesirable Consequences of Limited Liability

As opposed to the advantageous consequences of limited liability enumerated previously, of which only the contentions relating to contracting around liability and risk-taking are at all pertinent to the choice between entity law and enterprise principles in determining the legal relationships of the constituent companies of corporate groups, there are two major inherent disadvantages. Limited liability leads to excessively risky investments and impairs the efficiency of the capital markets, as discussed next. These inherent disadvantages are as applicable to corporate groups as to public investors.

In addition to the inherent disadvantages of limited liability, limited liability appears especially deficient when it serves to bar recovery for corporate injuries to certain creditors. Thus, whatever their views on the theoretical desirability of limited liability as a general rule, commentators increasingly agree that the doctrine creates serious externalities and inefficiencies in particular areas. These problems arise with respect to the claims of tort victims, employees, and certain trade creditors. These deficiencies in special areas are reviewed after the discussion of the inherent disadvantages.

Inherent Disadvantages
EXCESSIVELY RISKY INVESTMENTS

The introduction of limited liability into the calculation of risk and the feasibility or desirability of particular investments results in considerable distortion and leads to the increased likelihood of excessively risky investments. This is particularly true in the case of enterprises under economic pressure.

This problem can be severe and has led to numerous corporate insolvencies. In response, England and some Commonwealth countries have amended their winding up statutes to create a new statutory offense imposing personal liability upon officers and directors involved in certain excessively risky transactions. These "wrongful trading" provisions penalize such conduct as business management incurring indebtedness at a time when it was reasonably apparent that the indebtedness could not be repaid.[9]

The statutes represent a highly selective repeal of limited liability in an effort to respond to its tendency to lead to excessively risky behavior. Although the statutes impose liability on officers and directors, not upon shareholders as such, shareholder liability is also frequently involved. Thus, in the close corporation, it is common for the major shareholders to serve also as officers and directors, thereby becoming subject to the statute. Similarly, with respect to corporate groups and controlled corporations generally, the emerging "shadow director" doctrine seems likely to provide a route to imposition of statutory liability upon parent corporations or other controlling shareholders.[10]

Similar concern with excessively risky corporate investment has given rise to an Australian call for statutory law reform particularly addressed to the winding up of corporate groups. This has been led by Chief Judge Rogers of the Commercial Division of the Supreme Court of New South Wales.[11]

DEFICIENCIES IN NONMARKET SITUATIONS OR
IMPERFECT MARKETS

The economist's appraisal of limited liability as a societal tool to achieve efficiency relates to its role in market transactions. The analysis presupposes the existence of a bargain freely reached by independent parties of equivalent position, meaning, among other things, equal bargaining power, equal access to information, and an equal degree of risk aversion. It also assumes an absence of transaction costs. To the extent that such assumptions are not present, the market justifications for limited liability apply only in significantly reduced degree, if at all.

Thus, academic support for the doctrine in transactional controversies is sharply diminished when the issue arises in areas where serious market imperfections exist. These include not only involuntary transactions such as those giving rise to tort liability but those transactions that, while voluntary in form, do not represent genuine bargains or in which misrepresentation, fraudulent or otherwise, is present.

DEFICIENCIES FOR INVOLUNTARY CREDITORS

When the debate moves from the theoretical justifications for limited liability with respect to corporate obligations in general to consideration of the special problems presented by the claims of particular classes of creditors, the calculus of advantages and disadvantages is substantially affected.

Tort Creditors. Whatever their views on the general issue, most commentators agree that limited liability presents serious problems when applied in the case of tort and other involuntary creditors. Limited liability for shareholders of corporations unable to satisfy tort claims is inefficient because it causes externalities. Under limited liability, costs of a corporation's tortious behavior are costs of the business that are involuntarily imposed on the victims rather than on the business and then spread generally over those benefiting from the behavior, such as shareholders and consumers generally. Further, it frequently has the inhumane consequence of imposing costs that may be heavy or even catastrophic upon victims without adequate resources to meet them. Finally, insulation from shareholder liability defeats a primary objective of tort law by undermining the pressures deterring excessively risky conduct.

Thus, the economic commentary widely concludes that different liability rules should govern cases in contract and cases in tort. In the same manner, courts are increasingly recognizing that in the development of modern "piercing the veil jurisprudence" the standards for disregard of entity in tort should be less rigorous than in contract.

These concerns have come especially to the fore in the light of a series of catastrophic disasters giving rise to massive liability, including the *Amoco Cadiz* oil spill, the Bhopal disaster, the *Exxon Valdez* oil spill, asbestosis liability, and other major worker and consumer product liability litigations.

Because of increased management awareness of the exposure to liability from such events, reorganization of the corporate structure in corporate groups involving segregation of especially risky activity in selected subsidiaries has emerged as a legal technique to attempt to shield the group as a whole from tort liabilities of this kind. In such business planning, traditional entity law is being utilized to attempt to create a safe harbor for corporate groups seeking to externalize the costs of a subsidiary's negligence in conducting highly risky activities. This does not serve the economic values advanced in support of limited liability.

Involuntary Contract Creditors. In analyzing the reasons for distinguishing between tort and contract creditors, commentators arguing for different treatment generally emphasize the involuntary nature of tort creditors. In contrast, contract creditors are characterized as voluntary creditors who should be bound by the terms of the bargain that they have made. Although this distinction is sound as far as tort creditors are concerned, it is much too broad in treating all contract creditors alike.

Not all contract obligations represent bargains reflecting realistic negotiation. As has been increasingly accepted in the modern law of consent, the apparently voluntary feature of an act may mask the underlying reality, and it is necessary for the law to inquire further. Similarly, in determining the role of the limited liability doctrine in contract, the real question should be whether by nature of the transaction and the relative position of the parties, the contract in issue, including the provisions on liability, truly represents a bargain.

Thus, it is necessary to distinguish between contracts that represent actual bargains between parties with equivalent bargaining power and access to information and other contracts where these essential elements are not present. Where an actual bargain is involved, credit terms, including the identity of the parties obligated under the contract, are a material aspect of the bargain. As parties negotiate credit terms, the final price will be adjusted to reflect, among other factors, the bargain reached over credit. In a common example, the corporate borrower may borrow at one interest rate on its own credit and at a lower rate when its parent (or shareholders) assumes or guarantees the obligation as well.

Where such a genuine bargain occurs, there is no reason why the law should not respond to the expectations of the parties and enforce the bargain they have freely made. Indeed, a frequent theme of courts in rejecting creditor's efforts to "pierce the veil" or otherwise impose liability on parents and controlling shareholders in contract cases is the unwillingness of the courts to permit parties to remake their bargains.

In many contract transactions, however, the opportunity for bargaining over credit does not arise as a practical matter. This is particularly evident in employment contracts, retail consumer purchases, and in small trade contracts. In these cases, contracts are voluntary only in form.

Workers seeking employment, for example, are not typically in a position to incur the costs required to obtain credit information as to the financial resources of the employer. Even where such information is available, they lack the bargaining strength to refuse employment in the absence of appropriate adjustment of wage scales to reflect the credit standing of the employer. The assertion surprisingly made by a few (happily few) scholars that workers are free to bargain over such matters truly represents the limitations of the ivory tower. Similarly, retail consumers are rarely in a position to take credit considerations into account in purchasing products.

Finally, many trade creditors, particularly in smaller transactions, are similarly unable to bargain over credit and adjust their prices to an evaluation of credit risk. The imperfections in the market in which such creditors exist put these adjustments beyond their reach.

Many other trade creditors evaluate credit before entering into a transaction. They do so directly through the manufacturer's or supplier's own credit department or indirectly through a nonrecourse sale of the account to a factor who performs the credit evaluation before purchasing the account. Credit insurance is still another alternative. However, there is a threshold level of size below which such techniques are not practically available.

For these reasons, if perceived deficiencies of limited liability are to be corrected by special liability rules for designated creditors, the line of distinction should not simply be between contract and tort or between voluntary and involuntary transactions, but between transactions representing genuine bargains over credit and those in which such bargains did not realistically take place.

Limited Liability and Insurance

Limited liability may be viewed as a device for risk-shifting. It plays much the same role as insurance, the primary device for risk-shifting in modern society. Wherever insurance is economically available, the liability rule loses much of its relevance, except to determine the party under pressure to insure. Some commentators have, accordingly, suggested insurance as the preferred solution to the conceded deficiencies of limited liability, rather than abandonment of the doctrine. However, in many situations, insurance is not available at all or is more readily obtained by the business than by the party dealing with it. For example, a manufacturer can more effectively insure against product liability losses than can the purchasers of its products. Similarly, a taxi company can better insure against its traffic accidents than passengers and pedestrians. In such situations, insurance does not provide an efficient alternative, and the deficiencies of the liability rule remain to be addressed.

So much for the general discussion. Whatever the advantages and disadvantages of limited liability as a general rule and its deficiencies with respect to such special classes of claimants as tort victims, employees, consumers, and other contract creditors in transactions not representing genuine bargains, there are two major areas in which the inadequacy of limited liability is especially apparent. These areas include the severe limitations of the doctrine in the case of corporate groups and its complete inappropriateness in the construction and application of statutory law.

Limited Liability and Corporate Groups

When the discussion focuses not on limited liability in the economy generally but on the applicability of the doctrine to constituent companies of corporate groups, the problem changes dramatically. Many of the economic advantages advanced in support of limited liability simply become irrelevant, and the utility of such a legal rule becomes increasingly doubtful.

The problem must be considered in the light of the scale and operation of large corporate groups operating through scores, if not hundreds, of companies: parent company, subholding companies, and lower-tier subsidiaries throughout the world, functioning under common control and central direction or coordination. The complex corporate structure of the multinational group frequently includes two, three, or even four tiers of subsidiary companies. Thus, a reader will find increasing references to "multitiered" corporate groups in American judicial opinions, particularly those dealing in bankruptcy with problems of substantive consolidation.[12]

Under entity law and limited liability, each higher-tier company of the multitiered corporate group is insulated from liability for the unsatisfied debts of the lower-tier companies of which it is a shareholder. In the multitiered group, there are, thus, as many layers of limited liability as there are tiers in the corporate structure. Limited liability for corporate groups thus opens the door to multiple layers of insulation, a consequence unforseen when limited liability was adopted long before the emergence of corporate groups.

The firm is seen to exist because of its potentiality for internalizing economic activity, thereby reducing transaction costs that would otherwise arise from contracting out the activity. Such internalization has been generally perceived to be responsible for the rise of corporate groups, particularly multinational groups. Thus, most commentators agree that multinational groups pursue a policy of group profit maximization in which the interests of the individual constituent members of the group are subordinated to the interests of the parent, that is, the group as a whole.

Group profit maximization is reflected in many ways. One major area is the internal allocation of group funds to the sectors earning the highest rate of return for equivalent risk. This ability to internalize the capital markets has been seen as one of the significant factors contributing to the growth of multinational corporations.[13]

A second major area is the persistent utilization by multinational groups of distorted transfer pricing of intra-enterprise transactions as a technique to manipulate or circumvent national regulatory and revenue statutes. The opportunity and temptation to utilize transfer pricing to accomplish such objectives are great. The U.S. Department of Commerce estimates that intrafirm transactions represent around thirty percent of all American exports and around forty percent of all imports.[14]

This phenomenon is apparent in skewed, that is, nonmarket, transfer pricing, in efforts to move income from high-tax countries to low-tax countries or to reduce the aggregate impact of export and import duties. A related technique appears in the possibilities for multinational enterprises, through skewed transactions and transfers of funds, to evade or reduce the impact of national capital repatriation or currency exchange controls or to help resist trade union wage demands. Similarly, it has been suggested that in vertically integrated enterprises, distorted transfer pricing is employed to concentrate profits in areas of least competition in order to deter competition at other stages.

Such skewing of income has been thought to reflect political factors as well. In the case of a particularly profitable subsidiary, shifting accounting income from the subsidiary to its affiliates or parent located in other countries may avoid local resentment and such disadvantageous local responses as increased tax burdens or increased labor demands.

Reflecting the extent of these practices and the concern of many countries, particularly undeveloped countries with less sophisticated statutory structures, the United Nations has been particularly active in studies of the problems and possible solutions. Transfer pricing in an effort to maximize group profitability has become an international problem of considerable significance.[15]

Still another example of group profit maximization is the common practice of interchange and movement of personnel through group subsidiaries as part of the education of group personnel for assuming control of the coordination and direction of group policies for the subsidiaries of the group.

In all these areas, the economic performance of a particular subsidiary is not the determinative standard. Instead, the maximization of group performance is the objective. Where the apparent performance of a group subsidiary is distorted by skewed transfer pricing to achieve the objectives reviewed above, increased monitoring and information costs may arise to reduce the savings from sidestepping onerous government and other restrictions or imposts. However, such transfer pricing should continue so long as the savings exceed the costs.

Judge Posner raised an argument for extension of limited liability to component companies of corporate groups, even in the face of its deficiencies in particular areas. While conceding the lack of efficiency in limited liability in tort, Posner suggested that unlimited liability is undesirable because it would adversely affect the competitive position of subsidiaries with parent companies unprotected by limited liability that were seeking to operate in the same market with independent companies whose shareholders were insulated from company debts. Presumably, the latter companies would be somewhat freer to engage in riskier transactions. He illustrated his analysis by reference to the celebrated decision in *Walkovszky v. Carlton*,[16] which involved the application of "piercing the veil jurisprudence" to individual investors in the New York City taxi industry.

He assumes, quite unrealistically, that the parent corporation is no more than an investment company (or pure investor) and is not itself engaged in the operation of an integrated taxi business collectively being conducted by a number of companies under common control. As reviewed in Chapter 4, however, the taxi industry cases involve a very different reality. In these decisions, the controlled corporations are typically only fragments of a larger integrated business, with formal legal lines drawn between them in an effort to compartmentalize exposure to liability. The taxis of the various companies comprising the group typically operate from a common garage, are served by a common maintenance staff, and use a common source of fuel supply. They may share the same logo, telephone number, and trade name.

In these circumstances, the courts have imposed enterprise liability on the companies comprising the group, but not on the controlling shareholders or investors not themselves engaged in the business. The reality of the industry is that the group, not the individual subsidiaries, is the effective competitor in the marketplace, and the shareholder-investors of the parent (or the shareholder-investor of affiliated companies operating under common ownership and control), like the shareholders of its corporate competitors, are protected by limited liability.

Special Problems Presented by Corporate Structure

The foregoing discussion has related to corporate groups with wholly owned subsidiaries conducting integrated businesses. Although most large American corporate groups function through wholly owned sub-sidiaries,[17] the number of partly owned subsidiaries seems to be increasing, reflecting, among other matters, the growing popularity of including local investors as a technique for foreign investment. A number of groups also conduct conglomerate or other less than fully integrated enterprises. Finally, some groups, particularly in Japan, appear to be organized as networks with a high degree of decentralization. These classes of corporate groups present special problems that require special consideration.

Partly Owned Subsidiaries

The threshold issue presented by shareholder liability rules for partly held subsidiaries is the treatment of the public minority shareholders of subsidiary corporations. If enterprise liability means liability for all shareholders, the calculus of the theoretical advantages and disadvantages of a limited liability policy changes dramatically. The advantages of limited liability that had been irrelevant in the case of corporate groups with wholly owned subsidiaries suddenly become relevant. These would cast a significant weight in any comparative evaluation of the relevant advantages and economic feasibility of the alternative theoretical liability regimes.

Further, if one were to conclude that because of the relevancy of the full panoply of the disadvantageous consequences of an unlimited liability regime different rules than those for wholly owned subsidiaries should apply to partly held subsidiaries, with limited liability available for the latter and not for the former, the resulting legal system would become unworkable. Parent corporations could then routinely avoid unlimited group liability by converting wholly owned subsidiaries into companies with small minority interests. Confronted with this problem, professors Hansmann and Kraakman abandon a corporate law solution in this area, completely eliminating limited liability for all corporate groups. Instead, they argue for a tort law solution restricted to elimination of limited liability in tort.[18]

However, there would appear to be an alternative that the law already seems to have followed. As reviewed previously, judicial decisions imposing liability on partly owned companies that rely on "piercing the veil jurisprudence" or enterprise principles have typically imposed liability *in full* on the parent corporation (or controlling shareholder) for the obligations of a *partly owned* subsidiary (or controlled) corporation. At the same time, those shareholders not part of the control group have been held not liable at all. Under this principle of having liability follow the control group, rather than shareholder status generally, the rule for intergroup liability is the same without regard to whether the subsidiary is fully or partly owned. In a regime of unlimited liability, this principle would seemingly avoid the problem. However, Hansmann and Kraakman contend that this would distort corporate behavior by providing an incentive to corporations to dispose of their hazardous activities to small publicly traded companies that are thinly capitalized. How significant this might be remains to be seen.

The existence of minority shareholders in partly owned subsidiaries introduces still another element requiring consideration. Under traditional doctrines of Anglo-American corporation law, parent corporations (and controlling shareholders) have fiduciary obligations to minority shareholders. Under these fiduciary principles, the parent corporation (or other controlling shareholder) and the subsidiary's board of directors are to conduct the affairs of the subsidiary in the best interests of the subsidiary and maximize the return on investment of the subsidiary without regard to the interests of the group. Further, the parent corporation and the subsidiary's board of directors must respect fiduciary standards of fairness in all transactions between the subsidiary and the parent corporation and other companies of the group. They may not impose transactions on a subsidiary that are disadvantageous to the subsidiary and advantageous to the parent. Although these fiduciary obligations to minority shareholders manifestly constitute an important constraint on the direction of the subsidiary's business and affairs, the standards are loose and not fully effective.[19]

Nevertheless, fiduciary standards do exist and must be considered to some degree in the management of the group, particularly with respect to programs concerned with group profit maximization. This represents an element of cost that may become undesirable for a particular group. Thus, a recurrent feature in corporate restructuring through freeze-outs to eliminate minority shareholding is the adverted desire to avoid the costs and difficulties of policing intragroup transactions to avoid breach of fiduciary obligations to minority shareholders.

Although such fiduciary obligations play some role in shaping the direction of the subsidiary's affairs, they relate only to the internal governance of the subsidiary and do not involve the rights and liabilities of third parties. Accordingly, they have little relevance in considering whether in a particular case enterprise principles should be employed to impose liability upon a parent corporation or on the group by reason of dealings between the subsidiary and third parties. Thus, the limited number of decisions considering the use of enterprise principles or "piercing the veil jurisprudence" to impose liability in cases involving partly owned subsidiaries or other controlled corporations properly do not give this feature any particular significance.[20]

Conglomerates and Other Less Than Fully Integrated Groups

Conglomerates and other less than fully integrated groups present a more complex problem. In the formulation of enterprise principles, the economic integration of the group has played a significant role in the evolution of the law thus far. In economically integrated groups, the group may accurately be said to be collectively conducting a common business that has been fragmented among the various constituent companies of the group. In the event of the application of enterprise principles, the business enterprise and the legal unit (the economic entity and the legal entity) for the purposes at hand would be the same.

In conglomerates, the group conducts businesses that are in different industries. Although their production and distribution functions may not be integrated, the subsidiaries are, nevertheless, integrated in other important respects. In financial matters, conglomerate groups function much like other groups, with a high degree of financial interdependence among the affiliated companies. The economic potential from internalization of the capital market function through substitution of the group for the market for financing purposes has in fact been recognized as one of the major incentives for the existence of conglomerate organizations in the first place.[21]

In addition to financial interdependence, conglomerate groups similarly use the same patterns of administrative interdependence evident in other groups, with the constituent companies utilizing group resources providing an extensive series of essential supporting services.

Financial and administrative interdependence provide opportunities of importance for economies of scale and other advantages of internalization.

The constituent companies in diverse industries organized in a conglomerate group constitute a "firm" because of the opportunities for economies of scale and scope through financial and administrative interdependence. Nevertheless, conglomerate groups present at least two special difficulties for application of enterprise principles different from those presented by integrated enterprises. These are the impact on entrepreneurial risk-taking and the possible externalization of costs.

One of the important advantages of limited liability is its encouragement of entrepreneurial risk-taking and new investment. Application of enterprise principles to impose liability in the case of conglomerate groups, thus, might have undesirable consequences in tending to discourage expansion by the group into new businesses. This is a factor not present in the imposition of enterprise principles and the resulting loss of limited liability in the case of an integrated group, where a single business has been fragmented among the members of the group who continue to conduct it collectively under common control. In the latter case, entrepreneurial venturing into a *new* business is not involved at all. However, whatever the possible impairment of risk-taking by conglomerate diversification, the fact remains, as some commentators have noted, that the various companies are not truly independent from a financial and commercial perspective, and that investments in them do not represent a full diversification of risk.[22]

A final problem in applying enterprise principles in the case of conglomerate groups is the possible externalization of costs. In tort law, the application of enterprise principles has been recognized as particularly appropriate because it means the imposition of the costs and risks of an undertaking on all the operations responsible, with the ultimate social and individual costs of the product spread over the consumers of the products in question. In integrated enterprises, enterprise law appropriately makes all assets held by the subsidiaries conducting the fragmented parts of the business available for payment of the tort liabilities of the enterprise. The goal is to prevent externalization of the losses arising from such risks from the activity producing them.

The question arises as to whether conglomerate enterprises present a different situation. Where a group conducts a number of unrelated businesses, does the imposition of enterprise principles and elimination of limited liability within the group result in the automatic imposition of costs arising from the economic activity of the acquired company upon unrelated activities in other areas? If this were to occur, the imposition of enterprise principles with the objective of preventing externalities would in fact be creating other externalities for conglomerates.

This important question has two parts. The first is whether the costs are being imposed outside the "firm." This inquiry has already been discussed. As noted, although the component corporations of conglomerate groups lack the economic integration of the productive and distributive processes of integrated groups, they are tied to the group by both financial and administrative interdependence. Such linkages provide the necessary economies of scope and scale that make it economic for conglomerate enterprise to exist. Thus, despite the different industries served, the conglomerate enterprise is, none the less, a "firm."

A second, and independent, question is may such costs in fact be imposed on consumers of the products of the other unrelated subsidiaries? In the conglomerate, externalization could still arise if any of the costs imposed on the parent or sister subsidiaries arising from the exercise of enterprise principles were passed along to consumers of those affiliates, consumers of a different product or in a different geographical market. Whether this would occur, however, will depend on the extent of competition in the relevant markets. In the absence of monopoly elements, prices in such markets would be determined by the collective impact of costs of the various sellers in the industry and the nature of the demand. Any allocation of enterprise liability costs to the affiliate in the market would be irrelevant. The imposition of costs on the affiliates would affect their profitability but it could not affect prices unless the affiliates possessed monopoly power. In such a case, however, the answer would appear to be the need for correction of the monopolistic elements in the market rather than a change in the sweep of enterprise law for this particular consequence.

Thus, in summary, while conglomerate groups present a somewhat different balance of the comparable advantages and disadvantages of limited liability and unlimited liability from those presented by integrated groups, they do not appear to justify different liability rules on the basis of theoretical analysis. Nevertheless, it is necessary to observe that many of the reported decisions involving intragroup liability give considerable emphasis to the existence of economic integration as a factor of significance justifying employment of enterprise principles or "piercing the veil jurisprudence." This, at the least, suggests that conglomerate corporations may present some unique aspects and that courts may distinguish even more sharply between conglomerate and integrated groups in the further development of enterprise law. To date, the cases on this aspect are simply too few to provide any guidance.

Inapplicability of Market Analysis to Statutory Law

Economic analysis looks to legal rules for transactions in the marketplace. Although this represents a substantial portion of the legal problems of an industrialized society, it does not represent all of them. Government regulation is an increasing reality in American business life; as aptly described by Dean Calabresi, this is an "Age of Statutes."

The history of American statutory law has demonstrated the increasing acceptance of enterprise law in regulatory statutes as essential for fuller implementation of the statutory objectives and to defeat the manipulation of corporate structure through the organization of subsidiaries to evade statutory policies. Where the legislature has drafted the statute in terms of general application without specifically addressing the problem presented by corporate groups, the courts have the burden of determining whether construction of the statute according to enterprise principles is appropriate. In such a concern, the courts are increasingly making it clear that legal rules, such as entity law and limited liability, developed in litigation involving common law controversies between private parties, have limited application. Market efficiency is not an appropriate legal standard in cases involving the construction of statutory law and determination of the outer boundaries of a statutory regulatory regime.

Summary

The academic debate over the general theoretical desirability of limited liability for investors continues to boil over. Scholars disagree on whether limited liability is theoretically essential for a modern business society or desirable as a general rule. Some conclude that the doctrine is not necessary, while others would retain it intact. Still others, while not prepared, at least for the moment, to attack the doctrine generally, would carve out particular areas in which it would be inapplicable. Thus, as noted, important areas of consensus seem to be developing, particularly with respect to the treatment of tort claimants. Other scholars would extend such special treatment to employees as well. Although the limited liability doctrine presents much the same deficiencies for many trade creditors that it does for tort claimants and employees, this area has attracted less attention; even here, however, some note the inapplicability of the doctrine.

When the focus turns from public investors to the responsibility of parent and affiliated corporations for the obligations of other companies in the group, the fundamental nature of the problem changes and much, but not all, of the commentary becomes irrelevant.

In a world economy in which multinational corporate groups of enormous size and power predominate, enterprise principles have been increasingly accepted in national legal systems in the areas where they appear to implement the underlying legal policies and objectives more effectively than traditional entity law. Many of these areas in statutory law, and some at common or procedural law, do not involve the imposition of liability at all. For such problems, this discussion is quite irrelevant. In other areas, however, the imposition of intragroup liability contrary to traditional doctrines is at the heart of the controversy. In such litigation, limited liability frequently plays an important, if not decisive, role in determining whether enterprise principles or the traditional entity law concept of the separate corporate personality will prevail. In these cases, the choice is between an enterprise view or an entity view strongly reinforced by the limited liability doctrine.

Thus, evaluation of limited liability is a major element in any analysis of enterprise law relating to the areas involving imposition of liability. Although the advantages of limited liability for shareholders generally are inapplicable in many of the legal situations in which intragroup liability is in issue, some advantages remain, and American law today is obviously not ready to abandon the principle of limited liability generally, even in the case of corporate groups. However, in selected intragroup areas — particularly tort law — the principle plays a significantly reduced role.

In the numerous other legal issues that do not involve imposition of liability at all, the doctrine, of course, does not apply. Thus, by reason of these factors, in selected areas of the law — of which certain doctrines of procedural law; some areas of bankruptcy, property, and tort law; and most prominent of all, much of the area of statutory law are the leading examples — American law of corporate groups is emerging with growing emphasis on enterprise principles, while rigorously preserving limited liability as a protection for the public shareholders of the group.

Although the discussion is increasing on the academic level, there is no sign of any political activity toward reconsideration of the doctrine in the United States. The European Community presents quite a different picture. Influenced by the German *Konzernrecht*, the Community staff has attempted, through early drafts of a number of proposed directives on corporate law, to impose general liability on parent corporations for the liabilities of all companies in the group. Although such attempts have not prevailed to date, there is no indication that the pressures for increased utilization of enterprise principles in Community law may not grow in the future.[23]

This is the challenge to world legal systems presented by corporate groups, particularly the giant multinational corporations dominating world business. The inadequacies of nineteenth-century entity law for dealing with the legal problems presented by such enterprises is evident. In consequence, the world is seeing increasing adoption of enterprise principles and the rejection of entity law in selected areas to deal effectively with the economic realities in the cases presented for decision.

In many cases, limited liability and entity law are intertwined, and except in matters of statutory law, procedure, or in tort, enterprise principles are less likely to be adopted. In these remaining areas, concern for limited liability plays an important role in the jurisprudential struggle between entity law and enterprise law, fortifying the continued acceptance of traditional entity legal principles, notwithstanding the transformation of the economic society. In many other cases, as enumerated previously, limited liability is not involved at all and, accordingly, is not available to reinforce entity law. In such areas, enterprise principles have achieved their greatest success. The problem is dynamic. Although acceptance of enterprise principles appears to be accelerating, it is much too soon to foretell the ultimate sweep of the development and the extent to which discrete areas of entity law and limited liability will ultimately survive in a world of corporate groups.

III

World Dimensions

7

European and British Commonwealth Experience with Enterprise Law

Reflecting their common Roman origins, the legal systems in Europe, as well as in the United States, are firmly grounded on entity law. The separate existence of the corporation, with rights and responsibilities distinct from those of its shareholders, is deeply embedded in the legal order on both sides of the Atlantic. Similarly, in Europe as in the United States, the separate legal identity of the corporation is everywhere accompanied by the corollary principle of limited liability.

The economic development of the corporate society, like the evolution of its legal concepts, has been much the same in Europe and the United States. Multinational corporate groups have come to play a leading role on the world scene. Thus, in the United States and the United Kingdom, they account for between eighty and ninety percent of all exports.

The multinational corporation is no longer mainly an American phenomenon. It is a worldwide one. Of the 500 largest industrial multinational enterprises in 1991, ranked by sales, only 157 are American. Europe, headed by Britain with 43, Germany with 33, and France with 32 companies, had a total of 171 companies. Asia, led by Japan with 119, had 141 companies. The remainder were distributed among Australia, Canada, Latin America, and Africa. By 1985, western European enterprises were providing over fifty percent of worldwide foreign direct investment flows, whereas the United States was providing only twenty-two percent and Japan eleven percent.[1]

As in the United States, the challenge facing European legal systems arising from the inadequacies of entity law in dealing satisfactorily with the problems presented by the interrelationships of parent and subsidiary corporations of corporate groups has, not surprisingly, led to some acceptance of enterprise principles in selected areas. Although on the whole, the development is clearly not as pronounced as in the United States, to date, there are many parallels in the experience, as well as signs that the evolution may be accelerating.[2]

Unlike the United States, in which the courts as well as Congress have made major contributions, European acceptance of enterprise principles is largely represented by statutory law. Judicial "piercing" or "lifting" the corporate veil is far from unknown,[3] but its application has been relatively sparse in comparison with the continued outpouring of American cases that rely on the doctrine. On the judicial level, entity law essentially remains supreme.

The United Kingdom

Notwithstanding isolated decisions and selective instances in statutory law, England, followed by its Commonwealth spin-offs, remains among the nations most firmly committed to traditional entity principles.

Judicial Decisions

Rigid adherence to entity law in the English-language jurisdictions is the legacy of the 1896 decision of the House of Lords in *Salomon v. Salomon & Co.* This much criticized decision, with its rigid respect for the separate entity of the nineteenth-century one-man company, continues to dominate English and Commonwealth law,[4] even with respect to the legal relationships of multinational groups of enormous size doing business all over the world. In the *Salomon* decision, the House of Lords refused to impose liability upon the controlling shareholder of an insolvent one-man corporation for the unpaid obligations of the company. It reached this result although the corporation had replaced the shareholder's individually owned business with a capital structure overwhelmingly consisting of debt to the shareholder.

For a time, as cases involving corporate groups emerged, it appeared that the *Salomon* decision and traditional entity law were beginning to yield, at least in some areas, to the application of enterprise principles. In fact, a leading authority on English company law, Professor L.C.B. Gower, concluded in 1969 that English courts were "coming to recognize the essential unity of a group enterprise rather than the separate legal entity of each company within the group." Soon thereafter, Lord Denning, in *D.H.N. Ltd. v. Tower Hamlets*, citing Gower among others, applied enterprise principles in a condemnation case involving compensation for a taking of land held by one of two subsidiaries of a grocery chain. However, this trend soon came to end, and the subsequent development of the law gives no sign of change from continued application of the *Salomon* doctrine and unyielding fidelity to entity law. As recently as the major decision of the House of Lords in the 1989 *International Tin Council* case, Lord Oliver asserted: "The decision of this House in *Salomon* is as much the law today as it was in 1896."[5]

Salomon and entity law have rendered English courts impotent to deal with the problems presented by corporate groups under statutes of general application where Parliament has not specifically addressed the issue. This is at its most visible in the series of English decisions discussed below, which virtually nullified the application to corporate groups of English remedial statutes seeking to protect employees and unions in such areas as sex discrimination and secondary boycott.

Statutory Law

English statutory law shows some variation. In isolated areas of company, corporate tax, and antitrust laws, and, to a minor degree, in selected areas of labor law, English statutory law, while firmly grounded on traditional principles of entity law, embraces principles of enterprise law in dealing with some of the problems presented by corporate groups. Although these various provisions of enterprise law merely constitute isolated fragments in the entire English legal order, they collectively form a mosaic of significant dimensions, revealing, in this area at least, some visible penetration of enterprise law into English statutory jurisprudence.

COMPANY LAW

In a comprehensive revision of English company law, The Companies Act of 1985 introduced enterprise principles only in three carefully delimited areas: group accounts, the prohibition against a company's purchase of its own shares, and the prohibition against company loans and guaranties to directors. For these purposes, it referred to the "holding company" and the "subsidiary," which it defined in terms of the power to appoint a majority of the board or the ownership of more than half in nominal value of the equity shares.

Four years later, reflecting its obligation to harmonize English company law with the requirements of the Seventh Council Directive on Consolidated Accounts of the European Community (EC), which dealt with group accounts, Parliament amended the 1985 Act by enacting The Companies Act, 1989. To conform to the EC directives, the 1989 Act introduced a new definition, the "subsidiary undertaking," while retaining an amended definition of subsidiary for other purposes of the statute. In contrast to the somewhat simplistic definition in the 1985 Act, the 1989 Act, following the lead of the EC, in more sophisticated terms defines "subsidiary undertaking" to include not merely the holding of shares with a majority of voting rights or the power otherwise to appoint a majority of the board, but also as any company in which the holder (a) has a "participating interest" *and* (b) either "actually exercises a dominant influence" or "manages" itself and the "subsidiary undertaking" on a "unified basis." Thus, in 1989, the English, at the urging of the EC, gave statutory recognition to the paramount significance of de facto control in the large public company.

This concept of a "participating interest" has no American parallel. Resting on an EC innovation, it is defined as an interest in another undertaking held "on a long-term basis for the purpose of securing a contribution to its activities by the exercise of control or influence arising or related to that interest." The Companies Act, 1989, provides that holding twenty percent or more of the shares gives rise to a rebuttable presumption of the existence of a "participating interest."[6] The EC directives permit, but do not require, member states to define "participating interest" to mean not less than twenty percent of the equity. Because its presumption is not conclusive, the English statute has not taken full advantage of this option.

The acceptance in the 1989 Act of a sophisticated standard of "control" embracing de facto control was not without precedent in English statutory law. The Fair Trading Act, 1973, dealing with mergers, had realistically expanded its scope by adoption of a functional, rather than a conceptual, standard for acquisition of "control." It provided that for purposes of the act, a party had "control" if it was "able, directly or indirectly, to control or materially to influence the policy of a body corporate, or . . . any person in carrying on an enterprise . . ." even when a party lacks a "controlling interest."[7] Although the *existence* of a controlling or material "influence" suffices for the Fair Trading Act, by contrast, the Companies Act, 1989, requires proof of its "actual exercise."

These standards have a striking resemblance to those employed in the American statutes utilizing enterprise principles as the basis for pervasive industry-wide regulation. These include the Bank Holding Company Act, the Public Utility Holding Company Act of 1935 (PUHCA), the Savings and Loan Holding Company Act, and the Investment Company Act of 1940. As discussed in Chapter 5, the American models similarly utilize as their standard the *existence* of a "controlling influence" (without requiring proof of its *exercise*) or, in the alternative, a rebuttable presumption of control arising from ownership or control of twenty-five percent (ten percent in the case of the PUHCA) of the voting shares. The English standards also closely resemble other European models. These include "controlling influence," as in the German *Konzernrecht*; "dominant influence" as elsewhere in The Companies Act, 1989, the original proposed EC statute for a European Company, and the proposed EC Ninth Directive; or "decisive influence," as in the EC regulations dealing with restrictive trade practices and in the Swedish Company Law.

Nonstatutory regulatory programs provide two interesting, additional examples. The United Kingdom, New Zealand, and Australia accounting standards for nonconsolidated or equity accounting of investments in associated companies of a group employ a "significant influence" standard.[8] This appears to be a somewhat more inclusive standard reaching relationships that conceivably could fall short of "dominant," "decisive," or "controlling" influence.

The English City Code on Take-overs and Mergers utilizes, for its special purposes, standards related to "control." Its procedures apply upon the acquisition of shares with thirty percent or more of the voting rights, without requiring any further proof of the acquisition of de facto control. Acquisitions by all "associated" companies are to be aggregated for this purpose. An "associated" company is one linked by ownership of twenty percent or more of the equity shares.[9]

TAX LAW

The Income and Corporate Taxes Act, 1988, provides in elaborate detail for enterprise treatment in selected tax law areas dealing with such matters as group (or consolidated) returns, intragroup transactions, and controlled foreign corporations. These provisions utilize a series of definitions, including the "51 percent subsidiary," the "75 percent subsidiary," and the "90 percent subsidiary," for different purposes.[10] It is interesting to note that unlike the American models, the English definitions apply these percentages of stock ownership to *proprietary* ownership and do not turn on the percentage of voting power at all.

As reviewed in connection with the American tax laws, the need for clarity and certainty to assist in tax planning and administration makes the use of objective numerical standards in tax statutes almost inevitable, except in the sections dealing with taxpayer manipulation of intragroup or related party transactions.

Thus, the Act abandons any objective, numerical standard and turns to an expansive definition of "control" when it deals with the tax consequences of certain intragroup transactions. It defines "control" for such purposes to mean the *exercise* or *the ability to exercise* "direct or indirect control over the company's affairs." Like the comparable provision in the Internal Revenue Code (§482), the English statute employs a general, functional standard rather than a rigid numerical one that would invite ready evasion. Similarly, in dealing with controlled foreign corporations, the Act defines "control" even less restrictively to mean when "affairs are conducted in accordance with the wishes" of the controlling party.[11]

LABOR LAW

The Employment Protection (Consolidation Act), 1978, provides a final illustration of the penetration of enterprise principles into English law. For purposes of redundancy or severance payments, this act treats the businesses of "associated" employers as one. "Associated," for these purposes, rests on "control" as defined under The Company Law of 1989, that is de jure control arising from ownership or control of majority voting power.[12]

However, the response by English courts to the problems of application of remedial labor statutes to corporate groups is quite another matter. In two prominent cases, English courts have given the most literal and rigid construction of statutory provisions involving secondary strikes and sex discrimination. Tenaciously clinging to entity law, these courts have insisted on the unwavering application of entity law under circumstances that completely ignore the economic realities, frustrate the statutory objectives, and permit ready evasion of the statutes by corporate structuring.[13] The readiness of English courts to confine themselves to the literal provisions of these statutes in the face of such consequences contrasts sharply with the prevailing doctrine in the United States that remedial statutes are to be given a "broad" or "liberal" construction in order to implement the underlying objective of the law and to prevent evasion.

The British Commonwealth

Australia

The judicial response in Australia is mixed. In most areas, including company and tax law, entity law and the *Salomon* doctrine still prevail, with Australian courts reported to show a "rigid and unwavering attitude" that is "deeply entrenched."[14] Even in the judicial decisions construing the tax law, Professor Baxt describes the courts as showing "more technical rigidity" than in the other English-language jurisdictions. However, in such areas as torts and the winding up of insolvent companies, there are judicial decisions that evidence a degree of unrest and uncertainty very different from the undisturbed state of entity law elsewhere in Australian or English law. Chief Judge Rogers of the Commercial Division of the New South Wales Supreme Court has thus described the tort law as being in "a state of flux."[15]

Nor is there significant difference in Australian statutory law. The principal recognition of enterprise principles in Australian statutory law has been with respect to the preparation of group accounts and in isolated provisions of the tax laws.[16] Although there are some instances of enterprise principles in the company and securities laws, typically using the familiar standard of "control," these are isolated and highly restricted references.

Canada

Although more than a decade ago Canadian tax law was described as showing that "the corporate veil is in tatters,"[17] later commentators still describe Canadian statutory and decisional law as departing from traditional entity principles only in limited areas or in "exceptional" cases.[18]

The Canadian Business Corporation Act contains isolated provisions relying on enterprise law. In a few sections modeled after the English law, it contains provisions dealing with loans and guaranties between "affiliated" companies, with statutory definitions of "affiliate," "holding body," and "subsidiary." The Act utilizes the standard of "control," defined in simplistic terms as the ownership of voting shares sufficient to elect a majority of the board.[19]

The Canadian Bankruptcy Act has more notable provisions dealing with voidable preferences for insiders. The Canadian statute deals with transactions between "related" parties linked by "control," which the statute does not define, leaving the content of the terms to judicial decision. The response of the Canadian courts has been highly restrictive. In contrast to the wide-ranging emphasis on de facto control in American law, the Canadian courts have construed "control" under this provision of the Bankruptcy Act to mean only de jure control, that is ownership of fifty percent of the voting shares.[20]

New Zealand

New Zealand presents a somewhat different picture. The New Zealand Companies Act, as amended, contains wide-ranging applications of enterprise law in winding up proceedings that go beyond the law of any other nation. One provision grants open-ended authority to courts in the winding up proceedings of a subsidiary or controlled company to impose obligations on parent companies and other controlling shareholders whenever it is "just and equitable" to do so. This focus on enterprise principles in insolvency law may be spreading.

Hill reports that the Australian Law Reform Commission has recommended much the same in Australia.[21]

Using the same expansive standard of "just and equitable," another provision of the New Zealand statute authorizes extension of a winding up proceeding of an insolvent subsidiary to include its parent and the winding up of both companies. A third provision provides for recapture of any consideration in "excess of value" between the company being wound up and persons in "control." For this purpose, "control," "parent," and "subsidiary" are defined by reference to the power of a member to control the composition of the board of directors or ownership of more than half in nominal value of equity share capital.

Finally, as in England, Australia, and the EC, the New Zealand Companies Act utilizes enterprise principles in requiring group accounts from all companies with one or more subsidiaries.[22]

Continental Europe

Germany

The 1965 German Stock Corporation Act[23] constitutes one of the outstanding examples of enterprise law for public stock corporations in world corporate legal systems. Its enterprise concepts have influenced the development of enterprise doctrines in European Community directives and Commission decisions, providing further models of enterprise law for consideration.

In its regulation of corporate groups, known as the *Konzernrecht*, the German Act divides groups into three classes, depending on the nature of the link between the constituent companies. These include groups resting on control contracts in which the parent is liable for annual deficits and may be required to post security for creditors (§§ 291–310); groups resting on de facto control in which, much like American law, the parent is liable to minority shareholders (but not to creditors) for any disadvantageous transaction imposed on the controlled company (§§ 311–318); and groups resting on an "integration" resolution adopted by a ninety-five percent-owned subsidiary for which the parent is fully liable (§§ 319–328).

Although the Act employs terms of "control," "controlling," and "controlled," and contains a presumption of control for companies holding a majority of the voting shares, it defines "control" as when "the controlling enterprise can exert, directly or indirectly, a controlling influence." This is a functional standard of "control" focusing on the economic realities, and it is borrowed almost in *haec verba* from the Public Utility Holding Company Act of 1935 (see Chapter 5) and the Investment Company Act of 1940 (see Chapter 2). Similarly, the determination of the existence of de facto control under German law, as under American law, is a question of fact.

Although the *Konzernrecht* is clearly the most extensive adoption of enterprise principles in Western world legal systems, with enormous influence over the evolving law of the EC, its immediate impact on German law is, in fact, somewhat confined. Thus, of the three types of groups with which the Act is concerned, only the group resting on de facto control plays a prominent role in the United States and other legal systems. "Control" resulting from contract or "integration" resolutions does not often arise and, consequently, is of lesser concern to foreign observers.

As to de facto control, the concept at the heart of much of the enterprise law developments, the German experience has little to contribute. One commentator describes it as a "dead letter."[24] Further, Dr. Gleichmann, who is the chief EC advisor on corporate groups, advises that the German Supreme Court has held that the *Konzernrecht* rules for de facto dependency relationships apply only to groups in which the parent only occasionally intervenes in the dependent company, but does not apply to so-called "virtual groups" in which the dominant firm exercises unified management over the dependent company and virtually integrates it into the dominant firm's business.[25]

Even with respect to the protection of minority shareholders in the subsidiary or controlled company, the German statutory provision for de facto groups does little more than restate existing fiduciary principles of American law.[26] Further, it protects only minority shareholders, not creditors. By contrast, in the cases involving corporate groups in the United States and elsewhere, the position of creditors holds the center of the stage and presents the most challenging problems. On this vital matter, German enterprise law has little to offer.

Finally, the *Konzernrecht* does not apply to all groups. It only includes public stock corporations or *Aktiengesellschaft* (A.G.).

However, most German subsidiaries are organized as private companies, or *Gesellschaft mit beschrankte Haftung* (G.m.b.H.), and the act does not apply. This further weakens its impact.[27]

There has been some development of "lifting" or "piercing the corporate veil" jurisprudence in the German courts. The most notable case, *Autokran*, involved a G.m.b.H. and, therefore, was not subject to the *Konzernrecht*. In *Autokran* and its companion case, *Tiefbau*, the German courts held that where parent corporations were "permanently and extensively" involved in the management of G.m.b.H. subsidiaries, they would be liable to creditors in bankruptcy unless they could sustain the burden of proof and show that the losses were beyond their control.[28]

Finally, German law also widely utilizes enterprise principles in its labor laws pertaining to work councils and co-determination. These recognize the parent corporation as the source of control and central direction and provide for worker participation at the level of the parent companies of the group.[29]

France

The most notable French movement toward the introduction of enterprise principles has been in French bankruptcy law. Sections 101 and 180 (formerly 99) of the French Bankruptcy Act provide for the extension of the bankruptcy of a subsidiary to its parent where the parent has committed acts familiar to American students of "piercing the veil jurisprudence." These include, among others, excessive intrusion into the management of the subsidiary and failure to use due care, utilization of the subsidiary as a facade for the conduct of its own business, and disposition of the assets of the subsidiary as if they were its own.[30] Through this technique, French bankruptcy law achieves very much the same result as the judicial devices of substantive consolidation that has become an increasingly prominent feature in American bankruptcy law or traditional "piercing the veil jurisprudence."

The French commercial law similarly imposes liability on parent corporations under the doctrine of *confusion des patrimoines* for debts of subsidiaries where the activities of the companies have been integrated to an impermissible degree, leading to a de facto intermingling of assets. These include such cases as where the subsidiary has been a dummy or facade, or lacks separate books and records, or lacks its own decision-making machinery, or is completely dependent economically on the parent as a result of joint operations.[31] This application closely resembles American "piercing the veil jurisprudence."

French courts have ventured on isolated occasions into disregard of entity. Thus, several foreign controlling companies have been held liable for the obligations of a bankrupt French controlled company because of excessive exercise of control, including, in one case, a parent's appointment of a representative in the subsidiary to report on its activities.[32] Excessive exercise of control has led, in isolated cases, to the imposition of liability on parent corporations and other controlling shareholders elsewhere in Europe, including The Netherlands, Belgium, and Germany.[33]

Finally, there are some instances of the introduction of enterprise concepts into French labor law. As in Germany, French works councils participate at the level of the parent company of the group. The theory of the group as an "economic and social unit" is said to have become a "central concept of [French] labour law."[34] Further, where a parent plays a role in the conduct of the labor policies of its subsidiary through participation in hiring or work instructions, French law makes the parent liable for the subsidiary's severance and other obligations to its employees.[35]

Sweden

The Swedish Companies Act, 1975, as amended, deals with corporate groups in isolated areas, including group accounts, distributions of dividends, cash loans to directors and officers, and a subsidiary's acquisition of its parent's shares. To define corporate groups, the act uses not only the familiar standard of ownership of shares with a majority of the voting rights, but also includes an unusual formulation as an alternative standard: the existence of a "decisive influence" *and* possession of "a considerable share in the results."[36]

Although "decisive influence" is unusual, it is not unique. It is also used in the EC regulations dealing with restrictive trade practices. "Decisive influence" appears to be the equivalent of "controlling influence" in American and German law and "dominant influence" in English and some EC law. However, the Swedish statute supplements "decisive influence" by also requiring possession of a "considerable share in the results." This unique formulation would appear to demand some substantial participation in equity, but a Swedish commentary advises that "nobody really knows" how much participation is required.[37] "Considerable share" is not without parallel elsewhere. It has some similarity to the concept of the "participating interest" in the EC Fourth and Seventh directives pertaining to group accounts, which has been enacted into English law as well.[38]

Swedish jurisprudence also employs enterprise principles in selected areas of labor law that provide for representation of subsidiary employees on the board of directors and on the supervisory councils of parent companies. Finally, the Swedish act imposing sanctions on South Africa applies to all group affiliates, including foreign subsidiaries of Swedish parent corporations.

The European Community

Largely influenced by the German model, the EC has adopted enterprise principles in a series of important actions.[39] Such terms as "parent," "subsidiary," "control," "dominant influence," "decisive influence," and "participating interest" play a crucial role in widely diverse areas. These include regulations and decisions affecting banking, services, air and road transport, and restrictive trade practices. They also include a number of directives on company law, including the Seventh Directive, which requires consolidated accounts for subsidiaries, including those outside the EC; the proposed Ninth Directive (or Vredeling proposal), which provides for fuller disclosure to workers in the event of plant closings as well as protection of creditors and minority shareholders; and the proposed Regulation on a Statute for a European Company. Although the initial draft directives for the latter two proposals originally made bold attempts to introduce far-reaching principles of enterprise law, these engendered considerable resistance, and the later drafts, still awaiting approval, while not entirely abandoning enterprise principles, employ them in a much more tentative manner.

The Seventh Directive on group accounts applies to parent and subsidiary undertakings. The original proposal defined the group relationship in functional terms as existing "if the dominant undertaking exercises in practice its dominant influence to the effect that all such undertakings are managed on a central and unified basis by the dominant undertaking."[40] As noted, this definition went beyond de facto control to require as well its exercise to the point of managing the group components in a unitary manner.

In the end, in the form finally approved, the Seventh Directive substantially retreated from the functional approach of the original proposal. Consolidated accounts are required for majority-owned subsidiaries. The parent undertaking must have a majority of voting power, or be a shareholder and either have the right to appoint a majority of the board or have elected a majority of the board "solely by exercise of its voting rights." Consolidated returns are also required where the shareholder has the right to exercise a "dominant" influence by contract or provision in the articles. However, such contracts or provisions are rare outside of Germany. Finally, the original proposal survives in modified form in authorizing member states to require consolidated returns where the parent holds a "participating interest" and either "actually exercises a dominant influence" *or* manages the parent and subsidiary on a "unified basis."[41]

The proposed Regulation on a Statute for a European Company and the proposed Ninth Directive would utilize a somewhat different approach. They define "dependency," or "control," as the ability "directly or indirectly, to exercise a dominant influence" and presume its existence from ownership, control of a majority of the share capital, control of the voting rights, or the ability to appoint at least half of the members of the board. Whereas the substantive provisions of the original proposals in each of these instances went very far indeed, providing generally for the imposition of liability on the controlling undertaking for the debts of dependent companies of the group, such far-reaching proposals for eliminating limited liability with the group have been dropped in later, revised drafts.

Approval has still not been achieved for either the regulation or the directive. The Ninth Directive appears irretrievably "bogged down." Its prognosis is far from favorable, even though the revised proposal would not apply to subsidiaries organized as close corporations, thereby excluding a large proportion of groups. On the other hand, the Statute for a European Company is still undergoing negotiation among the member states, and prospects for its ultimate adoption after several decades of controversy are distinctly brighter.[42]

The EC Merger Control (antitrust) Regulation uses the term "decisive influence," rather than "dominant influence." Although it would appear that a "decisive influence" standard is somewhat more demanding than "dominant influence," it is far from clear how it will differ in practice, if at all.[43]

In the area of restrictive trade practices, the EC Commission and the European Court of Justice have firmly adopted an enterprise view of groups. Through the doctrine of the "economic entity," they have applied enterprise law to multinational groups as the means of extraterritorial application of EC regulatory policy upon the foreign parents of multinational groups with subsidiaries in the EC. Although some of the decisions may be explained in other terms, such as the direct participation of the foreign parent in the prohibited conduct, the doctrine clearly applies to foreign components, even where this alternative basis for application is absent.[44]

Summary

Although less advanced than in the United States, the European and British Commonwealth experiences in extending governmental regulation over activities of corporate groups are striking in the extent of their similarity to the development of American law. Throughout the Western world, legal systems are recognizing, in varying degrees, the importance of implementing regulatory programs over corporate groups by proceeding in selected areas on an enterprise basis, rather than by continued reliance on entity law. These regulatory programs over major business enterprises are utilizing a number of familiar variations of the fundamental concept of "control" to accomplish this result. In many cases, they do not restrictively define "control" in terms of ownership or control of a majority of the voting shares, but instead, significantly expand the concept through use of such functional terms as "controlling," "decisive," or "dominant" "influence."

8

National Law and
Multinational Business:
Enterprise Law and Extraterritoriality

Enterprise concepts generally seek to impose legal obligations of one component of a corporate group upon the other components of the group; occasionally, enterprise principles are used to attribute legal rights of one group component to another. In the case of multinational corporations with component corporations in several, if not many, countries, the use of enterprise principles by a nation invariably involves extraterritorial application of the doctrine to foreign affiliates, thereby frequently precipitating a clash with the national legal systems of the other countries in which the group operates. This is particularly likely when the group operates in other nations that continue to rely on entity principles.

This serious problem is inherent in national legal policies that seek to govern world business. A regulatory program resting on entity law reaches only the local part of a worldwide business. The existence of foreign affiliates free of the restrictions of a national program inevitably leads to ready evasion of the national program and frustration of the objectives of the statute. Thus, in the case of multinational groups, utilization of enterprise principles is frequently essential for full implementation of the national regulatory program over the domestic business. However, such extraterritorial application of the law of the regulating nation runs the risk of clashing with conflicting governmental policies of every nation in which the constituent companies of the multinational group are conducting business. Where such conflict arises, retaliation is likely, with high political costs to the country asserting its law extraterritorially and heavy economic costs to its corporations. As illustrated by the American experience in attempting to enforce its embargoes on trade with China and the Soviet Union, reviewed in this chapter, the trade-off is direct and severe.

Extraterritoriality falls into two basic classes, depending on whether enterprise principles are being applied to a parent corporation or to a subsidiary. The use of enterprise principles in executing a nation's political or legal policies with respect to the domestic parent corporation of a multinational group means extraterritorial application of the national program to the foreign components of the group. This is *home country extraterritoriality*. Such extraterritorial application necessarily means extension of the scope of the home country's laws to foreign subsidiaries that are subject as well to the laws of the host country under which they are incorporated or have their *siège*. Such overlapping application is an irritant under all circumstances. Where, however, the policies that are served by the domestic governmental program being applied extraterritorially conflict with those in the foreign nations concerned, home country extraterritoriality means not merely irritation, but conflict that can assume prominent dimensions and lead to international confrontations of magnitude. Thus, the United Kingdom is only one of several countries to enact statutory procedures to prevent the extraterritorial assertion of American law, particularly in such areas as antitrust, assertion of in personam jurisdiction, and discovery.[1]

In contrast to home country extraterritoriality, a very different type of problem arises when a host country applying enterprise principles to a domestic subsidiary of a foreign-based multinational group asserts jurisdiction over, or imposes liability upon, the foreign parent or affiliates of the group. This is *host country extraterritoriality*. The consequence of extraterritoriality, whether exercised by the home or host countries of the group, is the inevitable clash of conflicting national legal policies applied to worldwide business enterprises.

In a world economy where developed countries jostle for competitive position in world markets and developing countries compete for capital investment, it is clear that extraterritorial application of national law may involve very serious economic, as well as political, costs. These costs affect both the world-power home countries attempting to export their own national interests and foreign policy concerns through attempts to regulate the conduct of national-based worldwide businesses and to host countries striking out at alleged exploitation by foreign multinational enterprises. While wealthy, developed home countries may more readily absorb such self-imposed costs, underdeveloped host countries are particularly vulnerable. For the capital-hungry host country, fearful of creating disincentives to local investment, the costs may well be insupportable, and such policies may be reversed if the reaction in the developed world is severe.

In the marketplace, disincentives to capital investment are not the only deterrent operating in this arena. The loss of competitive position in the international economy is a factor to be reckoned with as well. World business operates in a world market, and the economic pressures from domestic law may render a local industry simply noncompetitive in the world market. In such a posture, a society may well have to choose between giving up on its worldwide application of domestic law that is in conflict with the law of other powerful market factors and exposing local industry to serious impairment of its competitive position in the world market.

It is the goal of international law to develop legal principles to avoid or resolve such disputes. However, the principles of international law developed thus far are grounded on entity law, and they therefore utterly fail to address the underlying legal problems presented by multinational corporate groups. Nations, particularly the United States but including a number of other countries as well, have accordingly have felt free to act in ways contrary to past concepts of international law, and the international world is in urgent need of the emergence of commonly acceptable, newer principles reflecting more accurately, and responding more adequately to, the underlying economic realities.

The problem presented by enterprise law and extraterritoriality is a formidable part of the major challenge to the legal systems of the world arising from the prominence of multinational enterprise in world business.

International Law

The imposition of national legal obligations on the foreign subsidiaries of domestic corporations, as is increasingly occurring in a number of important areas in American law, presents serious questions under international law. To avoid such clashes of national sovereignties, international law, in the quieter period before the full intertwining of the economies of the developed world, developed a series of principles based on entity law to determine when a nation may apply its own laws.

The most important of these are the *nationality principle* and the *territorial principle*, including the latter's corollary, the "effects" doctrine. What, then, under the traditional principles of international law and its attempted reformulation by the Restatement (Third) of Foreign Relations Law of the United States is a nation's jurisdiction to prescribe, that is to impose its regulatory programs and other legal rules upon the foreign subsidiaries of domestic corporations?

The Nationality Principle

Reflecting the dominance of entity law in the centuries during which international law was being formed, for jurisdictional purposes the nationality of a corporation has traditionally been characterized solely by reference to the state of incorporation so long as the corporation and that state have some sufficient connection. (Although some civil law jurisdictions look to the principal place of business, or the *siège sociale*, even these countries require incorporation in the same state, so that in the end, the test is much the same.[2])

With the state of incorporation determining nationality, other factors — such as the nationality of the controlling shareholders, the circumstances of the exercise of control, and the operation of a subsidiary as part of the integrated business of a corporate group conducting a common business under central direction — have all been dismissed as irrelevant.[3] A foreign subsidiary, accordingly, has foreign nationality, and does not acquire the nationality of its parent corporation.[4] In consequence, the home country of the parent corporation of a group cannot justify extending its regulation of the group to its foreign subsidiaries by appeal to the traditional nationality principle.

These doctrines became firmly accepted at a time when corporations typically confined their operations to a single country. This was long before the emergence of multinational corporations as the predominant element in the conduct of economic activity in most industrialized countries. Such enterprises, organized and operating on a worldwide scale, present difficult problems for the legal systems of each country in which they operate. With national legal systems no longer co-extensive with the areas of operation of the enterprise, the effectiveness of the national law of the home country of the group, if confined to the parent and subsidiaries organized under its laws, would severely suffer. Foreign components of the group would then not be subject to the national controls, and the group could evade *any* national law by having the proscribed activity conducted by a foreign component.

National control over world business, however, involves ultimate conflict between nations. National policies will inevitably differ, and there is no machinery to iron out the differences. Effective and internationally harmonious legal control over multinationals requires the establishment of international legal controls co-extensive with the geographical scope of the activities being controlled. The contemplation of such a development on the international scale is still visionary. Regional action, as in the European Community, or multilateral national action represent useful, although limited, approaches to the problem.

In the meantime, the problem of assuring the effectiveness of national policy creates an enormous pressure for the assertion of extraterritorial jurisdiction over foreign subsidiaries and affiliates of domestic multinational groups. In recognition of this pressure, the American view of jurisdictional doctrines has advanced well beyond the traditional principles of international law doctrines. For the United States, concerned with imposing its policies on American-owned foreign subsidiaries, the traditional view that corporate nationality is determined by the state of incorporation is becoming only the starting point of analysis, not the final answer. However, other nations have not yet significantly joined in such a reformulation.

American Modification of the Nationality Principle

The American Law Institute, in its Restatement (Third) of the Foreign Relations Law of the United States (the "Restatement"),[5] has recognized the need for the evolution of older doctrines of international law into a modern one that will reflect the challenge to effective national regulatory programs presented by an economic world in which transnational enterprises predominate. Although the Restatement makes an attempt to provide a comprehensive framework for the resolution of the problem, its standards are controversial and at best provide only very general guidance. Furthermore, the Restatement is a comprehensive statement of *American foreign relations* law, a statement that differs in important respects from generally accepted principles of international law.

Although the Restatement accepts the traditional standard of the state of incorporation as the starting point for corporate application of the nationality principle, it supplements it with a newer, more complex doctrine. It has approved significant modifications of the nationality principle in selected cases to include the exercise of national jurisdiction over foreign subsidiaries under situations of particular importance to the implementation of the home country regulatory program.

Acknowledging that "multinational enterprises do not fit neatly within traditional concepts of nationality and territoriality," the Restatement recognizes "exceptional cases" in which control of domestic corporations or persons over foreign corporations may, contrary to the traditional principles, serve as a link analogous to nationality, and support the assertion of home country jurisdiction over the foreign subsidiary.[6] However, such assertion is permissible only where it satisfies a balancing standard attempting to "accommodat[e] overlapping or conflicting interests of states, and affected private interests."

The Restatement has replaced the "rigid concepts" of the traditional doctrine by "broader criteria embracing principles of reasonableness and fairness." It utilizes a "search for the center of gravity" of the situation as the appropriate standard to supplement traditional principles of international law.[7] The balancing standard of Section 403(2) embraces a number of major factors, and is sufficiently important to justify extensive quotation. It includes the following elements:

> (a) the link of the activity to the territory of the regulating state, *i.e.*, the extent to which the activity . . . has substantial, direct, and foreseeable effect upon or in the territory;
> (b) the connections, such as nationality, . . . or economic activity, between the regulating state and the person principally responsible for the activity . . . or . . . those whom the regulation is designed to protect;

(c) the character of the activity to be regulated, the importance of the regulation to the regulating state, the extent to which other states regulate such activities, and the degree to which the desirability of such regulation is generally accepted;

(d) the existence of justified expectations that might be protected or hurt by the regulation;

(e) the importance of the regulation to the international political, legal, or economic system;

(f) the extent to which the regulation is consistent with the traditions of the international system;

(g) the extent to which another state may have an interest in regulating the activity; and

(h) the likelihood of conflict with regulation by another state.

Where foreign subsidiaries are concerned, Sections 414(1), (2)(b) and (c) provide that the exercise of such jurisdiction "for limited purposes" is not unreasonable, depending on all relevant factors, including the extent to which the regulation is "essential" for advancing a "major national interest"; or the extent to which the national program of which the regulation is a part can be carried out "effectively" only if applied also to foreign subsidiaries; and the extent that the regulation conflicts, or is likely to conflict, with the law or policy of the state where the subsidiary is established. Section 414 concludes by stating that the burden of establishing reasonableness is heavier when the direction is issued to a foreign subsidiary than when it is issued to the parent corporation.[8]

Thus, as reformulated, the nationality principle no longer bars *every* application of American foreign trade and investment law to foreign subsidiaries of U.S. corporations. All the circumstances, rather than a "rigid concept" turning on the place of incorporation or the corporate *siège*, will determine whether an application of domestic law to foreign subsidiaries is valid in a the particular case. This is an authoritative American view, but, of course, the United States cannot unilaterally establish principles of international law; these rest on the assent of the world community. As will appear, other nations, including its closest allies, do not share the same view.

A foremost factor in the evaluation required by the reformulated standard is whether a "major national interest" of the regulating state is at stake. In the event of a war or other threat to the national security of the regulating state, the view that domestic law may be validly applied under principles of international law to foreign subsidiaries or enterprises owned or controlled by domestic corporations or other domestic nationals is most compelling.[9] However, where governmental action reflects only the implementation of peacetime foreign policy objectives, the case for extraterritorial application of domestic law to foreign subsidiaries is distinctly less persuasive. Thus, the Restatement provides for an exception to the traditional view only where extension of a regulatory scheme to include foreign subsidiaries is "necessary to prevent evasion of controls through incorporation or establishment abroad."

Where the application of American law to a foreign subsidiary of an American corporation conflicts with the law of the state in which the subsidiary is organized or located, the contradictory commands of the two sovereigns introduce still another dimension of the problem. Recognizing the difficult, if not impossible, problem facing the subsidiary, Section 441 of the Restatement provides that in such a case, the domestic law may "generally" not be applied to the foreign subsidiary. This is the "foreign compulsion" doctrine.

The Territorial Principle and the Effects Doctrine

The other major principle supporting the exercise of national jurisdiction to prescribe is the territorial principle, including its corollary, the effects doctrine. Under the territorial principle, a state has jurisdiction to prescribe with respect to conduct substantially taking part within its territory.[10] In this form, this principle has little, if any, application to assertion of extraterritorial jurisdiction.

However, this straightforward notion has been supplemented by an ancillary principle, the effects doctrine, extending territorial jurisdiction to include "conduct outside of [a nation's] territory [with] substantial effect within its territory."[11] This doctrine has been particularly utilized to support American enforcement of American antitrust, foreign investment, and securities regulation laws to reach conduct abroad with impact in the United States. Because such extraterritorial control over conduct abroad that may be lawful under the applicable foreign law has high potential for international confrontation, the Restatement confines the principle to cases where the effects are "direct, foreseeable, and substantial" and where the rule is not inconsistent with "principles of justice generally recognized."[12]

The application of American foreign trade and investment controls to the activities abroad of foreign subsidiaries of American corporations is by definition extraterritorial. It is, accordingly, unable to look to the basic territorial principle for support. Nor does the supplementary effects doctrine provide help. Although the foreign activity may impair important national security, foreign policy, or economic objectives, it lacks any territorial link to activities within the United States, except in one disputed area. In its imposition of export controls, the United States, relying on the territorial principle, has asserted jurisdiction over the re-export of U.S.-origin goods, data, or technology, either by foreign subsidiaries or by unrelated foreign purchasers. Whether such an application of American law to U.S.-origin items is supported by the territoriality principle has been vigorously disputed, particularly by Europeans.

The Protective Principle

The protective principle provides still another basis for the exercise of extraterritorial jurisdiction. International law recognizes a state's exercise of jurisdiction over a limited class of offenses outside of a nation's territory by foreign persons where vital interests are at stake. The Restatement includes "offenses directed against the security of the state or other offenses threatening the integrity of governmental functions that are generally recognized as crimes by developed legal systems."[13]

Foreign trade and investment laws have not generally been regarded as falling within this principle. After all, the regulated conduct is not "generally recognized as crimes." Although the Restatement's language is not entirely clear and could be read to restrict the reference to crimes to the "integrity of governmental functions," and not to modify the reference to "security of the state," the fact of the matter is that the limitation to crimes has been almost universally applied to both.

However, there is some contrary authority. In the *Sensor* litigation discussed in connection with the Siberian pipeline embargo, (see the section in this chapter entitled "The Soviet Union and the Siberian Pipeline Controversy"), a Dutch court held that the protective principle did not support the extraterritorial application of the American export controls involved in the embargo. However, in dictum, the court indicated that the protective principle could support extraterritorial exercise of jurisdiction in the case of matters that "jeopardize the security or credit-worthiness" of the foreign nation.[14] Such recognition would extend the protective principle from the tightly restricted class of "generally recognized crimes" to include economic controls of paramount importance to the foreign country. This expanded version of the traditional protective principle awaits future development.

As noted, in the most extreme threat to national security, such as war, there is widespread recognition of the legitimacy of stretching traditional concepts to enable belligerent powers to implement more fully restrictions on trade with the enemy. Such conduct has generally been justified by reference to the "link" or "substantial connection" to the enemy state as providing an analogy to nationality to support application of the nationality principle. It could be alternatively viewed as an application of the protective principle, in which event it could provide a basis for further expansion to include other threats to the security of the state, short of war. However, the question then arises: What lesser threat to security, short of war, would also suffice? In such an inquiry, the elaborate balancing standard proposed by the Restatement for extension of the nationality principle would seem fully applicable and conceivably could achieve greater international acceptance in that context than in the nationality context in which it has been advanced.

Home Country Extraterritoriality in the United States

Of the two areas of extraterritoriality — home country and host country — the more prominent is the imposition of legal mandates by the home country of the group's parent corporation upon its foreign subsidiaries. In this area, the home country is determining legal standards for companies all over the world that are organized under the laws of other nation-states and subject to local laws. The home country is attempting worldwide application of its regulatory program in order to achieve full implementation of the national policies involved, often ones of great importance that represent national security, foreign policy, or economic policy objectives. When the home country law conflicts with the national laws under which the foreign subsidiary is organized and where it is conducting its part of the multinational business, bruising international controversies are apt to develop.

In trade controls and a number of other regulatory law areas, American statutory law has moved aggressively. It has adopted enterprise principles as the keystone of the regulatory apparatus. It applies such principles extraterritorially, even though such application may violate generally accepted principles of international law. Further, it requires the foreign subsidiary to comply with American law, even when it violates the law of the nation in which it was organized and is conducting business. Although international law forms an essential element of the American legal system and is generally to be applied by all American courts, federal and state, Congress has the power under American law to enact statutes inconsistent with international law. All that American law requires is that Congress clearly express its intention to override international law. When Congress has done so, the federal law governs.[15]

The imposition of trade controls over foreign concerns owned and controlled by American corporations and persons has evolved from simplistic and ineffective beginnings in World War I to a highly sophisticated and effective legal structure, reaching American-controlled multinationals around the world. These statutes constitute a major segment of the American statutes of specific application of enterprise principles to corporate groups. They are not confined to trade with designated countries in times of war or national emergency, but include foreign trade in peacetime, as well. Similar statutes include the Age Discrimination in Employment Act of 1984, the Anti-Boycott Act, and the Foreign Corrupt Practices Act among others. The regulatory apparatus of all these statutes typically rests on the existence of "control" by an American corporation (or other American shareholder) of any foreign corporation, and thereby includes all foreign components of American corporate groups.

Often involving the leading powers of the Western world, the international controversies surrounding the extraterritorial application of some of these statutes illustrate dramatically the inevitable consequences of national efforts to deal with the economic and social problems of worldwide business. Such controversies have been the recurrent experience of American attempts to utilize the foreign trade of American-based groups as a tool of American national policy. These efforts have proved costly both in terms of the disruption of relations with nations normally closely allied with the United States and the economic losses directly and indirectly sustained by American businesses.

International law based on the nineteenth-century entity principles of national states is inadequate to resolve the problems presented by world business. To deal with the threat to the effectiveness of regulatory programs of national importance arising from the limitations of entity law in the face of multinational enterprise, the United States has declined to comply with established doctrines of international law and has turned to enterprise principles, notwithstanding the breakdown in the international order that necessarily results.

World War I: Entity Law

In the Trading with the Enemy Act of 1917, enacted after the entry of the United States into World War I, Congress authorized the President to seize assets of Germany and its allies and to impose an embargo on trade with Germany and the other Central Powers. The Act was naively drafted. It applied only to "person[s] in the United States" and it defined "enemy" in simplistic fashion to include only corporations incorporated in an enemy country and corporations incorporated in a neutral country that were trading with an enemy country.[16]

Utilizing the state of incorporation as its standard, the statute completely ignored enemy ownership or control of businesses incorporated within the United States or neutral countries. When the issue eventually came before the Supreme Court, well after the immediate passions of the war had cooled, the Court unanimously refused to expand the literal boundaries of the statutory coverage to include enemy-controlled enterprises. The Court held that a New Jersey subsidiary of a German parent corporation and a Straits Settlement corporation, in which Germans held a majority of the stock, were not "enemies" within the statutory definition and were therefore beyond the reach of the statute. State courts reached a comparable result.[17]

Entity law and strict construction prevailed in these cases, even though they made frustration of the fundamental national objectives represented by the legislation inevitable. Only the fact that World War I had been over for a number of years made such harsh results politically acceptable.

The British judicial system faced a similar question while the war was at its height. In 1916 in *Daimler Co. v. Continental Tyre & Rubber Co.*,[18] the House of Lords reached a very different conclusion. Although it held that a British subsidiary of a German corporation with a board of directors comprised solely of German nationals was an "enemy" corporation for purposes of British law, the Law Lords divided sharply on the basis for the decision.

A majority of the judges avoided the issue of corporate nationality. They inferred the enemy status of the corporation from the German residence of those in control. Another judge concurred on the alternative ground that the subsidiary had German nationality because it was controlled by German nationals. Two judges dissented, concluding that incorporation in Britain was decisive, notwithstanding the German nationality of its shareholders and directors.

World War II and Postwar: Enterprise Law

In the First War Powers Act of 1941, enacted on the eve of the entrance of the United States into World War II, Congress enacted a comprehensive regulatory program authorizing the President in time of "war" or "national emergency" to prohibit or regulate economic activity and to seize "foreign property" or "property in which any foreign country or any national thereof has . . . an interest."

The statutory program was of very broad scope. Instead of being limited to "persons within the United States," the statute applied to "any person . . . subject to the jurisdiction of the United States." The regulations expressly included foreign subsidiaries and affiliates of American corporations among those "subject to the jurisdiction of the United States" and subject to the Act. The Supreme Court approved.[19]

Although neither the Act nor the regulations defined the term "control," the Office of Foreign Assets Controls interpreted it in de facto terms to include "any type of effective control, actual or potential"; lack of fifty percent stock ownership was not fatal.[20]

Thus, the United States abandoned the traditional nationality standard of the state of incorporation as determining the outer perimeter of American regulation of economic activity abroad. This was an enormous step forward in providing the executive branch with the flexibility to deal in a sophisticated manner with the complexities of international trade and capital movements involving multitiered corporate groups.

By 1941, Congress had at last learned that comprehensive federal regulation of economic activity was inherently defective unless the scope of the regulatory program was determined by economic realities, not by jurisprudential concepts vulnerable to manipulation by corporate structuring. Commencing with the Emergency Transportation Act of 1933 and the ensuing wave of New Deal reform statutes, Congresses during the New Deal era regularly defined the scope of their regulatory statutes in enterprise law terms, utilizing standards turning on "control," rather than on traditional concepts of entity law.

During World War II, with the Western world united against Hitler, extraterritorial trade controls directed against Germany presented no problems. After the war, as the foreign policies of the allied powers diverged, the picture changed dramatically. Extraterritorial trade controls inevitably mean international conflict when the trade policies of countries, particularly those of the great powers, differ. This is best illustrated by episodes of American attempts to enforce extraterritorial controls against the profound opposition of its closest allies. These episodes include American embargoes on trade with China following the Korean War and on trade with the Soviet Union following the 1981 invasions of Poland and Afghanistan.[21]

THE CHINA EMBARGO

With the invasion of South Korea in 1950 by North Korea, later joined by China, President Truman issued a Proclamation of National Emergency, and the United States responded with economic and military measures. The Foreign Assets Control regulations promulgated under the 1941 Act prohibited unlicensed financial and commercial transactions between the United States and North Korea and China; in addition, they froze North Korean and Chinese assets in the United States.[22] Both embargoes survived long after the Korean War came to an end.

So long as the Korean War continued, enforcement of these regulations did not lead to significant disputes with the European allies. After the conclusion of hostilities with the signing of the Pact of Panmunjom, American antagonism toward North Korea and China continued unabated for many years, and economic measures forbidding trade with China and North Korea remained in force. In most Western countries, however, animosities in time subsided, and foreign trade policies in time swung around to renewal of trade relations with China. This difference in national policy objectives over continuance of the China embargo led to celebrated confrontations between the United States and its closest allies: the United Kingdom, France, and Canada.

United Kingdom: ITT-Standard Electric Affair. Standard Electric, an English subsidiary of a U.S. parent corporation, had contracted to supply a British manufacturer with radio equipment for aircraft being built for China. The Treasury Department forbade the transaction, insisting that because an American subsidiary was involved, the transaction was subject to the embargo. However, by this time, the British government had abandoned its previous policy and favored trade with China. Not surprisingly, the British strongly resisted the assertion of American jurisdiction over business operations in the United Kingdom to enforce a policy contrary to British policy.

A tense period of confrontation followed until the two governments papered over the dispute. Standard Electric did not perform the disputed contract, and American policy seemed to prevail. However, the reality was otherwise. The British government itself supplied the necessary equipment out of its own military stockpile, ordering replacement sets from Standard Electric to replenish the stockpile.[23] Thus, in the end, the territorial sovereign had its way, and the United States had to yield.

France: The Fruehauf Controversy. An equally stormy confrontation with France, with much the same result, involved a French corporation (Fruehauf-France), two-thirds of which was owned by an American parent corporation (Fruehauf-USA).[24] Fruehauf-France had contracted with the largest French truck manufacturer, its most important customer, to produce Fruehauf semitrailers and couplers for trucks to be exported to China.

Pursuant to a Treasury Department order, Fruehauf-USA instructed Fruehauf-France to cancel the contract. After the French president-general manager resigned in protest, Fruehauf-USA sought to remove the French directors of Fruehauf-France and to replace them with American directors in order to implement the Treasury order.

The French directors, however, refused to yield and instituted legal proceedings in the French courts. They succeeded in obtaining both the appointment of an administrator to operate Fruehauf-France and a court order directing the administrator to carry out the contract. In granting the application, the French court pointed to the economic loss to Fruehauf-France and the layoff of six hundred French employees. At this point, noting that rejection of the contract would "definitively injure the financial equilibrium and credit of Fruehauf-France," the United States Department of Commerce had enough and decided not to enforce the export regulations against Fruehauf.

Thus, in both the *Fruehauf* and *Standard Electric* controversies, French and British policy, not American, prevailed. After causing confrontation and ill will with its close allies and imposing heavy costs on American and American-controlled enterprises, strenuous attempts to achieve extraterritorial application of American law to foreign subsidiaries of American groups failed.[25]

Canada. The experience with a weaker power, Canada, was quite different. Canada was also seeking to develop trade with China. When the United States took measures to prevent Canadian automobile, oil, and grain companies owned by American concerns from supplying China in violation of the embargo, the two nations came into direct conflict.[26]

Although Canada, like the United Kingdom and France, resisted the American program, it was unable to make its will prevail. The United States persisted in largely enforcing the embargo while purporting to accommodate Canadian concerns through the establishment of a procedure of "full consultation" to reduce or avoid confrontation between Canada and America.[27] However, notwithstanding a few Canadian successes in obtaining approval of major transactions with China, Canadian efforts, in practice, were largely unsuccessful.

The United States accomplished its objective by utilization of "indirect" controls, making its policy less visible and less controversial, but no less effective. It enforced the embargo through pressure against the American parent corporations, rather than by direct order to their Canadian subsidiaries. American multinationals simply caused their Canadian subsidiaries to refer export orders to the parent companies for decision. Orders to China one way or another rarely received final approval at the American headquarters of the group.

The Canadian government was apparently unable or unwilling to defy the United States and aggressively pursue its China trade policy in this particular instance. American political and economic power cast a heavier shadow over Canada than over the United Kingdom or France.

THE SOVIET UNION AND THE SIBERIAN PIPELINE CONTROVERSY

Soviet repression of Poland during 1981 evoked a strong hostile reaction in the United States and led the Reagan administration to intensify its program of economic pressure against the Soviets, particularly in their efforts to construct the proposed Siberian Oil pipeline. The Pipeline Embargo Order (the embargo), issued in January 1982 and amended in June 1982, required prior governmental approval of exports to the Soviet Union by any person "subject to the jurisdiction of the United States," including foreign subsidiaries and licensees of American firms.

The extraterritorial nature of the controls produced a "storm of criticism and outrage" from numerous nations, including such close American allies as the United Kingdom, West Germany, and France. The controls were also condemned by the European Community as representing "sweeping extensions" of American jurisdiction "repugnant to international law."[28]

The embargo gave rise to a number of celebrated controversies involving foreign subsidiaries of American corporations obligated under major supply contracts for the Soviets. In both France and the United Kingdom, foreign subsidiaries of American groups were again simultaneously threatened with sanctions by the United States government in the event of a delivery under an embargoed contract and by sanctions from the foreign host country if it complied with the American direction. At the same time, foreign governments did not challenge the application of the embargo at home to American subsidiaries of foreign multinationals. Application of American regulatory controls over American subsidiaries of foreign parent corporations, including subsidiaries owned by a foreign sovereign, is an accepted aspect of American law.[29] It complies with the nationality principle of international law.

France: The Dresser Industries Controversy. At the time of the imposition of the embargo, a wholly owned French subsidiary of Dresser Industries, an American corporation, had contracted to manufacture compressors for use by the Soviets in the transmission of natural gas. After the embargo, Dresser-France stopped production of further equipment but readied three already completed compressors for shipment on a Soviet freighter. The United States government threatened sanctions if the compressors were loaded for shipment to the Soviet Union, and the French government responded by threatening its own sanctions if Dresser-France did not honor the contract.

Faced with this intolerable predicament, Dresser Industries and Dresser-France instituted in the United States a declaratory judgment action seeking to declare the embargo invalid and restraining its enforcement. The court refused to rule on the merits and referred the Dresser companies to administrative remedies. Before there was any ruling on the merits, the embargo was lifted, and the case became moot.[30]

The United Kingdom. The United Kingdom also resisted the Soviet embargo. The British government ordered affected companies with major pipeline contracts—three British subsidiaries of American multinationals and a British concern using U.S.–origin parts and technology to disregard the embargo.[31] The United States and the United Kingdom were again in head-on confrontation, but as in France, the impasse came to an end with the lifting of the embargo several months later, before decisive action was taken by either government. Although the companies affected were then able to complete performance under their contracts, the American policy imposed "great long-run economic and political costs" on them.[32]

The Netherlands. The *Sensor* litigation in The Netherlands led to the only European judicial adjudication of the legal effect of the embargo. In compliance with the embargo, Sensor, a Dutch subsidiary of an American parent corporation, had refused to comply with its contract for equipment intended for the Soviet Union. When sued by the Dutch purchaser in Dutch courts for breach of contract, the subsidiary unsuccessfully sought to defend by pleading the illegality of performance under American law.

The Dutch court held that Dutch law governed the contract and that under Dutch law, the subsidiary had Dutch nationality because it had been incorporated in The Netherlands. The nationality principle of jurisdiction under international law was accordingly not available for the defendant. The court similarly held that because there had been no "direct or illicit effects" within the United States, the territorial principle and the effects doctrine were inapplicable. Finally, the court held that the protective doctrine was not applicable because it was available only for situations that "jeopardized the security or credit-worthiness of the state" and did not include trade controls of this nature. The embargo accordingly did not comply with international law and could not provide a defense for the subsidiary.[33]

Opposition to the pipeline embargo was not confined to Europe. Business opposition at home was as vociferous as the political opposition abroad. Although the administration strenuously attempted to make the embargo effective, it abandoned the effort a few months later. The political disruption arising from the controversies with American allies was severe, and the economic losses to American and world enterprise were enormous, particularly if the loss of future sales is included. It has been noted that the true costs of imposing export controls are long-term and substantially hidden.[34]

SUMMARY

As an international political matter, the effectiveness of these trade controls has depended on the degree of congruence between American foreign policy or national security objectives and the objectives of other foreign nations with respect to the countries against which the American trade policy is directed. Where such congruence exists, as, for example, in the case of the World War II controls and many sanctions in the postwar world, the program has been highly successful. Thus, the NATO powers (excluding Iceland), Australia, and Japan effectively coordinated their efforts to keep strategic goods and technology from moving to the Soviet Union during the Cold War, through an ad hoc agency called the Coordinating Committee (CoCom). Although Europeans have perceived CoCom as primarily an American vehicle, it has served as a model of the international apparatus that can reach accommodation and avoid national confrontation in the political administration of world trade.

Where, however, foreign nations have different objectives and confrontation, rather than cooperation, occurs, as, for example, in the American trade embargo against China and the Soviet Pipeline, the controls proved much less successful and in the end had to be abandoned. In brief, where other great powers are concerned and where the issue is sufficiently important for such powers to adopt an adamant position, their territorial control over the American subsidiaries located within their borders in the end is likely to prevail over American extraterritorial controls and pressures.

Thus, assertion of foreign policy through extraterritorial assertion of jurisdiction over foreign subsidiaries of American corporations has frequently not been successful. In addition, it has involved the United States in costly controversies with its closest allies, ending in abandoned controls and impaired relations with powers whose support and cooperation in other areas of foreign affairs were of grave importance.

Host Country Extraterritoriality

Although both home country and host country extraterritoriality involve the extension of national law over foreign corporations, the two differ sharply in the nature of application. Home country extraterritoriality regulates foreign acts by foreign subsidiaries of domestic parent companies; it represents extraterritorial application of jurisdiction to prescribe. Host country extraterritoriality involves the use of enterprise principles to assert national law over foreign corporations not operating within the country by asserting jurisdiction over them and imposing liability upon them by reason of the activities of their local subsidiaries. This is extraterritorial application of jurisdiction to adjudicate. However, this is only the initial chapter. There are rarely enough, if any, local assets of the foreign parent or affiliates to satisfy the judgment within the host country, and the confrontation with the national legal system of the parent will arise in the courts of the country — home country or neutral country — in which the plaintiff, successful in the host country, seeks to enforce the judgment. This introduces still another dimension of the complex problem: Under what circumstances will one nation recognize or enforce the judgments of another?

Argentina: The Deltec *Litigation*

The outstanding example of the exercise of host country extraterritoriality reflecting enterprise principles is the *Deltec* litigation in Argentina during the Peronista era. This episode, which occurred at a time of strident hostility toward Western capitalism, provides a dramatic example of the application of enterprise principles in bankruptcy by host country courts to impose worldwide liability on a major multinational enterprise for the liabilities of its bankrupt domestic subsidiaries. This important development is best understood as the product of a society in political ferment controlled by a third-world government expressing intense hostility to foreign investors and to perceived exploitation by multinational business. Political pressures transcending purely jurisprudential considerations contributed to a dramatic formulation and application of enterprise law.[35]

The *Deltec* litigation involved the reorganization of Cia-Swift, the largest Argentine meat-packing company, which had been acquired long before by Deltec, a Canadian multinational conglomerate group. After Deltec had unsuccessfully tried to sell off Cia-Swift, the company was placed in reorganization. The company-appointed referee originally found that Cia-Swift assets substantially exceeded outside liabilities and indeed exceeded liabilities when intercompany debts were included as well.[36] A reorganization plan calling for payment of all debts in full, with interest over four years, received the support of eighty-six percent of the creditors. Nevertheless, at the instance of a minor creditor with a mere $4,000 claim, the court rejected the intercompany claims and "extended" the liabilities of Cia-Swift to other Deltec companies. The court relied on the "unified structure of decision and interest which makes it a single unit" and "penetrates the corporate personality." On appeal, the intermediate appellate court upheld the bankruptcy order but reversed the enterprise ruling that had extended liability to group affiliates.

The case then went to the Argentine Supreme Court, whose entire membership had changed after the election triumph of the Peronista regime. Applying enterprise principles and finding that the Deltec group comprised a "unified socio-economic entity," the Supreme Court reinstated the lower court decree and remanded for a determination of the other Deltec companies "compris[ing] an economic unit" with the bankrupt company to be subjected to its liabilities. As perceived by the court, grave national interests were at stake in the relation of multinational enterprises in their "interdependence, linkages, and their multinational nature" to the "paramount interests of [Argentine] society."[37] On remand, the lower court decree included the Deltec parent and subsidiaries in entirely different industries than meat-packing. The conglomerate nature of the multinational did not prevent enterprise treatment of these foreign affiliates.

The enterprise principles of the *Deltec* litigation were thereupon incorporated into Argentine statutory law. In a provision without parallel elsewhere in the world, the Argentine Foreign Investment Law of 1973 made foreign affiliates of multinational enterprises liable for the obligations of their Argentine companies.

In 1976, the Peron regime was ousted, and Argentina began to restore normal relations with the Western economic world. The 1973 Act was promptly repealed and replaced by the much more conventional Argentine Foreign Investment Law of 1976, reflecting entity law concepts and treating Argentine subsidiaries as legally separate from their foreign affiliates.[38]

This episode illustrates, in some degree, the economic restraints of world markets on the national legal policies of developing nations. The Argentine introduction of extraterritorial enterprise principles in a highly charged atmosphere created significant disincentives to foreign investment, contributing to a severe economic downturn. The Peron government subsequently fell, and the new government returned to the conventional legal principles of the developed nations in order to restore the flow of capital and business opportunity to Argentina.

The *Deltec* decision, coming against a highly politicized background, evoked severe international hostility. Whether an application of enterprise principles under stable political conditions through ordinary legislative or judicial procedures would have the same effect remains to be seen. However, it would seem clear that, on the margin, the adverse economic impact would inevitably have to be taken into account in investment decisions. So long as world legal systems are overwhelmingly based on entity law, the introduction and application of enterprise principles in the legal system of any developing country is bound to make investment opportunities in the country less attractive to groups otherwise operating under entity law.

India: The Bhopal *Litigation*

According to Indian sources,[39] more than 2,500 people were killed and more than 200,000 were permanently injured as a result of the December 1984 disaster at the Bhopal, India, plant of the 50.9 percent-owned Indian subsidiary of Union Carbide Corporation. The government of India and numerous private plaintiffs brought suit both in the United States and in India against the Indian subsidiary and its American parent corporation. Although five of the six causes of action asserted direct liability on the part of the parent for its own tortious acts, a sixth cause relied on enterprise doctrines, seeking to impose intragroup liability on the parent for torts of its Indian subsidiary. In the United States, the federal courts refused to assume jurisdiction on the ground of forum non conveniens on conditions not material for purposes of the discussion.[40] The litigation thereupon proceeded in India. The Supreme Court of India ultimately upheld a $470 million settlement judgment against Carbide, resting on both its direct negligence and on intragroup liability under enterprise law. The litigation, at least in its civil dimensions, has come to an end.[41]

The settlement has made unnecessary any attempt by the plaintiffs to obtain extraterritorial enforcement of any contested Indian judgment in the event, not unlikely, that Indian assets of Carbide and its Indian subsidiary would be insufficient to satisfy the judgment. Such an attempt would have presented an interesting ultimate question: To what extent would the courts of other nations still wedded to entity law enforce a foreign judgment resting on enterprise law? (However, in view of the fact that such a judgment might have also rested on the direct liability of Carbide, the issue of enterprise liability conceivably might not have arisen.[42])

The *Deltec* and *Bhopal* litigations present very different circumstances. *Deltec* broke new jurisprudential ground, resting solely on a bold assertion of enterprise law. It also involved a questionable reorganization proceeding in which the Deltec subsidiary in question had been transformed from a company with assets substantially exceeding its liabilities but suffering from cash-flow problems into a hopelessly insolvent company. *Bhopal*, shorn of its catastrophic dimensions, was simply a case involving the assertion of enterprise principles to impose parent company liability for a subsidiary's torts, a result frequently reached in the United States through "piercing the veil jurisprudence."

Belgium: The Badger Case

The *Badger* case in Belgium, although brought to conclusion by other than strictly legal measures, provides a third illustration of host country extraterritoriality. It shows effectively how, in addition to national law, the climate of public opinion and voluntary international guidelines for the conduct of multinational businesses play an important role in the governance of corporate conduct. In the *Badger* affair, these factors combined to obtain parent company compliance with the extraterritorial application of host country labor law without any judicial determination of the underlying legal questions.

The Belgian second-tier subsidiary (Badger-Belgium) of an American subholding company (Badger-USA) of Raytheon, an American multinational group, became bankrupt. The group refused to pay the unsatisfied debts of Badger-Belgium, including the severance pay for Belgian employees required under Belgian law.

Matters developed into an international cause célèbre. The Belgian government and trade unions contended that Belgian statutory law requiring severance pay applied extraterritorially to Badger-USA. The Organization for Economic Cooperation and Development similarly pressed Badger to comply with its voluntary Guidelines for Multinational Enterprises. In the end, Badger-USA capitulated and paid the severance pay, but not any of the other obligations of Badger-Belgium. Governmental and public pressures in the end had succeeded in imposing an obligation on the multinational parent for the statutory labor obligations of its Belgian subsidiary. This was a victory for the Belgian government and Belgian workers, but not for Belgian creditors generally. Badger-USA did not assume responsibility for the nonlabor obligations of Badger-Belgium.[43]

Foreign Enforcement or Recognition of Host Country Judgments

In the event a plaintiff has obtained a host country judgment imposing liability on foreign affiliates of foreign-owned local companies, it faces the problem of collecting it. Levying on assets of the group within the country may present little difficulties, but, as in *Deltec*, they will usually be inadequate to satisfy the judgment. The plaintiff must seek to enforce the judgment abroad. It may seek to do so in the home country of the group parent, where it may well expect to find the courts to be hostile. Alternatively, it may seek a friendlier forum in neutral countries in which affiliates of the group are conducting operations.

Although nations generally are prepared to enforce foreign money judgments, there is a well-developed body of the law establishing the standards to be satisfied. The party seeking to enforce the judgment must demonstrate that the foreign judicial process conformed to the forum's own standards, including such matters as jurisdiction, notice, and opportunity to be heard. Further, the judgment must not offend the "public policy" of the forum. As stated by Judge Cardozo, it must not "violate some fundamental principle of justice, some prevalent conception of good morals, some deep-seated tradition of the common weal."[44] Thus, in the American follow-up on the *Deltec* Argentine judgment, a New York court, while dismissing the action on other grounds, made a passing disparaging observation that the Argentine action might amount to "confiscation of property."[45]

Under the so-called reciprocity rule, there is still another hurdle to enforcement of the foreign judgment. Some nations, including Belgium, the Netherlands, and Luxembourg, will not enforce a foreign judgment, even one meeting the foregoing procedural standards, unless the substantive rules of law responsible for the result applied by the foreign courts are identical with those of the country involved.[46] Under such a rule, courts in jurisdictions continuing to apply entity law to matters such as those involved in the case at hand would deny enforcement to foreign application of enterprise law.

There appears to be only one appellate court opinion considering the enforceability of a foreign judgment based on enterprise principles. *Tahan v. Hodgson* involved an Israeli default judgment imposing liability for a corporate obligation upon its sole individual shareholder under traditional "piercing the veil jurisprudence."[47] On appeal, the Court of Appeals for the First Circuit upheld a lower court order enforcing the Israeli judgment. The court pointed out that Israel, like the United States, has a policy against lightly "piercing the veil" and that much of its law was English common law. It did not otherwise discuss the standards determining when foreign judgments resting on enterprise principles would be enforced.

Other Applications of Extraterritoriality

Extraterritorial application of national law is an inevitable response to the problems presented by world business. It has occurred in a wide range of areas, including antitrust and restrictive trade practice, securities, and tax laws, and those laws restricting foreign takeovers of domestic companies.

The United States has not been the only country that has asserted extraterritorial jurisdiction over foreign components of multinational corporations in the further implementation of national policies with respect to the domestic components of multinational groups. Although more limited in ambition and scope, other governments of developed countries have also resorted to extraterritorial application of their national laws. These include Germany, Canada, Australia, the European Community, and Sweden, among others. Thus, the problem of dealing with the disruptive influences of extraterritoriality upon the international order is not simply an aberration arising only in the United States and reflecting an uniquely American view of the appropriate range for the exercise of American power. It is a phenomenon that is occurring across the world in nations in which components of multinational groups conduct business. In brief, extraterritoriality is an almost inevitable concomitant of national legal systems struggling with the problems presented by world business.

The United States

American policy has produced great international friction in the areas of antitrust and discovery. In the area of antitrust, the United States has attempted, over the years, to penalize conduct abroad constituting violations of American antitrust laws without regard to whether the conduct was lawful under the laws of the nation in which it was carried out. It has done so on the basis of the economic effect on markets. This is an application of the so-called effects doctrine, which expands the territorial principle of jurisdiction to prescribe. Since the decision of Judge Learned Hand in *United States v. Aluminum Corp. of America*, American courts have upheld such extraterritorial application of the antitrust laws, subject to a principle of reasonableness evaluated in terms of a balancing standard. In addition, American courts have upheld the use of federal discovery procedures to obtain documents from foreign subsidiaries of American corporations for prosecution of such antitrust violations, and for use in litigation, as well.

As noted, this assertion of extraterritorial jurisdiction in both its substantive and procedural aspects has been bitterly resisted by foreign nations through diplomatic measures and the enactment of "blocking statutes."[48] Notwithstanding the foreign reaction, the Restatement, as noted, has recognized the legitimacy of such efforts, provided, among other things, that the foreign conduct has "direct, foreseeable, and substantial effect" in the United States.

Although legal issues pertaining to corporate groups have not played a leading role in the extraterritorial application of antitrust law, corporate groups have frequently been involved in discovery litigation. American persistence on obtaining information from foreign subsidiaries has given rise to as "much friction" as any other area.[49] Rule 34 of the Federal Rules of Civil Procedure requires the production of all documents in the "possession or control" of a party. For domestic purposes, this language is uniformly construed to require parent corporations to produce documents in the possession of their subsidiaries because they are properly perceived to be subject to the "control" of the parent. No exception is made, either in the Rule or by the courts, in the application of the Rule for foreign subsidiaries. American law has developed to the point where it is clear that discovery extends not only to documents of foreign subsidiaries generally, but also to documents of foreign subsidiaries prohibited by local law from making them available in response to such an American judicial order. For this purpose, the "foreign compulsion" doctrine is ignored. However, the courts take the existence of the foreign prohibition or limitation into account in determining the appropriate penalty for a failure to produce.[50]

The intensity of this problem has led the international community to seek a common resolution of the conflicting policies of different nations. The Hague Convention on the Taking of Evidence Abroad in Civil or Commercial Matters has reduced conflicts, but its usefulness is limited by the reservations many signatories have placed on it. While the Supreme Court has held that the Convention does not supersede the discovery provisions of the Federal Rules, many lower courts still require the Convention procedures to be used before discovery under the Rules is permitted.[51]

Germany

American exercise of jurisdiction over foreign mergers with domestic antitrust effects is not unique. Germany and the European Community both do the same. Relying on the effects principle of international law, the German Cartel Office, acting under the Act Against Restraints of Competition, regularly asserts jurisdiction over the merger abroad of two foreign parent corporations where the merger has "actual, substantiated and noticeable" effects on the domestic market. Germany has asserted jurisdiction not only where each of the foreign parties to a foreign merger has German subsidiaries, but even under certain circumstances where only one of the merger parties has German operations.[52]

The European Community

Both the European Court of Justice and the Council of the European Community have similarly approved extraterritorial application of EC law to component companies of multinational groups based outside the EC. Such extraterritorial assertion of jurisdiction has included both foreign subsidiaries of EC parent corporations and foreign parent corporations of EC subsidiaries. In a series of cases involving integrated multinational groups arising under laws of the EC dealing with restrictive trade practices, the European Court of Justice has imputed activities of EC subsidiaries to their foreign parent companies on the basis of their ownership and control of the activities of those subsidiaries. It has regularly rejected challenges to such assertion of extraterritorial jurisdiction that rest on an alleged inconsistency with international law.[53]

Canada, Australia, and Sweden

Both a Canadian statute dealing with foreign acquisitions of Canadian enterprises and an Australian statute dealing with corporate takeovers have also been applied to transactions involving foreign companies acting outside of the country involved where the foreign transaction transferred control of a domestic company. Thus, a Canadian court upheld application of the Canadian Foreign Investment Review Act to a Delaware merger between two Delaware corporations because one company had a Canadian subsidiary.[54] Ironically, the United States, which has repeatedly asserted extraterritorial jurisdiction over foreign components of American corporate groups, protested in this case that the Canadian action was contrary to international law.[55]

The Supreme Court of New South Wales gave comparable extraterritorial construction to a New South Wales statute regulating acquisitions of more than twenty percent of the stock of a New South Wales company. The case involved Brierly Investments, a New Zealand corporation with a second-tier subsidiary holding, just under twenty percent, of Woolworth, a New South Wales company. Brierly purchased more than twenty percent of the shares of Rainbow, another New Zealand corporation. Rainbow had a fifth-tier subsidiary also holding just under twenty percent of Woolworth. The court concluded that Brierly's acquisition of twenty percent of the Rainbow shares would "carry substantial influence and perhaps decisive influence" over Rainbow, justifying attribution of the Rainbow subsidiary's shares to Brierly. With this attribution, Brierly held almost forty percent of the Woolworth shares and was, accordingly, held subject to the statute.[56]

Sweden provides a final example. It is one of the many countries that has adopted sanctions against South Africa. However, unlike American South African Transactions Regulations, the Swedish statute applies not only to Swedish corporations, but also to their foreign subsidiaries. To avoid international confrontation, the statute includes a "foreign compulsion" exception under which the statute is inapplicable when in conflict with local law to the contrary.[57]

Disclosure under Securities and Taxation Statutes

The realities of multinational operations have made for international acceptance of extraterritorial principles requiring disclosure in connection with security issues and taxation involving foreign subsidiaries of multinational groups. Such requirements play an important role in the regulatory and tax structures of a number of countries, including the United States, Great Britain, Germany, and the European Community, among others. In probably no other area has enterprise law received more general acceptance than in the area of disclosure, where the painful issue of imposition of liability contrary to traditional entity law and limited liability is not involved.

The United States. In its disclosure requirements for the issuance of securities and the conduct of annual meetings of shareholders, the Securities and Exchange Commission requires the submission of consolidated group accounts on a worldwide basis, without regard to the nationality of component subsidiary corporations. Further, American income tax laws require routine disclosure of economic information with respect to foreign subsidiaries, as well as with respect to transactions with foreign subsidiaries. In the area of state taxation, the American courts, as noted, have upheld the constitutionality of worldwide unitary tax apportionment statutes involving disclosure of the assets, sales, and income of the group, wherever situated.

Great Britain. In its disclosure requirements, English company law similarly applies enterprise principles to corporate groups on an extraterritorial basis. The Companies Act, 1985, as amended, requires group accounts, including those of foreign subsidiaries, in order to conform to EC requirements in the EC Seventh Council Directive on Consolidated Accounts, pertaining to corporate groups.

European Community. The Seventh Council Directive on Consolidated Accounts requires member states, among other things, to enact legislation providing that EC parent companies submit annual financial information with respect to their subsidiaries, including non-EC subsidiaries organized and operating outside the EC. The provisions in the proposed Statute for a European Company (*Societas Europaea*) would require the same.[58]

In the proposed Ninth Directive, which deals with worker consultation, the EC would similarly have required multinational enterprises with an EC component — either parent or subsidiary — at least once a year to disclose "a clear picture of the activities of the parent corporation and its subsidiaries," including its non-EC group components.[59] Although the ultimate fate of this proposal is highly doubtful, a European Commission Directive requires much of the same information with respect to foreign subsidiaries to be supplied to work councils in cases of certain shutdowns and plant relocations.[60]

Assertion of Jurisdiction to Adjudicate Over Foreign Affiliates

A final example of the exercise of host country power over the foreign parent or affiliated corporations of a multinational group is the widespread assertion by American courts of jurisdiction over the foreign components of a corporate group because of the local activities of a domestic component. Most of these cases involved a domestic subsidiary of a foreign group and thereby involve host country extraterritoriality. The same doctrines, however, are being applied to assert jurisdiction over foreign subsidiaries by reason of the activities of a domestic parent, thereby involving home country extraterritoriality.

Such assertions of jurisdiction to adjudicate over foreign components, whether based on the activities of a domestic parent or subsidiary, are, of course, contrary to traditional entity law, and most American courts still reject this outcome. However, as reviewed in Chapter 4, in an impressive number of cases, particularly in antitrust and tort matters, an increasing number of American courts are permitting American plaintiffs to sue foreign parent or affiliated corporations in American courts, although the activities of its domestic subsidiary or affiliate and their collective participation in an integrated business are the only link to the forum.

Some of these decisions rest on traditional "piercing the veil jurisprudence"; Many others rest essentially on enterprise principles. These cases rest their outcome on an evaluation of the familiar enterprise factors of the nature of the extent of the parent's exercise of control; the extent of group economic integration, financial and administrative interdependence, and employee assignment, training, and benefit programs; and use of a common group persona. Where the parent's exercise of control extends to the day-by-day decision-making process of the subsidiary, that feature will generally lead to assertion of jurisdiction, even by courts otherwise wedded to entity law.

The tort cases involving product liability represent the furthest advance of assertion of American jurisdiction over foreign components of multinational groups. In product liability cases, courts, under the "stream of commerce" doctrine, are increasingly asserting jurisdiction over foreign manufacturers or distributors. However, such assertion does not rest primarily on enterprise principles, but on the foreign company's own action in placing its products in the "stream of commerce" under circumstances where it can reasonably anticipate that the products will be used in the forum. In some such cases, however, courts also rely on enterprise concepts to provide further support for their conclusions. The activities of a local subsidiary, particularly if integrated with the foreign parent's business where it serves as a local distributor or provides warranty service, provide a further basis for supporting such assertion of jurisdiction.

In this area, where the United States is the host country, there is thus a widespread use of enterprise principles to subject foreign components of multinational groups to American law. This action, however, does not seem to have created any significant disincentive to foreign trade or investment. The advantages for foreign multinational groups of participating in the enormous market opportunities provided by the United States not surprisingly seem to outweigh this exposure to American judicial process and possible ultimate liability.

Economic Limitations to National Legal Policy

It is clear that there are serious costs, both to the world-power countries attempting to export their own perceptions of national interest and foreign policy concerns through attempts to regulate the conduct of national-based multinational enterprises, and to home countries striking out at what they have perceived as exploitation by the (foreign) strong of the (local) weak. In each case, economic as well as political costs may be very serious indeed. Policies establishing legal rules otherwise perceived as desirable may involve such economic costs in the world capital and product markets that they may not be feasible. Whereas wealthy, developed home countries may more readily absorb such costs, underdeveloped, host countries are much more vulnerable. For the capital-hungry host country fearful of creating disincentives to local investment, the costs may well be insupportable, and such policies may be reversed if the reaction in the developed world is severe.

The unsuccessful attempt of the United States one-and-a-half centuries ago to depart from international maritime customs in the formulation of liability rules for American ships provides a historic example of the limitations that the world market imposes on national policy. In the United States during the first half of the nineteenth century, the owners of maritime vessels were liable for negligence without limit in the operation of their vessels. By contrast, the European powers, particularly Great Britain, were following the age-old maritime custom of limiting owners' liability to the maritime vessel and its cargo. The ancient custom had deep historical roots. It was well established by the time of Grotius in the seventeenth century and has been traced back by Holmes and others to medieval and Italian maritime practices of hundreds of years earlier.[61]

American law did not conform to the international practice. American maritime interests exposed to tort risks without limitation were adversely affected in their efforts to compete with foreign shipping owners, whose risks were limited. In response to this impairment of their competitive position, American shippers were successful in inducing Congress in 1851 to limit maritime liability under American law to conform to the world model. The statute limits the liability of the owner of any maritime vessel to "the value of the interest of such owner in such vessel, and her freight. . . ."[62]

The 1851 statute has still another aspect of keen interest for a volume concerned with the corporate entity. The Act protects the "owner" of the vessel. *Flink v. Paladini* presented the question of whether the statute protected shareholders where the vessel was owned by a corporation. In a notable opinion, Justice Holmes, who had already written on the aberrational maritime liability usage in *The Common Law*, rejected the traditional conceptual approach of entity law. Instead, he utilized the newer twentieth-century technique of construing statutory language not in terms of its common law meaning, but in a manner implementing the statutory objectives.

Justice Holmes wrote:

> For this purpose no rational distinction can be taken between several persons owning shares in a vessel directly and making the same division by putting title in a corporation and distributing the corporate stock. The policy of the statute . . . must extend to both. [T]he words of the act . . . must be taken in a broad popular sense in order not to defeat the manifest intent.[63] [citations omitted]

This is an early example of enterprise law.

It should be evident that world trade plays a major role in the economies of all nations. Profound changes of legal principles by less than a critical mass (whatever that may be) of the players in the world economy will inevitably affect the international flow of capital investment, as well as trade. The adverse consequences of legal changes on the economy become a factor of significance in the calculus determining the relative desirability of the change.

Summary

The reality of the matter is that effective regulation of corporate groups or their activities inevitably requires control of all the components participating in the enterprise. Where multinational groups are concerned, this inevitably means extraterritoriality. It increasingly appears to be a world phenomenon rather than something primarily associated with American controls over foreign subsidiaries of American multinationals. From the viewpoint of effective economic regulation, it is not merely appropriate, it is essential that the legal structure match the economic structure of the enterprise subject to the regulatory system. However, the extraterritorial assertion of national law inherent in the application of enterprise principles to components of multinational groups inevitably will engender international confrontation and disrupt international trade and relations. This is the dilemma.

The challenge for the world order is the evolution over the years ahead of an international legal machinery to mediate, adjust, and reduce national conflicts and to emerge with a framework that will not only facilitate the imposition of effective governmental controls over the activities of multinational groups, but will encourage the harmonious development of international economic relations.

IV

Jurisprudential Implications

9

Legal Rights, Legal Responsibilities, and Recognition of the Legal Unit: Individuals and Physical Objects

The notions of the corporate entity that were developed to serve the needs of the simple economic society of nineteenth century and of earlier societies are archaic in the face of the emergence of giant corporate groups conducting worldwide enterprises. The traditional concept of the corporate entity to which the law attributes rights and on which it imposes responsibilities no longer matches the economic organizations conducting activities that the law seeks to recognize and to govern. In the modern world of transnational corporations, the economic actor is typically the corporate group; however, the law continues to focus on each component company, rather than on the group, as the legal actor.

The great challenge to the national legal structures of the Western world and to the emerging new world legal order is the pressing need for the formulation of enterprise principles and a new doctrine of enterprise law in order to deal with the legal problems presented by transnational enterprises. Such a reformulation requires a fresh look at the fundamental concepts of Western legal thought. It requires a reexamination of the traditional views of what has been referred to as the corporate entity, or the corporate personality, and a reconsideration of the fundamental principles of the legal system.

Legal Units, Legal Attributes, and Legal Personality

The legal system functions by recognizing certain basic units to which it attributes certain fundamental legal rights and upon which it imposes certain legal responsibilities. This basic legal unit has been variously described as a "legal person," a "legal personality," a "legal entity," a "right-and-duty bearing unit," or, as Roscoe Pound and my old teacher, Edward H. Warren, simply put it, a "legal unit."[1]

A number of the terms traditionally employed are unfortunate. They prejudge the nature of the unit and the rights and responsibilities to be attributed to it and are better avoided. Thus, the very use of the terms "person" or "personality" almost inevitably leads to an anthropomorphic view of legal existence, with accompanying notions of "personhood," that somehow mirrors for the unit in question much the same legal recognition as accorded to human beings. Criticism of such a usage is a prominent current in much of the American literature about corporate constitutional rights. The term "corporate personality," in addition, has the confusion of being used sometimes to refer to the corporation as a legal unit and sometimes to the rights and responsibilities attributed to it.

"Entity" has been firmly affixed to the traditional description of corporations generally, as in references to the corporate entity and entity law. Entity has also been used to refer to each constituent corporation, whereas enterprise has been used to refer to the group as a whole. A reformulation of "corporate entity" on enterprise principles and a description of the group as the *new* "corporate entity" would inevitably involve considerable confusion.

To avoid misunderstanding, references to person or personality (except when referring to individuals) and to corporate entity should be used guardedly, if at all. Neutral terms, such as legal unit or juridical unit, that sidestep such dangers are preferable.

The legal system requires a concept of a legal unit in order to formulate legal relationships. These legal units are the subjects in the society that the law recognizes as separate and distinct for some legal purpose and to which it grants legal recognition of some kind. Without recognition of the subject for some legal purpose, there can be no legal unit.[2]

Distinguished by their particular legal rights and responsibilities, each class of legal unit is unique. They include legal subjects as disparate as individuals, maritime vessels, physical objects, partnerships, associations, special accounts, funds, economic interest groupings, and governmental agencies, as well as the corporation and the corporate group. In each case, the attribution of rights and responsibilities demarcating the perimeters of legal recognition of the unit reflects all the factors that underlie societal lawmaking: the historical development of the law, changing values and interests, socio-economic and political forces, and conceptual currents.

There are certain fundamental points. First, neither legal rights nor legal units exist "in the air." Legal rights must pertain to a legal unit that can exercise them. Further, there is no comprehensive list of legal rights and responsibilities that automatically springs into existence upon recognition of a particular subject as a legal unit. Quite the contrary. It is the recognition of particular rights and responsibilities (principally rights)—one by one—that shapes the juridical contours of the legal unit for which they have been created.[3]

When the law recognizes a particular right or imposes a particular responsibility on a presumptive legal unit, this constitutes recognition as a legal unit to the extent of the attribution. Other rights and responsibilities may or may not exist, depending on whether such recognition of the unit in the view of the lawmaker—whether legislator, administrator, or judge—will fulfill the underlying policies and objectives of the law of the time in the area. Further, as the society changes, the concepts of legal identity and the legal consequences to be attributed to them inevitably change as well.

As the following pages illustrate, the jurisprudence of legal identity is dynamic, not static. The legal recognition given over the years to such older legal subjects as partnerships and unincorporated associations and to such newer subjects as "special accounts," funds, or economic interest groupings represents a process of continuing adaptation of legal status to reflect changing economic realities. The development of principles of enterprise law for the corporation appears to be undergoing a similar evolution.

Along with the concepts of the particular legal unit and the right/ responsibility attributes recognized historically in the particular case for a particular unit, there is still a third element at work. This element is legal theory as to the nature of the unit. The ideas in the heads of the judges, in Max Weber's expression, as to the nature of particular legal units on occasion influence the ultimate decisions in the law in action in determining the changing content of rights and responsibilities to be attributed to a particular legal unit. Not infrequently, particularly when precedent is not available to aid in the solution of a legal problem, judicial theory plays an important, or even decisive, role in the result.

There are other concepts, such as standing and capacity, that have sometimes been mistakenly introduced into discussion of the problems of legal existence. These matters are irrelevant because they do not consider the existence of legal identity: they assume it. Standing is concerned with the very different issue of whether a party recognized as a legal unit with the right to sue has a cognizable interest in a particular controversy, entitling it to institute or participate in the litigation. Capacity, another concept that has led to confusion, inquires whether a recognized legal unit is, for legal purposes, competent to manage its affairs. An assertion of lack of standing or capacity does not challenge either the legal existence of the legal unit in question or its legal right to act where it has a cognizable interest or is not incapacitated.

In summary, for legal purposes, the recognition of the separate juridical identity of a legal subject does not arise as a logical derivation from some legal or philosophical premise. It arises only when the law, case by case or statute by statute, attributes certain legal rights to, or imposes certain legal responsibilities upon, a particular legal subject. Then, at least for the purposes in question, the subject may properly be said to have a separate legal existence of its own, with the particular rights or responsibilities so attributed to it. As the law evolves, and attributes additional rights and responsibilities to a particular unit, its jurisprudential identity changes correspondingly.

The question arises: What are the legal attributes that the law at a particular time recognizes for certain legal subjects under certain circumstances?

Legislative and Judicial Recognition of Legal Units

Recognition as a legal unit means the attribution of certain fundamental legal rights and responsibilities. Different units typically have their own special bundles of rights and responsibilities. When some rights or responsibilities are recognized, the legal subject must be regarded as a separate legal unit for those purposes, but such recognition does not result in the automatic attribution of other rights or the imposition of other responsibilities. In brief, legal units are unique.

Accordingly, in considering the jurisprudential status of any legal unit, the threshold question is: What are the particular legal rights and responsibilities that have been attributed to it and constitute its recognition as a legal unit? These will include one or more of the following:

- the right to a name (and thus to have an identity);
- the right to sue and be sued;
- the right to acquire, hold, and dispose of property;
- the right to contract; and
- rights under various constitutional and legislative provisions

Legal responsibilities must be considered as well because they play an essential role in determining the full boundaries of legal existence for each subject. One must, therefore, also inquire to what extent the presumptive legal unit is subject to such legal responsibilities as amenability:

- to be sued (as a matter of pleading and practice)
- to be substantively liable under statute or common law for the unit's acts, giving rise to legal remedy against the unit

If one or more of the foregoing rights or legal responsibilities may be shown to exist for some purpose, then one can conclude that the subject is in fact a legal unit for that purpose and under the circumstances in question. Thus, federal statutes create federal legal rights in some cases, impose federal legal responsibilities in many other cases, and, on occasion, even invent novel federal legal units of a nature previously unknown to the law. These legal elements of the federal system form an important part of American jurisprudence, and the fact that they may be unrecognized under state law or common law is manifestly irrelevant. Legal identity, rights, and responsibilities are concepts pertinent to the particular matter at hand; they are not necessarily transcendental factors throughout the entire legal system.

At an irreducible minimum, the legal quality required for recognition as a legal unit is the right to sue and be sued, the ability to assert some right, or being subject to some legal responsibility in a judicial (or quasi-judicial) forum. Because it would be pointless to recognize a right to sue with respect to a legal unit that had nothing for which to sue (that is, had no other rights), the minimum concept of legal identity or recognition as a legal unit must also include some other recognized legal right. The right to sue must be associated with some other legally cognizable interest to be advanced by suit.

In the case of corporations and other organizations, certain aspects of legal identity have been advanced as primary legal attributes of the legal units in addition to the items previously specified. These include such matters as

- fixed duration of a term of years or perpetual;
- continued existence, notwithstanding a change in membership or share ownership;
- limited liability of members for organizational legal responsibilities; and
- central direction of management.

While enormously important as a practical matter,[4] these attributes are not fundamental for jurisprudential existence of the units. However, in a particular case, their recognition forms part of the jurisprudential contours defining the unit in the jurisdiction in question.

Still other types of legal rights are even further removed from the class of primary attributes. These include such matters for individuals as the right to vote, freedom of thought and movement, and other political rights. However important such rights may be in determining the degree of equality and participation in the society, they are far removed from the primary legal rights serving as the touchstones for recognition as a legal unit. Thus, individuals with the legal rights of access to the courts, to contract, and to acquire, own, and dispose of property are recognized legal units, whether or not they have the right to vote.

The rights and legal responsibilities enumerated previously determine recognition as a legal unit. This represents the product of a legal evolution over the years that recognizes and defines the legal identity of various classes of legal units.

The individual human being is the primary example of a legal unit. Each individual has his or her own legal rights and responsibilities that are separate and distinct from those of any other human being. Complexity enters when individuals organize into groups or organizations and present the problem of determining the respective rights and responsibilities of the organization on the one hand and of its members on the other.

In addition to organizations comprised of individuals, such as most unincorporated associations, and corporate groups comprised of constituent subsidiary companies, there are still other, very different types of legal units that have no constituent legal units. These are physical objects, particularly maritime vessels under admiralty law.

The following pages review briefly the evolutionary recognition of rights and responsibilities giving rise to the existence of juridical identity for these different classes of legal units. Among other things, this review will illustrate the extent to which the juridical nature of legal units has undergone dynamic change over the years. The boundaries of legal identity have been neither sharp, nor precise, nor unchanging.

Individuals

In all legal systems, individuals are the cardinal example of recognition as separate legal units with their own rights and legal responsibilities. However, it is not as simple as that. In the past, some classes of human beings have been deprived, in varying degrees, of the primary rights given generally to other human beings under the legal system. Concerning those periods of deprivation of certain primary legal rights for particular classes of individuals, as in the case of slavery, several questions may be asked. What was their legal status? In what respects, if any, did the law, despite such deprivation, recognize their existence as legal units?

The legal history of slavery in the United States during the period before the Civil War provides a vivid example of the interaction of the legal system and such a deprivation of primary legal rights. In the southern United States, slaves lacked primary legal rights. They could not own property; they could not sue or be sued; they could not contract; they could not testify against whites in court; they could not marry. They were the property of their masters and were not free to live their own lives free of direction from their masters.[5]

However sweeping the deprivation of such fundamental rights, it was not complete. Notwithstanding the very wide areas in which slaves lacked these rights, they nevertheless had some legal rights and were recognized as legal units for certain other purposes. They were legally capable of committing crimes and subject to criminal punishment, but only after trial, verdict, and sentence. Further, in the later days of slavery, slaves were protected in some jurisdictions in the South by a limited number of fundamental procedural rights, including the right to trial by jury, the right to counsel, and the right against self-incrimination in cases involving capital offenses. In some states, such rights extended beyond capital offenses to other criminal proceedings. Missouri and Texas recognized the right to trial by jury in criminal cases generally and Kentucky did so in cases of felonies. Georgia went even further. By 1850, it is reported that in criminal proceedings generally, Georgia law recognized rights for slaves equivalent to those of free persons. In Alabama and Arkansas, as well, the ordinary rules of the common law of crimes applied to slaves. The law of slavery also imposed obligations on masters to be humane and to provide food, clothing, housing, and care.[6]

However ineffectual these rights may have been in practice, and however much slaves were oppressed in other respects, slaves in the Confederate South clearly constituted legal units with certain recognized, albeit painfully limited, legal attributes.

The slavery experience demonstrates that existence as a legal unit with certain recognized rights and responsibilities is a very different question from determination of the totality of the rights and responsibilities that the law may recognize for a particular unit. The experience also illustrates how recognition as legal units and the extent of rights and the nature of the responsibilities imposed upon different classes of individuals reflect the values and power relationships of the society in question. The juridical attributes of legal units are thus malleable, and they change with evolving societal responses to social, political, and economic developments.

Maritime Vessels and Other Physical Objects

At an even more primitive level, the law has recognized physical objects as legal subjects that exist as separate legal units with rights and responsibilities separate and distinct from any other legal unit. The status of maritime vessels under the law of admiralty is the most prominent of these.

Maritime Vessels

The law of admiralty recognizes significant rights and imposes important legal responsibilities on maritime vessels as legal units separate from their owners or masters or other human beings. Thus, as the Supreme Court stated in *Tucker v. Alexandroff*, a vessel upon launching

> acquires a personality of her own; becomes competent to contract and is individually liable for her obligations upon which she may sue in the name of her owner, and be sued in her own name. Her owner's agents may not be her agents, and her agents may not be her owner's agents. She is capable, too, of committing a tort, and is responsible in damages therefore.[7]

In the case of *The Camanche*,[8] the Supreme Court similarly recognized the right of a vessel to institute salvage proceedings in its own name without any allegation that the suit was being prosecuted for the benefit of the master and crew or owner.

The recognition of a maritime vessel as a separate legal unit is even more clearly established with respect to the imposition of independent legal responsibilities. In admiralty, a vessel is "considered as herself the wrongdoer" liable for torts independently of its owner.[9] A vessel may be seized and forfeited under federal statute entirely without regard to any fault or acts on the part of the owner. In *The Little Charles*, a very early case arising under the embargo acts prior to the War of 1812, Chief Justice Marshall, on circuit, said:

> This is not a proceeding against the owner; it is a proceeding against the vessel, for an offence committed by the vessel, which is not less an offence, and does not the less subject her to forfeiture because it was committed without the authority and against the will of the owner.[10]

Two contrasting Supreme Court cases illustrate vividly the independent nature of the tort liability of the maritime vessel in admiralty in contrast to the common law. Thus, a vessel involved in a collision as a result of the negligence of a compulsory pilot required by local law was liable in admiralty, whereas neither such a vessel nor its owner was liable at common law.[11]

As a matter of admiralty procedure, the independent maritime liability of the vessel is pursued through use of in rem jurisdiction in the strict sense where the "proceeding *in rem* is one taken directly against property, and has for its object the disposition of property, without reference to the title of individual claimants."[12] This is very different from the more familiar use of in rem jurisdiction in the common law, where it serves only as a procedural device to assert a claim against the owner.

The Hindu Idol *Case*

Another example of the recognition of a physical object as a separate legal unit is the Privy Council decision, *Pramatha Nath Mullick v. Pradyumna Kumar Mullock*, involving the status of a Hindu idol under Indian law. Considering an appeal from an Indian court, Lord Shaw stated:

> A Hindu idol is, according to long established authority, founded upon the religious customs of the Hindus, and the recognition thereof by [Indian] courts of Law, a "juristic entity." It has a legal status, with the power of suing and being sued. Its interests are attended to by the person who has the deity in his charge and who is in law its manager . . . this doctrine, thus simply stated, is firmly established.[13]

Commenting on this decision, an English writer wisely stated:

> if the Privy Council says he is a juristic entity, then he is. . . . Much confusion might be served if lawyers using the word in argument always made it clear that by "legal personality" they mean simply capacity for rights and liabilities. . . . This would at any rate clarify some of the discussions on the real or fictitious nature of juristic personality.[14]

Forests, Oceans, Rivers, and Natural Objects

Fifteen years ago, Professor Christopher Stone argued in a "little discourse on the unthinkable" that legal rights be given to "forests, oceans, rivers and other so-called 'natural objects' in the environment."[15] Stone was moved to make his proposal because of the difficulties that environmental groups were having in satisfying the standing requirements of the courts for participation in environmental litigation. Underscoring the fears of Stone and other environmentalists, the Supreme Court, in *Sierra Club v. Morton*, refused to recognize the right of the Sierra Club to intervene and contest the building of a dam that had received the approval of the appropriate government agency, notwithstanding the contention that the litigation had not adequately tested the claim of substantial environmental damage. In his dissent, Justice Douglas adopted Professor Stone's suggestion and called for:

> fashion[ing] a federal rule that allowed environmental issues to be litigated . . . in the name of the inanimate object about to be despoiled, defaced, or invaded by roads and bulldozers and where injury is the subject of public outrage. . . .
>
> Inanimate objects are sometimes parties in litigation. A ship has legal personality, a fiction found useful for maritime purposes. . . . So it should be as respects valleys, alpine meadows, rivers, lakes, estuaries, beaches, ridges, groves of trees, swampland or even air that feels the destructive pressures of modern technology and modern life.[16] [footnotes omitted]

While this suggestion has not received legislative or judicial recognition, it is manifestly technically feasible. It illustrates in vivid fashion that concepts of legal entity exist to serve the needs of the law and, accordingly, must be flexible to respond to the changing needs of the society.

With this introductory discussion illustrating the wide variety of allocation of legal rights and responsibilities among different types of legal units, ranging from human beings to vessels and physical objects, it is now appropriate to consider the various degrees of allocation of legal rights and responsibilities to different types of organizations and their consequent recognition as legal units.

10

Legal Rights, Legal Responsibilities, and Recognition of the Legal Unit: Organizations

When the focus moves from individuals and physical objects to organizations, the law is confronted by a more complex problem. It must determine the legal distinction between the organization and its members. Of all organizations, it is the corporation that matured earliest and has had the most developed concept of organizational legal existence. Its jurisprudential roots go back to the twelfth and thirteenth centuries.

In contrast to corporations, which have for centuries been treated as separate legal units, organizations lacking incorporation are in a less mature state for legal purposes. The legal attributes shaping their legal identity are less advanced, but are still slowly continuing to develop. Under the older common law, partnerships and unincorporated organizations lacked independent juridical identity. As such organizations have grown in numbers, size, and significance, the law has struggled to adapt its older, increasingly unrealistic conceptual perceptions to the economic and social realities of the times. In the process, the traditional concepts have substantially yielded to increasing revision, and, for many purposes, the law has recognized the separate legal existence of unincorporated organizations. However, traditional notions continue to survive for other purposes, and partnerships and associations in some respects still lack the full recognition as separate legal units long ago achieved by corporations. Nevertheless, corporate and unincorporated organizations are more alike than is generally recognized.

Partnerships and Associations

Partnerships

The distinction between the partnership and its partners is still a subject of continuing debate in the law. Is the partnership an entity—a legal unit of its own—or is it only an aggregate of the partners who comprise it, with the partners themselves recognized as the legal units possessing the rights and responsibilities pertaining to partnership affairs and operations? American and English law are still ambivalent. For many purposes, they treat the partnership as a separate legal unit, whereas for others they treat it as the aggregate of its partners.[1]

THE PARTNERSHIP AT COMMON LAW

At common law, the partnership in all respects was an aggregate. Notwithstanding its economic significance, the partnership had no legal rights or responsibilities and accordingly was not recognized as a legal unit. The partnership could not sue or be sued; litigation had to be brought by or against the individual partners. The partnership could not acquire, hold, or dispose of property in its own name; the assets of a partnership for legal purposes were the collective property of the individual partners as tenants-in-partnership. The partnership could not contract; contracts made by a partner for the firm were the joint and several obligations of the partners.

The partnership was only a contractual understanding between the partners. It had no continuity or independent life of its own. It came automatically to an end whenever one of the partners withdrew, died, or became insane, or whenever the partnership agreement otherwise expired. Admission of a new partner could only be accomplished by termination of the existing partnership and the formation of a new firm.

As the scale of partnership enterprise grew, this view of the partnership as an aggregate of its individual partners that lacked independent organizational existence clashed with the obvious realities. For legal purposes, it was clumsy and inefficient. To deal with its limitations, the courts contrived to formulate technical legal solutions to the problems. However, these judicial measures were halting and essentially a patchwork in nature. The pressures to adapt the legal recognition of partnership existence to match its economic reality moved to the legislature.

STATUTORY EVOLUTION

Recognizing the prominent role of partnerships in the economy, statutory law has moved away from the traditional view. It has adopted an increasingly functional approach to partnerships, widely but not completely recognizing partnerships as separate legal units that are distinct from their partners. In brief, the law is gradually, although still imperfectly, coming to mirror the economic reality of partnerships.

In this process, which has not run its full course, state legislation, as in the Uniform Partnership Act, has given increasing recognition to partnerships as independent legal units. Thus, partnerships today generally have the right to sue and be sued and to contract. In some other respects, they have rights that they may assert directly, rather than being dependent on their members to do so on their behalf. In these particulars, partnerships have achieved an extensive degree of recognition as separate legal units. For other purposes, however, they continue as they have over centuries past. In those respects, even today, they are without legal existence of their own and are no more than an aggregate of the members that compose them. The members continue to possess jointly the remaining rights and legal responsibilities pertaining to the partnership that statutory law has not yet allocated to the partnership itself.[2]

The Uniform Partnership Act inconsistently embraces both views of the partnership, and courts and scholars alike disagree to this day whether on balance the Act mostly reflects an entity or an aggregate point of view. For example, in the Act, the partners themselves own the property of the partnership as tenants-in-partnership, reflecting an aggregate view. However, the property may be held and conveyed in the firm name as an entity. Perhaps the plainest demonstration of an aggregate view is that the partnership technically dissolves on the death or withdrawal of any member, but it nevertheless may continue its business after such technical dissolution, which reflects an entity view. Judicial decisions widely acknowledge that in various jurisdictions partnerships are treated as independent entities for some purposes and as an aggregate of the partners for others.[3]

The Internal Revenue Code illustrates much the same duality. The Code treats a partnership as an entity for purposes of filing a return but imposes tax liabilities on the partners on an aggregate approach. For most other federal statutory purposes, however, the partnership is treated as a legal unit. For example, the Bankruptcy Code treats the partnership as a separate entity and empowers it to file as the debtor under the statute. Finally, as noted, many statutes, including the provision governing the construction of federal statutes, generally provide that a partnership is a "person," that is a legal unit for purposes of the statute in question.[4]

This debate over functional recognition of the partnership as a separate legal unit revolves around the desirability of the further attribution of *rights* to the partnership as a legal unit, not the imposition of legal responsibilities. In contrast, with respect to corporate groups, the challenge of the times relates not to rights, but instead to the imposition of legal *responsibilities* upon a parent corporation or other group constituent by reason of the activities of a subsidiary or other affiliate of the group. There is little, if any, interest in recognizing the *right* of the parent corporation or group to sue on claims of its subsidiary corporations or to have a property interest in the assets of its subsidiaries.

JUDICIAL CONSTRUCTION

The choice between conceptualism and functionalism in partnership law is most sharply presented in cases arising under statutory law of general application in which Congress was unclear whether it was imposing responsibility on partnerships. The Supreme Court has twice faced such a choice in partnership law in recent years.

United States v. A & P Trucking Co., decided in 1958, involved the validity of the indictment of a partnership for criminal violation of the Motor Carrier Act under circumstances where the partners themselves were not criminally liable.[5] The statute and regulations imposed liability on any "person" violating certain safety regulations and, in fact, defined "person" to include partnerships. Writing for the Court in a five to four decision, Justice Harlan avoided the conceptualistic debate. Relying on the principle of statutory construction — that statutes be construed in the manner which would most fully implement their underlying objectives — Justice Harlan upheld the indictment of the partnership. He noted that the policy of the Act was to assure compliance with safety regulations and concluded that the jurisprudential nature of the organization violating the regulations was irrelevant: "The mischief is the same." He concluded: "True, the common law makes a distinction between a corporation and a partnership, deeming the latter not a separate entity for purposes of suit. But the power of Congress to change the common-law rule is not to be doubted." Congress had specifically included partnerships within the definition of "person" in this particular case, as well as in a number of other major regulatory acts, thus showing an intent to treat partnerships as legal units under federal regulatory law. He accordingly construed the statute as imposing criminal liability on the firm. The partnership was viewed as a legal unit for this purpose and was criminally liable, although the individual partners were not culpable.[6]

Justice Douglas, writing for the dissenting justices, took a very different approach. He would have dismissed the indictment largely on conceptual grounds, contending that:

> In this country the entity theory has not in general been extended to the partnership. . . . We should therefore assume that this criminal statute, written against this background, reflects the conventional aggregate, not the exceptional entity, theory of the partnership.[7]

In his view, only the individual partners, not the partnership, were subject to indictment in absence of a clear indication in the statute to the contrary.

Four years later, in *Blau v. Lehman*, the Court faced the question of whether a partnership should be deemed as a legal unit to be a "director" and subject to the prohibition against short-swing trading in Section 16(b) of the Securities Exchange Act of 1934. A majority held that, at least on the facts presented, only the individual partner involved was subject to the statute and that it did not cover the partnership as an entity.

Justice Douglas again disagreed with the Court's construction of the statute. Ignoring his invocation of the aggregate view of the partnership in his dissent in *A & P Trucking*, Douglas abandoned conceptualism and turned to a functional view. He strenuously contended in pragmatic terms that application of the short-swing provisions of the

Act was essential in order to implement the statutory objective and prevent evasion by the "great Wall Street trading firms." He dismissed conceptualism, stating: "In partnership law a debate has long ranged over whether a partnership is an entity or an aggregate. Pursuit of that will-o'-the-wisp is not profitable."[8]

Although the Court applied a functional view of the partnership in *A & P Trucking* and a conceptual view in *Blau*, the different results in the two cases should be seen as reflecting the Court's views as to the different objectives of the two statutory programs, not as any inconsistency or ambivalence in deciding on the "true" aggregate or entity nature of a partnership.

The inconsistent opinions of Justice Douglas in the two cases vividly illustrate how, on occasion, judges seem ready to use concepts to serve the ends of the moment in arguing for a particular resolution of the case before them.

Although the inconsistent usage of aggregate and entity concepts in partnership law has been strongly criticized, this type of criticism really misses the point insofar as these two cases are concerned. The law is not a philosophical construction that strives for uniformity, tidiness, and elegance. It resolves controversies. The courts do not set out to build philosophical or jurisprudential edifices. They decide cases, and cases will inevitably present very different clashes of interests and values in different areas of the law. Twentieth-century jurisprudence is increasingly concluding that the solution of such controversies should reflect the policies of the law in the particular area in question and the interests and values at stake, rather than universal principles of law. It is rejecting the formalistic jurisprudence of the nineteenth century, which aspired to resolve legal problems scientifically by logical derivation from universal concepts. When courts wisely reject the transcendental application of concepts in order to achieve the underlying objectives of the law in the particular area, they are inevitably going to be reaching decisions consistent with one concept in one area of the law and with an opposing concept in another, all as will best serve the law in the particular case at hand. However, this logical "inconsistency" reflects only the fundamental nature of the law, which seeks to achieve different objectives in different areas, such as in torts compared to contracts, in substantive problems compared to procedure, and in public law matters compared to private controversies.

Unincorporated Associations

As in the case of partnerships, recognition of the legal existence of unincorporated associations as separate from that of their members has lagged decades behind the increasing prominence of associations in society. Notwithstanding the realities of their de facto organizational existence, traditional law focused on their lack of incorporation and did not recognize their separate legal existence. Like partnerships, under common law they lacked such primary legal rights as the right in their own name to sue and be sued, to contract, and to acquire, hold, and dispose of property. Whatever their separate economic, political, or social significance, they were only aggregates of their members for legal purposes.[9]

Notwithstanding its lack of primary legal rights that traditionally accompanied existence as a legal entity, the association for some purposes had certain rights that reflected a legal identity of its own. Although suit to enforce the right had to be brought in the name of the members or by a member acting in a representative capacity, the association could obtain judicial relief to protect its integrity and interests against third parties. Thus, it could enjoin interference with the association or the misappropriation of the association's name or insignia.[10]

Through technical measures, the law gradually adapted to the realities of associational existence. Although the association was traditionally unable to sue or be sued directly, the individual members, acting on behalf of the association, could institute suit or be sued with respect to association matters. Similarly, although the association could not own property directly, members acting on behalf of it could acquire and jointly own property for the association as tenants-in-common.[11]

Notwithstanding the obvious functional resemblance between organizations described as partnerships and those described as associations, there are at least three fundamental differences in their traditional legal treatment.

Most important of all, for recognition under Anglo-American law, a partnership must be organized for profit, with the partners sharing profits and losses. By contrast, some associations are created for profit purposes, whereas others are not-for-profit organizations. Thus, many associations operate in noncommercial settings. These include such widely disparate groups as trade unions, clubs and social institutions, charitable agencies, professional organizations, and others representing a myriad of interests and objectives.

Second, partnerships and associations differ fundamentally in the internal conduct of their affairs and with respect to the legal responsibilities reflecting such conduct. Under partnership law, the partners are empowered to act as agents for the partnership and for each other. By contrast, members of an association have no inherent right to act for each other or the organization. Further, where the terms of its organic instrument so provide, an association may provide for central management and designate certain officers as the sole persons with power to act on behalf of the association. The lack of agency status and the possibility of centralized management are distinctions of great practical, as well as legal, significance.

Finally, in the very important respect of organizational existence, the association fundamentally differs from the partnership. In traditional partnership law, the existence of a partnership is completely tied to a particular roster of partners. The admission of a new partner, or the death, withdrawal, or incapacity of an old partner automatically brings the firm to an end. Although the partners may agree that in such event the firm is, nevertheless, to continue with its new membership and to conduct the same business under the same name, the continuing firm is, for legal purposes, a new firm legally distinct from the preceding one.

In marked contrast to partnership existence turning on the identity of particular partners, associations continue without change, notwithstanding turnover in their membership. As a practical matter, associations are typically substantially larger than partnerships. Indeed, some associations have millions of members. Such organizations could hardly function if their existence were affected by every change in their membership, events that in some cases could be expected to occur frequently, perhaps even daily. In this respect, the legal treatment of associations is entirely comparable to that of corporations, where corporate existence continues, despite changes in membership. As noted, this corporate attribute was hailed centuries ago as one of the outstanding characteristics of corporate existence.

The traditional common law view of associations is, of course, largely, but not entirely, a matter of the past. As in the case of partnerships, state statutes in most jurisdictions have responded to the realities of contemporary society. They have empowered the association with the customary attributes of separate juridical existence, permitting it to operate independently of its members. These attributes of the association (as provided in its organic instruments), recognized in most states, include such matters as

- the power to sue and be sued in its own name;
- the power to contract in its own name;
- the power to acquire, hold, and dispose of property in its own name; and
- to fix its own term of existence.

In these respects, the modern legal treatment of the association closely resembles that of the corporation. The most dramatic remaining difference relates to a matter not originally associated with the primary attributes of corporate identity: limited liability of members. The rule on liability of association members differs sharply, depending on whether or not the association is operated for profit. In such event, as in the case of partnerships, the liabilities of the association continue to be the liabilities of the members. However, in the case of nonprofit associations, the members are not liable, except where under the laws of agency they have authorized the acts giving rise to the liability.[12]

Although modern law has widely recognized the independent juridical existence of associations in many respects, recognition of the particular association rests on the underlying reality of its existence in the real world. To qualify for the legal recognition available, the association must have a "distinct identifiable membership" linked by a common purpose or interest.[13]

Statutory Creation of Novel Legal Units

With the increasing complexity of the worlds of finance and commerce and of governmental regulatory and revenue programs, modern society has seen the emergence of new forms of organizations in response to the challenges presented by contemporary needs. As with partnerships and associations, these newer forms of organizations present fundamental juridical problems of identification as legal units of their own.

Statutory law in the United States and in the European Community provides several prominent examples of recognition of newer and less familiar types of organizations as legal units. These include the "separate account" created by the Investment Company Act of 1940 for the marketing of variable annuity and insurance products and the myriad types of "funds" and other organizations qualifying for tax exemption under the Internal Revenue Code. Statutory law both in the United States and abroad has similarly created a variety of governmental instrumentalities presenting important questions concerning their juridical nature for constitutional and other purposes. Finally, the European Economic Interest Grouping created by the European Community provides still another example of a newly created legal unit.

"Separate Accounts" under the Investment Company Act of 1940

The "separate account" is a unique legal concept created by the Investment Company Act of 1940. Described as "a fascinating exercise in jurisprudence," it serves as a highly sophisticated allocation of regulatory responsibilities in the federal system. The "separate account" is a statutory device for restructuring the regulatory framework supervising the insurance industry. It enables insurance companies to sell variable annuity and variable insurance policies under federal regulation while state regulation continues to govern the other, more traditional activities of these companies.[14]

In many important respects, the Investment Company Act of 1940 treats a "separate account" as a legal unit apart from its sponsoring insurance company. For purposes of the Act, the "separate account" is recognized as a "person" subject to the Act, as an "investment company," and even as the "owner" of its assets. The "separate account" possesses the power to sue and be sued, to acquire, hold, and dispose of property, to contract, and to have indefinite existence. Insurance carriers are required to segregate in "separate accounts" all assets supporting their various classes of variable contracts, annuity contracts, or variable life insurance policies. The segregated assets of the "account" are restricted to the account and may not be "charge[d] with liabilities arising out of any other business."

Further, the Investment Company Act and the Securities Act of 1933 treat the "separate account," not the sponsoring insurance company, as "the issuer" of its variable contracts for statutory purposes. They relegate the insurance company to secondary status as a "co-issuer" or "guarantor" of the contracts and policies and as "sponsor" or "depositor" in the registration statement.[15]

As an "investment company," the "separate account" must have its own board of directors with the capacity to carry out specified actions. In addition, the "separate account" and the insurance company are required to file separate financial statements. At the same time, even for federal purposes, the "separate account" lacks limited liability, a seal, and any internal organization other than a board of directors with limited functions.

Through this imaginative legal creation, widely known as the "ecto-plasmic theory,"[16] federal law has created an unique statutory classification giving statutory recognition of the "separate account" as a separate legal unit for purposes of the Investment Company and Securities acts. In so recognizing the "separate account" as a separate legal unit for their particular purposes, the two acts supersede the general conceptual boundaries of traditional law. However, to make the "separate account" feasible as an investment vehicle, adaptation of state regulatory law was necessary as well. In less sweeping fashion than the federal statutes, the state statutes typically give the "separate account" minimum recognition as a separate legal unit. The state statutes typically do no more than segregate the assets of a "separate account" from other liabilities of the insurance carrier; liberalize the limitations on authorized investments of the account to permit heavier investment in equity securities; prohibit certain types of self-dealing between the account and the sponsoring insurance company; and require a segregated accounting of the assets of the account.

In other respects not regulated by federal law, traditional state law continues to govern, and the "separate account" for those purposes has no independent legal existence. Thus, under state law, the insurance company continues as the legal and beneficial owner of the assets of the account.[17] Further, for state law purposes, the company is deemed the obligor under the annuity policies even though, as noted, the Investment Company and Securities acts look upon the "separate account" as the "issuer" of the policies for their special purposes.

From the jurisprudential point of view, the "separate account" is a development of significance. It illustrates to a fare-thee-well how twentieth-century law proceeds functionally and pragmatically to achieve its objectives, brushing aside, to the extent required, traditional conceptual or formalistic limitations. To seek to determine on a conceptual basis whether the "separate account" is a separate legal unit or has a separate legal personality "in the air," divorced from the implementing federal and state statutes, is patently a fruitless inquiry. For certain purposes of the federal statutes, the account has separate legal existence. For other purposes, the account is only one of the many contractual relationships of the sponsoring insurance company and lacks any independent legal existence of its own.

Noncorporate Tax-Exempt Organizations under the Internal Revenue Code

The Internal Revenue Code recognizes many types of organizations as qualifying for recognition of tax-exempt status for certain purposes. It uses neither incorporation nor any other formal organic test, requiring only some "written instrument by which an organization is created"; this may be as simple as a club constitution or any other memorandum of association. Any real-life organization falling into the very elastic description utilized by the Treasury regulations can qualify and thereby achieve recognition as a legal unit for purposes of the statute. In this manner, the Code and regulations recognize as separate legal units with their own juridical identity such diverse organizations as community chests; funds; labor, agricultural, or horticultural organizations; business and national professional football leagues; chambers of commerce; real estate boards and boards of trade; clubs; and fraternal societies, orders, or associations. For the Code, the extent to which these organizations are recognized as legal units for other purposes is irrelevant.[18]

Miscellaneous United States Statutes

As reviewed in Chapter 5, the federal regulatory statutes generally are typically drafted in expansive terms to reach out widely and sweep almost any type of organized activity under their provisions. With respect to the attribution of statutory rights to organizations, the courts have construed such statutes liberally and have focused on functional considerations, not on the common law requirements of traditional juridical existence. The courts require only a showing that an organization exists as a practical matter and that it has a discernible purpose and a reasonably well-defined body of members. On such findings, the courts have upheld the right of various types of noncorporate organizations to pursue remedies under federal constitutional and statutory law, either on their own behalf or on behalf of their members.[19]

European Economic Interest Grouping

In its Regulation on the European Economic Interest Grouping (EEIG), the European Community created a new legal unit. This new form of business organization authorizes the creation of a legal vehicle to conduct activity as a joint venture of companies and individuals of EC member states.

Among other matters, the Regulation provides that the EEIG "shall have the capacity in its own name to have rights and obligations of all kinds, to make contracts or accomplish other legal acts, and to sue and be sued." However, the Regulation leaves it to the member states to determine "whether or not groupings registered at their registries . . . shall have legal personality."

The Regulation further provides that the EEIG members are jointly and severally liable for its debts and that EEIG profits and losses are attributed directly to the members. Thus, as a jurisprudential matter, the EEIG has both aggregate and entity aspects.

All member states, other than Germany and Italy, have granted legal personality. In England and Ireland, for example, the EEIG is a "body corporate." Thus, in spite of Lord Oliver's conclusion in the *International Tin Council* case discussed in Chapter 7 that English law did not recognize a corporation without limited liability, it has done so in the form of the EEIG pursuant to the EC directive.[20]

Government Agencies

The problems involved in the legal recognition of state governmental agencies present some parallels to the ambivalence existing in the law with respect to the legal status of partnerships and associations. Under the United States Constitution, what is the status of the various state instrumentalities that are increasingly being established to implement the growing functions being assumed by state and local governments? When are state agencies regarded as "the state" and protected by the unique constitutional status of the states, and when are they regarded as separate legal units with different, and lesser, constitutional claims? Does the protection of the Eleventh Amendment granting the states immunity against private suits in the federal courts also protect state agencies? Is the agency a "citizen" for purposes of the provisions of Article III, which deals with diversity-of-citizenship jurisdiction?

In determining whether a state instrumentality is immune from suit under the Eleventh Amendment or is a "citizen" for purposes of the federal diversity jurisdictional standard, the courts analyze the objectives, functions, history, and experience of the agency, along with the primary legal attributes granted in the authorizing statute. In most cases, state agencies of significant scale are provided with such primary legal rights as the power to sue or be sued, the power to contract, and the power to acquire, hold, and dispose of property. Agencies granted such rights have manifestly achieved recognition as separate legal units for many general purposes, but such recognition does not answer the constitutional questions.[21]

The courts go beyond such primary matters to focus on the fundamental nature of the relationship of the agency and its mission to the state. Thus, the cases give primary emphasis to the degree of financial independence of the agency and the extent to which the responsibility of an adverse judgment would be borne by the state; the extent to which the mission of the agency relates primarily to local rather than statewide matters; and the degree of decision-making and operational autonomy.[22] Although courts frequently describe this analytical problem as a question of whether or not the instrumentality is the "alter ego" or the "arm" of the state,[23] it should be apparent that, like the metaphors of "piercing the veil jurisprudence," these are no more than futile conclusory generalizations.

Corporations

As noted, centuries ago the corporation achieved recognition as a legal unit, with its primary legal attributes firmly fixed before the time of Coke. Since those early days, these have been unchallenged. The legal debate has revolved around such very different issues as limited liability and the applicability to corporations of various constitutional and statutory provisions. Although corporations have most of the legal rights and responsibilities of individuals, they do not have all of them. However, corporations are the most mature form of organizations recognized by the law, and their legal attributes serve as a useful register for determining how far unincorporated organizations lacking any recognition at the common law have, by statute, since acquired equivalent legal attributes.

Although the nature of the core attributes of the corporation and its existence as a legal unit have been settled for centuries, the challenge of adapting the concept of the separate juridical identity of each corporation to evolving economic changes, particularly to the component corporations of a corporate group collectively conducting a common enterprise under central direction, is much more difficult.

This challenge is not concerned at all with the core attributes of separate corporate existence reviewed elsewhere in the volume. These are overwhelmingly concerned with the attribution of legal rights. By contrast, the major challenge facing the legal systems of the world is the establishment of a jurisprudential framework for the imposition of responsibilities on corporate groups.

The statutes and cases applying enterprise principles in dealing with the legal problems of parent and subsidiary corporations organized in corporate groups—the materials comprising the law of corporate groups—have several features of fundamental jurisprudential significance. First, although they are overwhelmingly concerned with imposing obligations on group affiliates by reason of the actions of a constituent company of the group, in a number of instances enterprise principles attribute certain rights as well. Second, enterprise law is not transcendental. It is applied only in selected areas of the law where it more effectively implements the underlying purposes and objectives of the law. In other respects, entity law continues unaffected. These two distinguishing features play a fundamental role in shaping jurisprudential analysis of the juridical nature of the corporate group and the application of enterprise principles. These problems are reviewed in the next and final chapter of the volume.

11

The Jurisprudence of Enterprise Law

As multinational groups have come to dominate the world economy in the twentieth century, the law is inevitably changing. The law is responding to the challenge presented by the fundamental transformation of the economy from the very different world of earlier centuries in which business was conducted by single corporations to one dominated by complex corporate groups.

Dealing with single corporations conducting a business, nineteenth-century corporate jurisprudence readily determined corporate rights and responsibilities arising from conduct of the business solely by reference to the corporation in question. Such recognition of the separate legal identity of the corporation distinct from the identity of its shareholders was then fully in accord with the economic realities: the corporation conducted the business and the shareholders were investors. The separate legal identities of the corporation and the shareholders fully matched the economic separation between the business and the investors. Similarly, when the concept of the separate corporate identity was powerfully reinforced by the adoption of the principle of the limited liability of shareholders to encourage investment, limited liability protected only the investors, not the business or any part of it.

With the development of corporate groups, continued application of nineteenth-century jurisprudence, which focused on the separateness of the corporation and insulated its shareholder or shareholders from responsibility, was in sharp contrast to the reality. Although the legal concept still matched the separate economic role of the parent corporation's shareholders—the ultimate investors in the enterprise—it longer matched the role of the parent corporation itself. Although the parent corporation is the sole or dominant shareholder of its subsidiaries, it is not merely an investor. The parent is itself engaged in the business. Along with its subsidiaries, it collectively conducts a common business under its central control.

In contrast to the single corporation and the earlier nineteenth-century law, recognition of limited liability for corporate groups has meant that limited liability no longer protects solely the ultimate shareholder-investors. It also protects each corporate layer in the multitiered corporate group from the liabilities of lower-tier subsidiaries. The concept is applied at each level of the multitier structure of the pyramidal group, even though the shareholder-investors of the business are not involved.

This contrast between the traditional legal conception and the new economic reality has led modern legislatures and courts in increasing numbers to deal with the legal problems of corporate groups by reference to newer principles of enterprise law. They are imposing collective group, rather than individual subsidiary, responsibilities, where such a departure from traditional law better serves the objectives of the law in the area in question.

The preceding chapters have described the growing emergence of enterprise principles in American corporate law and the development of what may be called the American law of corporate groups. If this, then, is enterprise law, what does it represent as a matter of jurisprudence? This is the ultimate question.

The Traditional Legal Entity and the Economic Entity No Longer Match

The Limitations of Traditional Corporate Theory

The concept of the corporation as a separate legal entity, a concept that originally had satisfactorily defined the economic entity as well as the legal entity, has failed to correspond to the modern realities of American and world business.[1] Early nineteenth-century law no longer serves the legal needs of the late twentieth-century economic order. In consequence, lawmakers—whether legislators, administrative agencies, or courts — considering problems involving corporate groups face the challenge of considering whether implementation of the underlying objectives of the law in the particular area before them requires redefinition of the legal boundaries of the business organization so that the legal entity will correspond once again to the economic entity responsible for the actions in question.

Accordingly, it is appealing to consider whether it is feasible to fashion a new legal unit, consisting of the affiliated corporations of a corporate group, as an "enterprise" to serve either generally, or in appropriate cases, as the conceptual basis for attributing the liabilities (and perhaps certain rights as well) of the component companies of a group to each other. Thus, when the European Court of Justice and the European Community Commission went beyond traditional entity law to apply enterprise principles in order to implement EC policies regulating restrictive trade practices and abuse of a dominant market position by corporate groups, it referred to a new concept, the "economic entity."[2]

In an effort to define the "enterprise" or the "economic entity," a starting point is the economist's theory of the "firm." To what extent does the theory of the firm cast light on the outer boundaries of the firm and contribute to the lawyer's understanding of enterprise law?

The Theory of the Firm and the Economic Entity

The theory of the firm aims to answer the economists' question: Why are production and distribution sometimes carried on by firms, rather than through market exchanges? The variant explanations focus on different aspects, but all embrace, to more or less degree, the work of Professor Ronald Coase.[3] They all agree that firms exist where they lower costs, particularly transactions costs, or otherwise improve economic performance.

Coase defines the "firm" as a system of production through internal coordination under the direction of an entrepreneur-coordinator within an organization instead of through a complicated market structure with exchange transactions involving contracts with independent contractors. As so perceived and as amplified by scholars building on the Coase contribution, the firm is the substitution of internal fiat, hierarchy, and bureaucracy for a network of contracts in the market.

Thus, vertical or horizontal integration is the organization of production through the firm, rather than through contract, because of the reduced transaction costs.

Starting with Coase, all students of the theory of the firm presuppose the exercise of some significant central direction or fiat over all components of the enterprise. This factor readily corresponds to the central role of "control" in the legal analysis of enterprise principles. Although subsequent studies make refinements and significant additions to Coase's theory, they all accept the central importance of "control" and build upon it.

Alchian and Demsets suggested that centralized direction and fiat were not a fully adequate explanation. They supplemented the concept of centralized direction with reference to the existence of "team use of inputs" arising from internal contracts. They emphasized both the organizational dimensions of the firm, describing it as a "centralized contractual agent in a team productive process," and the role of monitoring in joint team production.[4]

Jensen and Meckling further broadened the Alchian-Demsets contribution. Although they also emphasized the factors of agency costs and monitoring and regarded contract relationships as the essence of the firm, they included external contracts with customers, suppliers, and creditors, along with internal contracts with employees. They broadened the inquiry to include all contracting parties, not merely those directly concerned with joint production. In their view, the firm emerged as a "form of legal fiction which serves as a nexus for contracting relationships."[5]

Williamson emphasized the significance of hierarchies within the economic organization in reducing transactions costs.[6] He also suggested that integration or internalization of production, particularly in the case of so-called relationship-specific investments,[7] had the advantage of reducing vulnerability to opportunistic behavior by participants, as well as reducing the costs arising from limited knowledge.

These theories, resting on exploitation by the firm of such advantages as specialization and division of labor and economies of scope and scale, do not attempt to define the boundaries of the firm other than in terms of efficiency. Thus, Coase asserts that the firm will expand until the costs of using direct internal authority exceed the transaction costs of accomplishing production through a market exchange. In the end, the economists include under the firm all internalized activities, and the boundaries of the firm, accordingly, are simply located wherever the efficiencies of internalization no longer exceed market alternatives. Expansion eventually is brought to a halt by the increasing loss of information and difficulties of control as the firm grows in size.[8]

Since firms are seen to exist wherever internalization provides economies, conglomerate corporations are also readily accepted as firms. Although integration or internalization of production or distribution may be absent in conglomerates, the internalization of financial and administrative activities provides the necessary opportunities for economies. The firm rests on the superiority of internalization of inputs, and whether the efficiencies of such internalization arise from group productive or supporting activities is not vital. For example, as noted, substitution of internal group financing for the capital markets has been advanced as an explanation for the growth of conglomerate enterprises.[9]

Similarly, minority ownership of subsidiary corporations is also irrelevant so long as the subsidiary continues to be subject to central group direction and its operations are integrated with those of the group in important respects, which provide economies of scope and scale.

As is evident, the theory of the firm is still in its early stages of development. It has not yet been refined, for example, to the point of being applied precisely to public corporations.[10] Nor does it provide any significant insight from the legal viewpoint into determining the outer boundaries of the firm.[11] Accordingly, the materials do not provide a useful standard for lawmakers in defining the limits to enterprise law. Nevertheless, it is striking how closely the factors emphasized in the economic discussion parallel those utilized by the courts and legislators in formulating principles of enterprise law.

As noted, both the economists and the law start with the concept of control and the centralized direction of affairs. The economists all recognize the central role of the parent's fiat, and differ among themselves only on the extent to which it is tempered by the need to accommodate interests within the firm. Both the economists and the law emphasize the aspects of group or internalized operation that promote economies of scope and scale. Such major elements of legal thinking as economic integration of production or distribution, financial interdependence, administrative interdependence, interrelated group personnel and group persona are cardinal features of economies of scope and scale that underlie economic thinking. Although economic thinking does not solve the legal problems, it provides encouraging and legitimating support for the existing development of legal enterprise thinking. Further, by including conglomerate corporations and partly owned subsidiaries within the firm, the economists provide support for the similar inclusion of such subsidiaries within the enterprise for legal purposes in those cases where enterprise principles have otherwise been deemed desirable.

Enterprise Law as the Recognition of the Economic Entity as the Legal Unit

Enterprise law may be viewed as the formulation of the corporate group as a new juridical concept to serve as the right-and-duty-bearing unit for group rights and responsibilities. Such a development would parallel the older "piercing the veil jurisprudence," under which the application of liability on a parent corporation or controlling shareholder was viewed conceptually as resting on the telescoping of the parent (or controlling shareholder) and its subsidiary corporation (or controlled corporation) into a single entity for the purposes at hand, disregarding the separate incorporation of the companies. Under such a view, the new legal entity—whether termed the enterprise, the economic entity, the undertaking, or the firm—would then match the economic reality.

However, serious difficulties that exist with such a view make it difficult to accept. These difficulties arise from two fundamental deficiencies. First, the enterprise as a legal unit lacks the legal rights characteristic of every other legal unit. It would be unique. Second, enterprise law does not treat the enterprise as a legal unit for all legal purposes. It attributes certain rights or imposes certain responsibilities only when the requirements for application of enterprise principles are satisfied. It operates only for special purposes and under special circumstances. In all other respects, entity law continues to prevail. In brief, it would be a legal unit very different from all other legal units and having recognition only intermittently in sharply demarcated areas.

Lack of Legal Rights

As reviewed in the discussion of legal units, legal attributes, and legal identity, it is the attribution of certain primary legal rights to a subject that has traditionally given rise to its recognition as a legal unit. As noted, the legal identity of the corporation, the partnership, and the unincorporated association, and their existence in modern law as legal units, rest on attribution to them, by common law or statute, of the primary legal rights: the right in their own name to sue and be sued, the right to contract, and the right to hold property.

Although enterprise law does include some examples of the attribution of rights to a parent corporation (or controlling shareholder) by reason of its relationship to a subsidiary (or controlled corporation), they are relatively rare. Nor do these rights include any of the primary ones recognized for other legal units that are enumerated. Enterprise attribution of rights occurs only in isolated, peripheral areas, including res judicata and collateral estoppel; discovery; some aspects of set-off law in procedural law; severance condemnation damages in property law; and in some areas of statutory law, including bankruptcy, patent, and trademark law and the filing of consolidated returns in tax law. Enterprise law is overwhelmingly concerned with the imposition of responsibilities, and attribution of rights plays a relatively minor role.

Even for the courts applying enterprise law, the enterprise has no right to sue or be sued, the enterprise has no right to contract, and the enterprise owns no property. All such primary rights continue to be possessed by the constituent corporations, according to traditional entity law. Nor is there any economic pressure to attribute such rights to the enterprise. Although the law denies it such powers, the group functions efficiently, with its constituent corporations possessing all such powers in their own names, subject to the common control of the group. In brief, a legal unit without rights, particularly the rights traditionally recognized as fundamental in the case of all other units, is an odd unit indeed.

Treatment of a maritime vessel as a legal unit under the law of admiralty provides the closest parallel because of the importance of recognition of the juridical personality of the vessel as a route to the imposition of liability, just as in the case of corporate groups. However, unlike the enterprise, recognition of the legal identity of the vessel does not stop with the imposition of liability. Recognition includes such fundamental legal rights as the right to sue and to contract. Although it is difficult to speak of the enterprise as a "right-and-duty-bearing" unit when it lacks the right to sue and to contract, the treatment of the maritime vessel does not present such a paradox.

Selective Application

Furthermore, it would be incongruous to have an entity that has a recognized existence only for highly limited areas and under certain circumstances. Unlike other legal units, the enterprise, although recognized for some legal purposes, has no existence for other purposes. It may be a legal unit for certain statutes and not for others, in some private law areas and not for others. If recognized, its existence would concededly be evanescent or intermittent.

Although legal terms, once defined, can be utilized as one may choose, it is hardly profitable to do so unless the conceptualization contributes to a better understanding of the development. The concept of the enterprise as a legal unit does not appear to do so.

Enterprise Law as the Imposition of Derivative Liability

In view of the central role that imposition of liability plays in the overwhelming number of legal areas in which enterprise law has been recognized, is it profitable to consider whether instead of representing a new legal unit, enterprise law might better be viewed as a development of derivative liability?

Such a view would treat enterprise liability as a legal development very much like some examples of derivative liability. One such example would be the vicarious liability under certain circumstances where principals or employers are held responsible for the torts and crimes of their agents and employees. Under certain circumstances in these situations, the law seeks to accomplish certain purposes by imposing liability on one legal unit for the acts of another. It does so even where the acts were unauthorized or contrary to express instructions.

In tort law, for example, vicarious liability achieves such fundamental purposes as creating incentives for the controlling unit to use its control to deter risky conduct by the controlled unit, to spread loss as a cost of the undertaking on all dealing with it, and to provide victims with an additional source of recovery typically possessing a "deeper pocket" than an employee or agent.

The common features of the cases of derivative liability appear to resemble closely the very factors present in the case of corporate groups: the existence of a close economic interrelationship and the right of control to direct the conduct of the related unit on the part of the unit subjected to liability. Under such circumstances, the imposition of liability upon the controlling unit and its assets for obligations of the controlled unit arising in the course of the closely integrated relationship may achieve underlying objectives of the law.

Thus, insofar as the imposition of liability is concerned, enterprise law, with its similar emphasis on control and close interrelationship, appears to be hardly distinguishable from these examples of derivative liability as a matter of jurisprudential conception. One should hasten to point out, however, that although enterprise law resembles derivative liability in terms of jurisprudential process, it is very different indeed in the circumstances giving rise to liability.

Vicarious liability is unknown to Anglo-American law, except in the area of torts, statutory law, and crimes. It is applicable only to employees and agents. By contrast, the imposition of liability under enterprise law is much more wide-ranging; under certain circumstances, it may involve contract or statutory law as well. Further, enterprise law concerns subsidiary corporations, not employees or agents. Although a parent corporation may become liable for its subsidiary's acts that had been performed by the subsidiary's employees and agents, the latter remain the subsidiary's employees and agents. Judicial imposition of liability on the parent does not require the latter to be viewed as the parent's employees and agents. Finally, like the suggestion of the enterprise entity, the analogy of derivative liability utterly fails to explain those circumstances in which enterprise principles are utilized to attribute rights or other legal consequences, rather than the imposition of responsibilities, to, or upon, group affiliates. Thus, while derivative liability offers certain parallels, it, too, does not smoothly fit and satisfactorily explain the emerging enterprise law.

Enterprise Law as a Form of Agency Law

The imposition of liability under agency concepts also provides an appealing, although similarly flawed, resemblance to the imposition of enterprise law. Over the years, a few courts and commentators have attempted to explain enterprise law and "piercing the veil jurisprudence" as a manifestation of agency principles.

However, as reviewed in Chapter 4, the authorities agree that this variant theory does not rest on common law concepts of agency. With common law agency concepts unavailable, the suggestion that enterprise principle rests on agency becomes no more than another ill-defined, metaphorical variation of "piercing the veil jurisprudence."

Enterprise Law as a Partial Elimination of Limited Liability

Enterprise law may be alternatively perceived as being no more than a limitation on the application of limited liability. In this view, it simply directs that, under certain circumstances, the principle of limited liability developed to protect investors in the enterprise is inapplicable to insulate a parent corporation collectively conducting a common business with an integrated subsidiary from liabilities incurred by the subsidiary in the conduct of the business.

Under enterprise law, limited liability is confined to protection of ultimate investors. It does not extend to protecting the constituent companies of a corporate group from liability for the obligations of an affiliated corporation where all have been engaged in conducting fragments of a common business through adoption of separate corporate forms.

In this view, enterprise law may be seen as an effort by the legal system to find a way around the problems created by the late-nineteenth-century courts when they automatically extended limited liability to protect parent corporations as well as the shareholders of the parent. Such courts were apparently unaware of the significance of their application of the accepted doctrine for the protection of shareholder-investors to a newer and fundamentally different type of shareholder: the parent corporation or subholding company that was both a shareholder and a constituent part of the business.

On reviewing the relationship of traditional entity law and its corollary, "piercing the veil jurisprudence," one might not inappropriately describe entity law today as providing a presumption that a parent corporation or other group affiliate is not liable for responsibilities of its subsidiaries or other affiliates, a presumption that may be overcome in "exceptional" cases by satisfaction of the rigorous requirements of "piercing the veil." In the same way, when selective enterprise law gains fuller acceptance, it may also come to be expressed as providing the contrary presumption that the parent corporation or other group affiliate is liable for the responsibilities of its subsidiaries or other affiliates, a presumption similarly subject to rebuttal for good cause. An obvious example of such acceptable cause arises in contract where, as part of the bargain, the creditor agrees expressly to restrict liability under the contract to the particular subsidiary with which it is dealing.[12]

Although entity law and the concept of each corporation as a legal unit separate from its shareholders long antedated limited liability, it should be apparent that the doctrine of limited liability, resting on powerful economic and political considerations, rather than the jurisprudential concept of separate legal identity, provides the explanation for the tenacious survival of entity law as the still-dominant principle in corporation law. Accordingly, explaining the growth of enterprise law as a reformulation of limited liability is appealing.

However, like the other possible explanations reviewed earlier, this suggestion has disqualifying limitations. It does not begin to explain the use of enterprise principles to attribute legal rights as well as responsibilities from one group constituent to another. Accordingly, although the increasing acceptance of enterprise principles clearly reflects the desire to restrict the scope of limited liability, it does not help to explain the application of enterprise principles in areas where limited liability plays no role.

Furthermore, the doctrine provides no explanation for the many legal areas where entity law prevails and enterprise law is not applied to corporate groups, which results in group affiliates, continuing to enjoy the protection of limited liability. Thus, while it deals satisfactorily with an important part of the problem, it leaves other areas still open.

Enterprise Law as a Form of "Privity"

The concept of "privity" offers a further analogy that may be useful in considering the jurisprudential role of corporate groups. In traditional law, "privity" is a concept that, under certain circumstances, enables the courts to attribute certain legal rights to, or impose certain legal responsibilities upon, one legal unit by reason of the nature of its relationship to another legal unit. Because this term lacks precise definition, it has been properly criticized. It all too often serves as a convenient device for lazy courts and scholars to offer an explanation of a legal result without rigorous examination of the underlying factors that make for the application of the term in the individual case. Nevertheless, its established utilization in the law as a classification of circumstances in which legal rights and legal responsibilities are attributed from one legal unit to another because of the nature of their relationship—where such attribution and imposition implement the objectives of the law in the area—provides a striking parallel to the application of enterprise principles. It is of particular interest because some instances of the use of the "privity" concept include the attribution of rights, as well as responsibilities.

The concept of "privity" has been utilized in very different fields of the law, including both substance and procedure. Among many other areas, the concept of "privity" has played a role in judgments, res judicata and collateral estoppel, warranties in contract and in tort, product liability under older law, and adverse possession and covenants running with the land in real property. There is "privity of contract," "privity of estate," "privity of possession," "privity of knowledge," and "privity in representation." The label is applied in a myriad of quite dissimilar relationships, including assignor and assignee, trustee in bankruptcy and debtor, co-parties, husband and wife and parent and child, judgment creditor and debtor, estate representative and decedent, grantor and grantee, insurer and insured, lessor and lessee, shipowners and vessels, mortgagor and mortgagee, principal and agent, principal and surety, and successor and predecessor, among others. Although the term describes a wide variety of relationships that differ sharply from one another, it is employed as a conclusory description of the attribution of legal rights or the imposition of responsibilities to one party primarily by reason of that party's relationship to another party, and to the acts of the other, rather than by reference to any act or fault of its own.

Because the factors constituting "privity" differ in the various areas, the term is properly viewed as slippery. By seizing on the interrelationship as the basis for attributing rights or imposing duties, privity diverts attention from the underlying circumstances that so tie the separate legal units together. It thus obscures analysis of the legal objectives that are to be implemented. Further, the term is essentially used tautologically. The rights of parties are advanced, or responsibilities are imposed, by reason of their relationship to other parties, to whom they are said to be in "privity." The legal interrelationship is recognized, but the usage does not tell us why this is so. It is no more than a conclusory label describing, but not explaining or justifying, the result. This is why its use in so many areas has been justly criticized.

"Privity" appears to have still another feature. In many of the areas in which it is employed, it arises from the very existence of a relationship between certain legal units. The legal units are said to stand in "privity" with each other simply by reason of the type of legal unit or the existence of a certain legal phenomenon. The particular aspects of the relationship are quite irrelevant. The result flows from recognition of the essential identity of the parties.

In some areas of the law, enterprise law is similarly a relatively simple concept turning on a single factor: the existence of "control." This is the case in almost all regulatory statutes of specific application, revenue statutes, res judicata and collateral estoppel, and discovery. Here, recognition of enterprise law as a form of "privity" would be modestly useful so long as one did not overlook the fact that legal consequences were arising because of the existence of "control," not because a quality called "privity" was involved.

The problem with characterization of enterprise law as "privity" arises elsewhere. Except in certain special cases, the law of corporate groups involves a complex evaluation of a series of factors in the light of the underlying objectives and policies of the law involved in the particular case. The attribution of rights or imposition of responsibilities does not arise simply from the parent/subsidiary interrelationship and the existence of "control." It involves such other factors as economic integration, administrative and financial interdependence, common employee policies and utilization, and common group persona. Faced with this complex determination, the use of a term as conclusory and simplistic as "privity" to describe the jurisprudential nature of enterprise is inadequate. It can do little more than provide a loose characterization of the development.

Enterprise Law, Economic Interrelationship, and Relational Law

Relational Law

Writing almost three-quarters of a century ago, Dean Pound suggested in *The Spirit of the Common Law* that the common law included both Romanist roots emphasizing consensual elements and English feudal roots emphasizing what he called relational elements where parties derived certain legal responsibilities from their relational status to each other. He referred to a "tendency [of the law] to affix duties and liabilities independently of the will of those bound, to look to relations rather than to legal transactions as the basis of legal consequences" and noted that "Anglo-American law is pervaded on every hand by the idea of relation and of legal consequences flowing therefrom." He called this dimension of Anglo-American law relational law.

Pound's suggestion of a "juristic conception of rights, duties and liabilities arising . . . simply and solely as incidents of a relation" aptly describes the jurisprudential nature of the law of corporate groups.[13]

Professor MacNeil, in contracts, and Dean Green, in torts, have built on the concept of relational interests in the law.[14] MacNeil has suggested that, where appropriate, problems in contract law should be analyzed as a part of the relational process of parties with continuing business dealings, rather than as isolated events. This resembles enterprise analysis in at least two respects. First is its emphasis on the interrelation of the law with the economic setting in which the legal problem has arisen. The other is its attempt to achieve a sharper focus for legal analysis by moving from broad doctrines universally applied irrespective of the setting in which the problem has arisen into more specialized doctrines responding to the particular needs of the area in question.

Dean Green was searching for a description of the legal concept giving rise to tort liability when the defendant wrongfully interfered with the continuing business dealings between the plaintiff and another party. He termed such business dealings as giving rise to a relational interest that tort law would protect and called for its recognition as a legal interest deserving "a place alongside of personalty and property." This is another attempt to analyze legal problems in the light of economic realities and to recognize legal consequences because of an ongoing economic relationship.

In a number of areas of developing modern business law that are responding to economic developments, traditional concepts of consent and party, or entity, have similarly given way to newer doctrines of increasing prominence. Although these doctrines have received different labels, including enterprise law of corporate groups; related forms of enterprise law of franchisors/franchisees, licensor/licensees, and contractors/subcontractors; successor liability; lender liability; and product liability, they essentially rest on the same foundation.[15]

In these cases, the courts are attributing legal consequences from one legal unit to another by reason of the interrelationship that arises from participation in a common economic activity. Legal responsibilities are increasingly following the "business," rather than being confined to the legal unit.

Enterprise Principles: Corporate Groups

The jurisprudential significance of the law of corporate groups may be best understood as another manifestation of the increasing emergence of relational law. In this case, it rests on the economic interrelationship between the parent and subsidiary corporations. The affiliated corporations are collectively conducting a common business. In the areas recognized by the law of corporate groups, the attribution of rights and the imposition of liabilities may be seen as the law, unconfined by traditional notions of entity, following the business and allocating legal consequences to the business.

As has been seen, the law of corporate groups rests on two unifying factors that lead, in appropriate cases, to the application of enterprise principles to impose intragroup liability or other legal consequences in place of traditional entity law. These primary unifying factors are "control," typically arising from ownership or control of voting stock, and economic interrelationship. Economic interrelationship comprises not only vertical and horizontal integration of processes of production, distribution, or supply of services, but also such additional elements as administrative and financial interdependence of the affiliated corporations, integration of employee relationships, and use of a common group persona. In sum, these factors are the hallmark of a unitary enterprise that has been fragmented among the affiliated corporations as a matter of legal form, with the companies continuing in the collective conduct of the business under a central, coordinated control. In imposing liability or otherwise attributing legal consequences in the light of these symbiotic interrelationships, the law is being molded to match the economic reality.

Where a group does not meet these sharply defined conceptual boundaries, enterprise law does not apply. Thus, enterprise principles recognize and respond to the reality that the general class of corporate groups embraces a wide variety of operational and structural patterns. As Easterbrook and Fischel point out, corporations are sometimes hierarchies, sometimes dictatorships, and sometimes divisional profit centers with loose or missing hierarchy. Teubner notes the increasing importance of networks. Dan-Cohen distinguishes among organizations by reference to structure, permanence, decision-making capacity, size, formality, internal complexity, and goal order functionality.[16] Enterprise law takes these differences into account. Thus, while enterprise law is often directed at hierarchical groups resting on ownership of a majority or other percentage of voting shares, the concepts of de facto "control," controlling influence over the management or policies, "participating interest" and "dominant influence" are flexible enough to respond not only to hierarchical groups, but also to newer forms of groups such as networks or other interrelationships.

Enterprise Principles: Other Economic Relationships

Application of enterprise principles in place of traditional entity law for the imposition of liability or the attribution of legal consequences is most prominent in cases involving affiliated corporations of corporate groups. However, there are a number of other areas in the law where enterprise principles, strongly resembling those comprising the law of corporate groups, appear to be at work. These developments, resting on the same fundamental factors of "control" and economic interrelationship, include such areas as the imposition of liability on franchisors, licensors, and contractors for the acts of their franchisees, licensees, and subcontractors, respectively; and the liability of lending institutions for acts of a controlled borrower. Still another area may be the imposition of liability under the doctrine of inherent authority in agency law.[17]

Although stock ownership or control is the wellspring of "control" in corporate groups, it is not the only source of "control" in economic interrelationships. Contract may also provide one party with the ability to direct, in important respects, the business and affairs of another party that may be entirely unrelated insofar as ownership is concerned. This is particularly true where one party to the franchise contract, the license contract, or the loan agreement has dramatically stronger bargaining power, as is frequently the case.

FRANCHISOR/FRANCHISEES AND LICENSOR/LICENSEES

Thus, the franchisor and franchisee and the licensor and licensee relationships manifest much the same powerful unifying factors of "control" and economic integration of elements of a common business as are present in corporate groups. Although not far advanced, the law is responding in certain circumstances to the imposition of liability or attribution of other legal consequences to franchisors and licensors by reason of the activities of their franchisees or licensees, which sharply resembles developments in the law of corporate groups.[18] In both, the law is following the fragmented segments of a common undertaking to attribute legal consequences from one interrelated party to the other. The fragmented segments are intertwined in direction and operation, and it is irrelevant that they are linked by contract rather than stock ownership. The decisions proceed much as if parent and subsidiary corporations were involved. For example, the motor hotel chain consisting of franchised motels in which the franchisor has no stock interest may be treated for some purposes much as the hotel or motel chains of corporate groups. In each, the law is following the business.

CONTRACTORS/SUBCONTRACTORS

Isolated cases dealing with contractors and subcontractors provide still another example of the application of enterprise principles to otherwise unrelated parties linked by contract.[19] Subcontracting is a common example of a fragmented economic process collectively conducted by otherwise unrelated parties pursuant to contract giving the dominant party "control" over major elements of operations. With such factors as "control" and economic integration not fundamentally distinguishable from those operating in the case of corporate groups and franchisors/franchisees and licensors/licensees, the law has similarly responded in isolated cases with a comparable application of enterprise doctrines to contractors and subcontractors.

LENDER LIABILITY

Lender liability is still another area in which enterprise principles have been applied in appropriate cases. Although the lender and its borrower are not linked by stock ownership, these cases have imposed liability on the lender for the borrower's obligations to third parties. They have done so because of the lender's excessive exercise of "control" over the direction of the borrower's business, much as in the case of the application of enterprise principles to corporate groups, franchisors, and licensors. By assuming direction of the borrower's business in the "work-out" of the loan, the lender has, in effect, made the borrower's business part of its own business, and although full economic integration has not occurred, the law may again be said to be following the business to its components.

Lender liability is occurring in American law in cases involving the imposition of liability under statutory and environmental laws and in bankruptcy in the modified form of equitable subordination.[20] Unlike the application of enterprise principles to the legal problems of corporate groups, lender liability, as the term indicates, relates solely to liability and does not involve the attribution of rights or other legal consequences.

In contrast to each of the areas of economic relational law just discussed, there are two other areas of relational law that do not rest on "control": successor liability and product liability. Similarly, unlike corporate groups, these areas only involve the imposition of responsibilities.

SUCCESSOR LIABILITY

In a dynamically developing field of American law, successor corporations conducting businesses previously run by the predecessor corporations from which they were acquired are increasingly being held liable for obligations arising from acts of those predecessors.

The doctrine seeks to deal with corporate and contractual structuring that relies on entity law to attempt to insulate a company (the successor) acquiring the business of another corporation against liability for the obligations of the other corporation (the predecessor). Corporate acquisitions may be accomplished in several ways: purchase of stock, purchase of assets, or corporate merger. Under traditional entity law, the successor company is liable for liabilities of the predecessor firm in the case of acquisition involving a merger, and takes subject to the liabilities of the predecessor in the case of purchase of stock. However, it is normally not liable in the event of the purchase of assets, unless it expressly assumes the debts. Thus, although the availability of these alternatives strengthens the bargaining flexibility of the parties, it permits the successor to escape liability for the predecessor's unpaid obligations arising from the business.

When, under traditional entity law, the liabilities do not move with the business because the buyer and seller have so structured the contract, the successor liability doctrine intervenes under some circumstances to protect unpaid creditors of the predecessor firm. In brief, successor liability (and its variant, the de facto merger doctrine) seeks to achieve much the same legal protection for preexisting creditors in the event of a sale of assets as they would have had in the event of a merger or consolidation.

Because of its interference with the bargaining process between the seller and buyer and its possible hardship on the successor-buyer, successor liability is imposed only in certain well-defined areas and to accomplish strong policy objectives. It has become prominent in at least four areas: (a) in product liability law with respect to injuries suffered from products sold by the predecessor and causing harm (sometimes decades) after the acquisition;[21] (b) under the labor acts with respect to the continuance of union obligations of the predecessor corporation;[22] (c) under the Employees Retirement Income Security Act for imposition of pension or contribution liability;[23] and (d) under the environmental laws with respect to statutory liability for hazardous waste disposition and removal.[24] It has appeared in other areas, including contracts. Finally, it has a counterpart in the corporation law doctrine of de facto merger, under which the economic aspects of an acquisition supplant traditional concepts to give rise to imposition of liability.[25]

Torts. The successor liability doctrine is most advanced in the area of torts. The easiest case for imposition of successor liability, and the area where the doctrine originated, is when the successor and predecessor firms share common ownership. Where the proprietary interest of the owners and the economic aspects of the business remain materially unchanged, the transaction lacks independent significance and may be readily viewed as a paper restructuring in an effort to avoid liability for obligations, even those that are only inchoate on transfer. In such situations, the conventional "mere continuation" theory readily imposes liability. By reason of the continuity of ownership, this may alternatively be described as a variant form of traditional "piercing the veil jurisprudence."

Successor liability, however, also has been applied where there has been economic continuity of the business, notwithstanding a material change in ownership. This is a jurisprudential development of significance. Through such theories as the "product line" and the "continuity of enterprise" doctrines, a number of jurisdictions have significantly extended the perimeters of successor liability in tort to include successors lacking continuing proprietary ownership.

Under the "continuity of enterprise" theory, accepted in Michigan and a number of other states, liability, notwithstanding the absence of continuity of ownership, rests on a broad spectrum of factors, including continuity of assets, continuity of general business operations, continuity of employees and supervisory personnel, production facilities in the same location, continuity of products, and continuity of trade names. Under the "product line" theory, accepted in such states as California and Pennsylvania but rejected in many others, liability is similarly imposed on acquiring corporations that manufacture and distribute the same product under the same trade name without disclosure of the change of ownership. Many states, however, continue to adhere to traditional entity law and have rejected continuation of the business as a basis for liability where there has been no continuity of ownership.

Much of the impetus for the doctrine comes in situations where injury from the defective product sold by the predecessor comes years or decades after the transfer, when the predecessor has long since been dissolved and any effective remedy against it or its shareholders is not feasible. Thus, some courts have restricted application of the successor liability doctrine to these very cases in which an effective remedy against the predecessor is unavailable. Some of these courts go further and require, in addition, that there be a causal relationship between the acquisition and the unavailability of a remedy against the predecessor. Other courts, however, ignore the availability of a remedy against the predecessor and, accordingly, are applying the doctrine in its most sweeping form.

Statutory Law. Concepts of successor liability also have become prominent in three statutory areas. In such areas as labor relations and environmental matters, and under the Employee Retirement Income Security Act, courts and agencies have broadly construed remedial statutes embodying strong public policy and have readily imposed successor liability in order to implement statutory objectives and prevent evasion of the statutory controls. Although this is most apparent in cases involving continuity of ownership, numerous cases have applied the doctrine even though there has been an absence of any continuity of proprietary interest. In labor areas, the doctrine gives particular emphasis to the extent of continuity of the workforce, supervision, and the labor processes of production. In the environmental and retirement areas, courts applying the doctrine have emphasized the strong statutory objectives.

Miscellaneous Applications. The successor doctrine has also been utilized on isolated cases in other very different settings. Ignoring the tort origins of the doctrine, courts have applied it in contract as well. It has also arisen in the wake of a corporate recapitalization or reorganization.

Like enterprise liability, the foregoing developments—franchisor, licensor, contractor, and lender liability—may be seen as an increasing recognition by the courts that, in certain areas, it is desirable to transcend traditional legal conceptualizations to assure that the costs of the various corporate parts of a business that is being collectively conducted under common control may be imposed on all participants in the economic activity, notwithstanding the legal structures involved. Successor liability is a closely related doctrine resting on the continuity of the economic enterprise imposing costs of the business on successive owners, otherwise unrelated.

The legal process is still in ferment, and the ultimate contours of the successor doctrine, although still appearing to expand, are not firmly fixed. As with the other examples of economic interrelationship and "control" that rest on contract, rather than on common ownership, utilization of the successor concept has concentrated on the imposition of liability. It does not appear to have been employed for the attribution of rights or other legal consequences. Accordingly, however useful in explaining enterprise law in such terms in connection with the imposition of intragroup or other integrated enterprise liability, this view also has its limitations. It has nothing to offer to explain the intergroup attribution of rights or other legal consequences.

Summary

Each of these areas of relational law share important common elements. They make legal consequences turn on the economic activity in question. For about a century since the Sherman Act, the increasing imposition of duties on those conducting economic activity has become a paramount feature of the legal system. As part of this profound political process, the doctrines of relational law impose responsibilities by reference to the business and abandon, where necessary, accepted principles of traditional entity law. Each of the discussed relational doctrines focuses on the intertwined economic interrelationship of the parties. In addition, except for successor liability, each of these doctrines relies as well on the crucial element of "control." Thus, through the development of a number of related breaches in entity law, the law is moving forward with the acceptance of enterprise concepts to achieve its objectives in selected areas. It is refusing to permit legal responsibilities to be evaded by corporate restructuring or subdivision of economic activity among different entities. In the law of corporate groups, it has gone even further in some cases and supplemented such action with the attribution of legal rights from one group component to another. Although enterprise law, accordingly, cannot be explained solely by reference to any of these doctrines, they are closely related manifestations of a common or closely associated underlying legal development.

To avoid making it a relatively vacuous doctrine such as "privity," the courts must effectively apply relational law through relatively precise characterization of the features of the relationship between the related parties and their impact on the underlying objectives of the law in the area in question that justify the attribution of relational rights and responsibilities. As outlined in this volume and further documented in *The Law of Corporate Groups*, enterprise law fully meets this standard.

Conclusion

Enterprise law is the conceptual solution being developed by courts and legislatures to respond to the inadequacies of anachronistic entity law inherited from the small-business world of the nineteenth century. It seeks to formulate a legal system capable of dealing adequately with the activities of giant, worldwide corporate groups. It plays a role of increasing importance in the legal systems of the modern world.

The acceptance of enterprise law thus far has been incremental, selective, and supplemental. Enterprise law is not a transcendental doctrine reflecting the emergence of a new legal unit — "economic entity," "enterprise," or "undertaking" — corresponding to the complex corporate organism conducting the activity. It does not supersede entity law, except in discrete areas where it better serves the underlying policies and objectives of the law. Entity law continues unchanged in other respects.

Enterprise law is a pragmatic response of the legal and political system to changing political, social, and economic realities. It is best described as an aspect of relational law in which legal responsibilities (and in some cases legal rights) follow the exercise of "control" and the integration of economic operations. In a selective manner, where enterprise principles implement its underlying policies and objectives, the law is matching rights and responsibilities to the collective economic activity (the business). Like the evolution of such legal phenomena as derivative liability and successor liability, which it resembles closely insofar as the attribution of responsibilities are concerned, it is part of the continuing process of adaptation of older doctrines of law to accommodate the new challenges of changing realities.

Developed to serve the needs of a contemporary economic society so very different from that of the past, enterprise law is an evolutionary development moving beyond the outmoded doctrine of legal entity. Closely resembling other modern legal developments adapting older doctrines to accommodate economic developments, enterprise law is a product of the modern age, an age in which the law is increasingly concerned with multifactor factual analysis, rather than with transcendental legal constructs.

Notes

Chapter 1

1. For a historical review of these developments, *see* Carr, *Early Forms of Corporations*, in 3 Select Essays in Anglo-American Legal History 161 (1909); C. Cooke, Corporation Trust and Company (1951); 3 W. Holdsworth, History of English Law 469-90 (5th ed. 1942), 8 *id.* 192-222; L. Gower, Principles of Modern Company Law 25-41 (4th ed. 1979).

2. Williston, for example, asserts that the early English law of corporations was borrowed almost entirely from Roman law. *See* Williston, *History of the Law of Business Corporations before 1800* (pt. 2), 2 Harv. L. Rev. 149, 164 (1888).

On the Roman law of corporations, *see generally* W. Buckland, Roman Law and Common Law (F. Lawson ed. 2d ed. 1965); P. Duff, Personality in Roman Private Law 35-37 (1938, reprint 1971). The Handlins wisely counsel that "the paucity of material and the uncertainty concerning the general character of Roman corporations render the drawing of analogies hazardous." Handlin & Handlin, *Origins of the American Business Corporation*, 5 J. Econ. Hist. 1, 10 n.52 (1945).

3. *See* C. Cooke, *supra*, at 21, 34-35.

4. 2 E. Coke, First Part of the Institute of the Laws of England or a Commentary upon Littleton 250a (1st ed. 1628); Case of Sutton's Hospital, 10 Coke 23a, 77 Eng. Rep. 960, 970-71, 973 (1612); Anon., The Law of Corporations (1702); 1 W. Blackstone, Commentaries on the Law of England 467-68, 470, 472, 478 (1st ed. 1765); 2 S. Kyd, Corporations 103 *et seq.* (1793).

5. In order to simplify discussion, this volume will use the term rights to refer to all advantageous aspects of corporate legal existence, whether more meticulously classified for other purposes as rights, powers, privileges, or claims. Similarly, the term responsibilities will refer to all duties, obligations, liabilities, and similar legal burdens.

6. Case of Sutton's Hospital, 10 Coke 250a, 253, 303, 77 Eng. Rep. 960, 970–71 (1612). *See also* 1 W. BLACKSTONE, *supra*, at 467–68. Kyd cautioned about Sir Edward Coke's metaphysical references to the "invisible, immortal" corporation, warning that the terms were "bewildering and apt to mislead." *See* S. KYD, *supra*, at 15.

7. Bank of the United States v. Deveaux, 9 U.S. (5 Cranch) 61, 86–91 (1809) and Trustees of Dartmouth College v. Woodward, 17 U.S. (4 Wheat.) 518, 636 (1819).

8. *See* C. COOKE, *supra*, at 68; Williston, *supra*, at 117–21.

For its subsequent decline, *see* Laski, *The Personality of Associations*, 29 HARV. L. REV. 404, 409 (1916) (In thirty years in the nineteenth century, the seal fell from being "the only authentic evidence of what the corporation had done or agreed to do [to] a relic of barbarous antiquity.")

9. J. KENT, 2 COMMENTARIES ON AMERICAN LAW 353 (13th ed. 1884); 3 J. STORY, COMMENTARIES ON THE CONSTITUTION OF THE UNITED STATES 58 (1833 reprint 1970). *See also* Providence Bank v. Billings, 29 U.S. (4 Pet.) 514, 562 (1830) (Marshall, C.J.) ("The great object of an incorporation is to bestow the character and properties of individuality on a collective and changing body of men.")

10. Case of Sutton's Hospital, 10 Coke 250a, 77 Eng. Rep. 960, 973 (1612).

11. On the evolution of the imposition of tort and criminal liability on corporations, *see generally* Carr, *supra*, at 78–87; Williston, *supra*, at 123.

12. New York Central H.R.R. v. United States, 212 U.S. 481 (1909).

13. *See* C. COOKE, *supra*, at 49.

14. For the English experience, *see* 1 S. KYD, *supra*, at 13. For the American experience *see* 2 J. DAVIS, *Essays in the Earlier History of American Corporations, No. 4*, EIGHTEENTH CENTURY BUSINESS CORPORATIONS IN THE UNITED STATES 27 (1917 reissued 1965).

15. *See* 2 E. COKE, *supra*, at 540; R. FORMOY, THE HISTORICAL TRADITIONS OF MODERN COMPANY LAW 11–16 (1923); E. LIPSON, THE ECONOMIC HISTORY OF ENGLAND 431, 572–74 (12th ed. 1959); 2 A. SMITH, AN INQUIRY INTO THE NATURE AND CAUSES OF THE WEALTH OF NATIONS 724, 740–58 (1776) (Liberty Classics ed., R. Campbell, A. Skinner, & W. Todd, eds. 1976) (Bk. V, pt. III, art. I).

16. *See* 2 M. FARRAND, RECORDS OF THE FEDERAL CONVENTION 321–22, 324–25, 615–16; 2 J. KENT, *supra*, at 272 ("improvident increase of incorporations"); 1 V. CLARK, HISTORY OF MANUFACTURERS IN THE UNITED STATES, 1607–1860, at 281–82 (1929) (1826 protest of Philadelphia mechanics against grant of incorporation).

See also J. DAVIS, *supra*, at 12–14, 303–04; J. HURST, THE LEGITIMACY OF THE BUSINESS CORPORATION IN THE CORPORATION LAW OF THE UNITED STATES, 1780–1970, at 30 (1970); Barzelay & Smith, *The One Best System? A Political Analysis of Neoclassical Institutionalist Perspectives on the Modern*

Corporation, in CORPORATIONS AND SOCIETY: POWER AND RESPONSIBILITY 81 (W. Samuels & A. Miller eds. 1984).

17. H. HOVENKAMP, ENTERPRISE AND AMERICAN LAW, 1836-1937 (1991).

18. *See, e.g.*, Bank of the United States v. Deveaux, 9 U.S. (5 Cranch) 61, 86-91 (1809) and Trustees of Dartmouth College v. Woodward, 17 U.S. (4 Wheat.) 518, 642-44 (1819) (Marshall, C.J.); 17 U.S. (4 Wheat.) 668 (Story, J.).

19. MacLaine Watson & Co. v. Department of Trade and Industry, [1990] 2 A.C. 418, 506; [1989] 3 All E.R. 523, 549 (H.L. 1989). *But see* Lord Nourse, dissenting in the Court of Appeal. J.H. Rayner (Mincing Lane) Ltd. v. Department of Trade, Industry & Ors., [1989] Ch. 72, 205 (C.A. 1988), [1988] 3 All E.R. 257, 323 (C.A. 1988), *aff'd sub nom.* Maclaine Watson & Co. v. Department of Trade and Industry, *supra*.

20. Louis K. Liggett, Inc. v. Lee, 288 U.S. 517, 556, 589 (1933).

21. For discussion of limited liability in English corporation law, *see generally* L. GOWER, *supra*, at 39-49; B. HUNT, THE DEVELOPMENT OF THE BUSINESS CORPORATION IN ENGLAND, 1800-1867 *passim* (1936); C. COOKE, *supra*, at 127-75; Shannon, *The Coming of General Limited Liability*, 2 J. ECON. HIST. 267 (1932).

22. Dig. of Justinian, tit. iv, §7(1) in 3 S. SCOTT, THE CIVIL LAW 32 (1932).

23. *See* 3 W. HOLDSWORTH, A HISTORY OF ENGLISH LAW 484; 8 *id.* at 203 (5th ed. 1973), *citing* Y.B. 19 Hen. 6, Pasch., pl. 1 (Markham); Y.B. 20 Hen. 6. Mich., pl. 19 (Fortescue) (the property of members not subject to levy in execution against the corporation); L. GOWER, *supra*, at 26; T. HOBBES, LEVIATHAN 175 (M. Oakeshott ed. 1962).

The Kings Bench held in 1668 that the creditors of a *dissolved* corporation could not assert corporate debts directly against the former shareholders. Edmunds v. Brown, 1 Lev. 237, 83 Eng. Rep. 385 (1668).

24. A. DuBOIS, THE ENGLISH BUSINESS CORPORATION AFTER THE BUBBLE ACT 1720-1800, at 95-97 (1938).

25. Kenyon, Case and Opinion of Jan. 29, 1784, Boulton & Watt MSS., Birmingham Collection, Assay Office, *cited in* A. DuBOIS, *supra*, at 95-96 n.66; Russell v. Men Dwelling in Devon, 100 Eng. Rep. 359 (1788).

26. 1 Ch. Cas. 204, 22 Eng. Rep. 763 (H.L. 1671).

There is scholarly dispute on the exact significance of *Salmon. Compare* E. DODD, AMERICAN BUSINESS CORPORATIONS UNTIL 1860 85, 86, 369 (1954); Jenkins, *Skinning the Pantomime Horse: Two Early Cases on Limited Liability*, 34 CAMBRIDGE L.J. 308, 312-21 (limited application) *with* C. COOKE, *supra*, at 78-79; L. GOWER, *supra*, at 26, 8 W. HOLDSWORTH, *supra*, at 204; and Williston, *supra*, at 161 (broad application).

American courts, a century and one half later, broadly applied the doctrine in *Salmon. See infra* note 32.

27. For general discussion of the rise of limited liability in the United States, *see generally* E. DODD, *supra*; Handlin & Handlin, *supra*; Livermore, *Unlimited Liability in Early American Corporations*, 43 J. POL. ECON. 674 (1935); O. HANDLIN & M. HANDLIN, COMMONWEALTH: A STUDY OF THE ROLE OF GOVERNMENT IN THE AMERICAN ECONOMY: MASSACHUSETTS, 1774–1861 (rev. ed. 1969).

For works dealing with particular areas, *see* E. DODD, *supra* (Massachusetts and New England); O. HANDLIN & M. HANDLIN (Massachusetts); Blandi, *Maryland Business Corporations 1783-1852*, 52 JOHNS HOPKINS U. STUD. HIST. & POL. SCI. 301 (1934); J. CADMAN, THE CORPORATION IN NEW JERSEY BUSINESS AND POLITICS 1791-1875 (1949); E. GRANT, YANKEE DREAMERS & DOERS (1973) (Connecticut); L. HARTZ, ECONOMIC POLICY AND DEMOCRATIC THOUGHT: PENNSYLVANIA, 1776-1860 (1948).

28. J. DAVIS, *supra*, at 27.

29. *See* 1 V. CLARK, *supra*, at 266-67 (1929); HANDLIN & HANDLIN, COMMONWEALTH, *supra*, at 107-21, 127; Baldwin, *History of the Law of Private Corporations in the Colonies and States*, in 3 SELECT ESSAYS IN ANGLO-AMERICAN LEGAL HISTORY 236, 249 (1909); S. BRUCHEY, THE ROOTS OF AMERICAN ECONOMIC GROWTH 1607-1861, at 87-90 (1965, reprint 1968).

30. E. DODD, *supra*, at 227, 373, 398, 409, 412, 419; S. LIVERMORE, EARLY AMERICAN LAND COMPANIES (1939 reissued 1968); Livermore, *Corporations*, *supra*, at 677-81. For New York exceptions, *see* J. DAVIS, *supra*, at 260; LIVERMORE, LAND COMPANIES, *supra*, at 269-70. For a Maryland exception, *see* Blandi, *supra*, at 28.

31. E. DODD, *supra*, at 365; LIVERMORE, LAND COMPANIES, *supra*, at 683-84; Blandi, *supra*, at 18, 44-45, 51.

32. Hume v. Winyaw & Wando Canal Co., 1 Carolina L.J. 217 (1830). *See* Briggs v. Penniman, 8 Cow. 386, 395-96 (N.Y. 1826); Slee v. Bloom, 19 Johns. 456, 493, 499 (1850).

In Massachusetts, Chief Judge Parsons deplored the inability to impose indirect liability because of the lack of equity jurisdiction. Commonwealth v. Blue-Hill Turnpike Corp., 5 Mass. 420, 426 (1809).

33. E. DODD, *supra*, at 120; Handlin & Handlin, *Origins*, *supra*, at 16-17; J. DAVIS, *supra*, at 294.

34. Spear v. Grant, 16 Mass. 9, 12 (1819); Wood v. Dummer, 30 F. Cas. 435, 436 (C.C.D. Me. 1824) (No. 17,944) (Story, J.); Myers v. Irwin, 2 Serg. & Rawle 368, 371 (Pa. 1816).

See J. ANGELL & S. AMES, LAW OF PRIVATE CORPORATIONS 349 (1st ed. 1832). The Handlins report that an earlier treatise did the same. HANDLIN & HANDLIN, COMMONWEALTH, *supra*, at 147, *citing* N. DANE, A GENERAL ABRIDGMENT & DIGEST OF AMERICAN LAW 472 (1824).

35. *E.g.*, Franklin Glass Co. v White, 14 Mass. 286, 288 (1817); Andover

& Medford Turnpike Corp. v. Gould, 6 Mass. 39, 42–45 (1809). *See* HANDLIN & HANDLIN, COMMONWEALTH, *supra*, at 158; Dodd, Book Review, 61 HARV. L. REV. 555, 558–59 (1948).

36. Although New Hampshire did not enact a general limited liability statute until 1836, substantially all charters granted after 1816 provided for limited liability. E. DODD, *supra*, at 396–99.

37. *See* 1 C. BEACH, COMMENTARIES ON THE LAW OF PRIVATE CORPORATIONS §143 (1891); 1 W. COOK, A TREATISE ON THE LAW OF CORPORATIONS HAVING A CAPITAL STOCK 675 n.1 (8th ed. 1923); Vincens, *On the Demise of Double Liability of Bank Shareholders*, 12 BUS. LAW. 275 (1957).

38. CAL. CONST. of 1849, art. IV, §36; CAL. CONST. of 1879, art. XII, §3 (repealed 1930); CAL. CIVIL CODE §322 (repealed 1931).

39. Acts of 1853 and 1863 applicable only to mining companies had an interesting variation. Under the mining company statute, pro rata liability established only the maxiumum aggregate liability of the shareholder, and an individual creditor could collect the entire amount of his debt from any shareholder to the extent that it did not exceed the shareholder's maximum obligation. 1853 Cal. Stat. 87, 90, *as amended by* 1863 Cal. Stat. 736–37.

40. Thomas v. Matthiessen, 232 U.S. 221 (1914); Pinney v. Nelson, 183 U.S. 144 (1901).

41. *See* 2 H. MARSH, CALIFORNIA CORPORATION LAW §15.13, at 330 (2d ed. 1988).

42. 1837 Mich. Laws 285, 286; 1842 N.H. Laws 605, 607; Wis. Rev. Stat., ch. 51 §11 (1849); 1853 Pa. Acts 567, 571.

43. *See* J. ANGELL & S. AMES, *supra*, at 362, *citing* 4 AM. JURIST 307 (complaining that Massachusetts unlimited liability was driving "millions of capital into the neighboring states for investment."). *See also* Blandi for similar assertions in Maryland. Blandi, *supra*, at 55.

44. *See* E. DODD, *supra*, at 383; HANDLIN & HANDLIN, COMMONWEALTH, *supra*, at 162.

45. *See, e.g.*, Chief Justice Marshall, in Trustees of Dartmouth College v. Woodward, 17 U.S. (4 Wheat.) 518, 636–37 (1819); Justice Washington, concurring in the same, 17 U.S. at 657–58; Chief Justice Nelson of New York, in Thomas v. Dakin, 22 Wend. 9, 71 (1839).

Chancellor Kent even lamented that "the tendency of legislatures and of judicial decision is to increase the personal liability of shareholders" and give corporations "more and more the characteristics of partnerships." 2 J. KENT, *supra*, at 272–74.

46. Shannon, *supra*; 8 W. HOLDSWORTH, *supra*, at 221; Todd, *Some Aspects of Joint Stock Companies, 1840–1900*, 4 ECON. HIST. REV. 46, 50 n.40 (1932). With the corporate form not practically feasible for the new manufacturing ventures, corporations were overwhelmingly conducting banking, fire

and marine insurance, and water and canal businesses. *See* C. COOKE, *supra*, at 91. Adam Smith, for example, does not discuss manufacturing corporations at all in this connection. *See* 2 SMITH, *supra*, at 756.

47. 6 Geo. 1, ch. 18, §18 (1719), *repealed* 6 Geo. 4, ch. 91 (1825). There was a flurry of prosecutions under the Bubble Act from 1807 to 1811, and again in 1821. *See* HUNT, *supra*, at 17–21. *E.g.*, Rex v. Dodd, 9 East 516, 103 Eng. Rep. 670 (1808). *See* Shannon, *supra*, at 269.

48. *See* L. GOWER, *supra*, at 40; Diamond, *Corporate Personality and Limited Liability*, in LIMITED LIABILITY AND THE CORPORATION 22, 31 (T. Orhnial ed. 1983); Perrott, in *id.*, at 81, 96.

49. *See* DuBois, *supra*, at 223; HUNT, *supra*, at 110; Shannon, *The First Five Thousand Limited Companies and Their Duration*, 2 J. ECON. HIST. 396, 399 n.3 (1932).

50. Eventually, several cases from 1849 to 1852 upheld the enforceability as a matter of contract law of a clause in an insurance policy limiting liability under the policy to the capital of the company. *E.g.*, Halket v. Merchant Traders' Ship, Loan & Ins. Ass'n, 13 Q.B. 960, 116 Eng. Rep. 1530 (1849); Hallett v. Dowdall, 18 Q.B. 1, 118 Eng. Rep. 1 (1852).

51. *See* 3 F. MAITLAND, TRUSTS AND CORPORATIONS IN COLLECTED PAPERS, 321, 342 (H. Fisher ed. 1911, reissued 1975).

52. *See* Shannon, *General Limited Liability, supra*, at 269.

53. Veblen concluded that the English opposition to limited liability, rather than reflecting political or economic forces, was rooted in the English attachment to the principles of "natural liberty" and "free contract." Liability was viewed as a personal attribute of the member of the enterprise from which a person was not competent to divest himself. T. VEBLEN, THEORY OF BUSINESS ENTERPRISE 280 n.1 (1904, reissued 1973).

As for the economists, *see* Amster, Bartlett, & Bolton, *Thoughts of Some British Economists on Early Limited Liability and Corporate Legislation*, 13 HIST. POL. ECON. 774, 779–92 (1981); Ekelund & Tollison, *Mercantilist Origins of the Corporation*, 11 BELL J. ECON., 715, 729 n.7 (1980).

54. *See* L. GOWER, *supra*, at 43; Perrott, *supra*, at 100.

55. Although the acts excluded banks and insurance companies, banks were included in 1857 and insurance companies in 1862.

56. See C. COOKE, *supra*, at 102–03.

57. *See* T. HADDEN, COMPANY LAW AND CAPITALISM 12 (2d ed. 1977); HUNT, *supra*, at 105–12; Hahlo, *Early Progenitors of the Modern Company*, [1982] JURID. REV. 139, 155. *See also* 8 & 9 Will. III, ch. 32 (1697).

58. *See* C. COOKE, *supra*, at 111.

59. *See* HUNT, *supra*, at 102, 105–12. Hunt also points out that the speculation in railway shares in the 1840s led to some criticism of limited liability for railways as well. *Id.* at 126 n.65.

60. *See* Shannon, *General Limited Liability, supra*, at 286–87; Hicks, *Lim-*

ited Liability: The Pros and the Cons, in LIMITED LIABILITY AND THE CORPO-RATION, *supra*, at 11, 12.

61. *See* DODD, *supra*, at 62–64; Shannon, *General Limited Liability*, *supra*, at 290.

62. *See* HUNT, *supra*, at 153–55, 417. Trollope described the speculative fever as "dishonesty magnificent in its proportions, and climbing into high places." A. TROLLOPE, AUTOBIOGRAPHY 294–95 (1883 reissued 1947).

63. French Code de Commerce [C. COM.] art. 33 (1807); C. FREEDEMAN, JOINT STOCK ENTERPRISES IN FRANCE, 1807–1867, at 17 (1979); A. KUHN, COMPARATIVE STUDY OF THE LAW OF CORPORATIONS, 65–69, 85–86, 90 (1912, reprinted 1968); T. OWEN, THE CORPORATION UNDER RUSSIAN LAW, 1800–1917, at 10 (1991); D. SERUZIER, HISTORICAL SUMMARY OF THE FRENCH CODES 140–52 (D. Combe trans. 1979).

Chapter 2

1. *See generally* M. DAN-COHEN, RIGHTS, PERSONS, AND ORGANIZATIONS (1986); F. HALLIS, CORPORATE PERSONALITY (1978); A. NEKAM, THE PER-SONALITY CONCEPTION OF THE LEGAL ENTITY (1938); S. STOLJAR, GROUPS AND ENTITIES: AN INQUIRY INTO CORPORATE THEORY (1973); Dewey, *The Historic Background of the Corporate Legal Personality*, 35 YALE L.J. 655 (1926); Radin, *The Endless Problem of the Corporate Personality*, 32 COLUM. L. REV. 643 (1932); Smith, *Legal Personality*, 37 YALE L.J. 283 (1928).

For more recent literature dealing with the corporate personality in connection with constitutional rights, *see infra* note 35.

2. 1811 N.Y. Laws 111; 1836–37 CONN. STAT. (Boswell), ch. 53.

3. *See* J. HURST, THE LEGITIMACY OF THE BUSINESS CORPORATION 37 (1970).

4. It is possible, of course, to hypothesize two corporations that, through purchase of each other's shares, can ultimately be each other's shareholders. Such cross-circular share ownership is virtually unknown in the United States and is prohibited by law in some European nations.

5. *See* Wolff, *On the Nature of Legal Persons*, 54 L.Q. REV. 496 (1938).

6. Trustees of Dartmouth College v. Woodward, 17 U.S. (4 Wheat.) 518, 636 (1819). *See also* Bank of United States v. Deveaux, 9 U.S. (5 Cranch) 61, 86–91 (1809).

7. *See, e.g.*, G. HEINAN, OTTO GIERKE: ASSOCIATION AND LAW 27–33 (1977) (reviewing theories of Savigny). *See also* Machen, *Corporate Personality* (pt. 1), 24 HARV. L. REV. 253, 255 (1911).

8. These form various subsets of the theory, with different emphases, but as Dewey said in distinguishing between the fiction and concession theories: "in spite of their historical and logical divergence, the two theories flowed together." *See* Dewey, *supra*, at 655, 668.

9. *See infra* notes 54–56.

10. Bank of the United States v. Deveaux, 9 U.S. (5 Cranch) 61, 91–92 (1809) (Marshall, C.J.); Trustees of Dartmouth College v. Woodward, 17 U.S. (4 Wheat.) 518, 666 (1819) (Story, J.).

11. *See* R. DIAS & G. HUGHES, JURISPRUDENCE 300 (1957); F. HALLIS, *supra*, at 166–88 (1978); G. PATON, JURISPRUDENCE 267–68 (1946); L. WEBB, LEGAL PERSONALITY AND POLITICAL PLURALISM 10–11 (1958).

12. *See* Chief Justice Taney in Bank of Augusta v. Earle, 38 U.S. (13 Pet.) 519, 586 (1839) and text *infra* accompanying notes 30 to 32.

13. *See, e.g.*, The Railroad Tax Cases, 13 F. 722, 744 (C.C.D. Cal. 1882); Santa Clara v. Southern Pac. R.R., 18 F. 385 (C.C.D. Cal. 1883), *appeal dismissed as moot sub nom.* San Mateo County v. Southern Pac. R.R., 116 U.S. 138 (1885).

14. In his influential treatise, published in 1882, Morawetz flatly asserted: "the rights and duties of an incorporated association are in reality the rights and duties of the persons who compose it, not of an imaginary being." 1 V. MORAWETZ, LAW OF PRIVATE CORPORATIONS §1 (1882).

15. *See, e.g.*, Paul v. Virginia, 75 U.S. (8 Wall.) 168, 177 (1868).

16. *See* Bratton, *The "Nexus of Contracts" Corporation: A Critical Appraisal*, 74 CORNELL L. REV. 407 (1989); Butler, *The Contractual Theory of the Corporation*, 31 CORP. PRAC. COMMENTATOR 555 (1989–90).

17. *See* R. HESSEN, IN DEFENSE OF THE CORPORATION (1979); R. WINTER, GOVERNMENT AND THE CORPORATION (1978).

18. O. VON GIERKE, POLITICAL THEORIES OF THE MIDDLE AGE (1958); F. HALLIS, *supra*, at 138–65 (1978); G. PATON, JURISPRUDENCE 268–69 (1946).

19. *See* Teubner, *Enterprise Corporatism: New Industrial Policy and the "Essence" of the Legal Person*, 36 AM. J. COMP. L. 130, 138 (1988).

20. *See* W. BLACKSTONE, COMMENTARIES ON THE LAWS OF ENGLAND 468; S. KYD, CORPORATIONS 18. Heraclitus really said something quite different. Emphasizing change not stability, Heraclitus said: "You can't step into the same river twice." ON THE UNIVERSE. *See also* Plato, CRATYLUS, 402a.

21. 2 M. FARRAND, RECORDS OF THE FEDERAL CONVENTION 321–22, 324–25, 615–16. *See* G. HENDERSON, THE POSITION OF FOREIGN CORPORATIONS IN AMERICAN CONSTITUTIONAL LAW 19–20 (1918). Henderson states that the opposition in the Convention rested on the association of incorporation with monopoly.

22. *See generally* McGovney, *A Supreme Court Fiction: Corporations in the Diverse Citizenship Jurisdiction of the Federal Courts*, 56 HARV. L. REV. 853 (1943).

23. 9 U.S. (5 Cranch) 61 (1809).

24. *See* 2 F. Cas. 692, 693 (C.C.D. Ga. 1808) (No. 916).

25. Cases not involving federal questions or admiralty matters may be heard in the federal courts only under diversity-of-citizenship jurisdiction.

26. 9 U.S. at 86–91.

27. Louisville, Cincinnati & Charleston R.R. v. Letson, 43 U.S. (2 How.) 497 (1844); Marshall v. Baltimore & Ohio R.R., 57 U.S. (16 How.) 314 (1853). In *Letson*, the Court rejected the *Deveaux* standard. The Court held that for purposes of diversity jurisdiction a corporation was to be regarded as a "person, though an artificial one, inhabiting and belonging to" the state of incorporation and therefore "entitled, for the purpose of suing and being sued, to be deemed a citizen of that state." 43 U.S. (2 How.) at 555. This holding was controversial and provoked repeated dissent from the Court in subsequent cases. *E.g.*, Rundle v. Delaware & Raritan Canal Co., 55 U.S. (14 How.) 80, 95 (1852) (Daniel, J., dissenting). Eleven years later, in *Marshall*, the Court found it prudent to retreat in theory, but not in result. 57 U.S. (16 How.) at 327–29.

The modern codification appears in 28 U.S.C. §1332(c) (1988).

28. AUSTL. CONST. §75 (iv); Australian Temperance & Gen. Life Assur. Soc. Ltd. v. Howe, (1922) 31 C.L.R. 290.

29. 38 U.S. (13 Pet.) 519, 586–88 (1839). *See also* 75 U.S. (8 Wall.) 168, 181 (1868).

30. 38 U.S. (13 Pet.) at 586.

31. Notwithstanding the firm tilt towards limited liability climaxed by the adoption of a limited liability statute by Massachusetts in 1830, the issue was still not settled as Taney was writing. The political struggle continued for another two decades or so. As reviewed in Chapter 1, a number of states instead adopted unlimited liability from 1837 to 1853, before the controversy ultimately died away.

For an example of the continued pressures for unlimited liability, *see 1842 Gubernatorial Address of Governor Henry Hubbard of New Hampshire*, in THE PHILOSOPHY OF MANUFACTURES: EARLY DEBATES OVER INDUSTRIALIZATION IN THE UNITED STATES (M. Folsom & S. Lubar eds., 1982) (This condemned limited liability as "a fruitful source of the embarrassment and distress . . . now pervading our land.")

32. From the early days of the republic, suits involving corporate rights and duties were brought by or against the corporation, not by or against their shareholders. *E.g.*, Marine Ins. Co. v. Young, 5 U.S. (1 Cranch) 332 (1803); Bank of N. Am. v. McKnight, 2 U.S. (2 Dall.) 158 (Pa. 1792).

33. 75 U.S. (8 Wall.) 168, 177 (1868).

34. Pembina Consol. Silver Min. & Milling Co. v. Pa. 125 U.S. 181, 187–88 (1888). *Accord* Hague v. Committee for Indus. Org., 307 U.S. 496, 514 (1939); Western Turf Ass'n v. Greenberg, 204 U.S. 359, 363 (1907).

35. *See* Flynn, *The Jurisprudence of Corporate Personhood: The Misuse of a Legal Concept*, in CORPORATIONS AND SOCIETY: POWER AND RESPONSIBILITY 131 (W. Samuels & A. Miller eds. 1987); Graham, *An Innocent Abroad: the Constitutional Corporate "Person,"* 2 UCLA L. REV. 155 (1955);

Hager, *Bodies Politic: The Progressive History of Organizational "Real Entity" Theory*, 50 U. PITT. L. REV. 575 (1989); Horwitz, Santa Clara *Revisited: The Development of Corporate Theory*, 88 W. VA. L. REV. 173 (1985); Hovenkamp, *The Classical Corporation in American Legal Thought*, 76 GEO. L.J. 1593, 1597–1601, 1640–51 (1988); Mayer, *Personalizing the Impersonal: Corporations and the Bill of Rights*, 41 HASTINGS L.J. 577 (1990); Schane, *The Corporation Is a Person: The Language of Legal Fiction*, 61 TUL. L. REV. 563 (1986); Comment, *The Personification of the Business Corporation in American Law*, 54 U. CHI. L. REV. 1441 (1987); Note, *Constitutional Rights of the Corporate Person*, 91 YALE L.J. 1641 (1982).

36. 118 U.S. 394, 396 (1886). It is far from clear what the Court meant by its statement. *See generally* H. GRAHAM, EVERYMAN'S CONSTITUTION 567 (1968).

37. *See* Horwitz, *supra*.

38. 125 U.S. 181, at 189. The language is borrowed from Justice Story's concurring opinion in the *Dartmouth College* case, 17 U.S. (4 Wheat.) 518, 666, 667 (1819).

39. Southern Ry. v. Greene, 216 U.S. 400, 412–13 (1910).

40. In *Northwestern Life Ins. Co. v. Riggs*, decided in 1906, Justice Harlan stated flatly: "The liberty referred to in [the Fourteenth] Amendment is the liberty of natural, not artificial persons." 203 U.S. 243, 255 (1906). In Western Turf Ass'n v. Greenberg, 204 U.S. 359, 363 (1907), the Court reaffirmed this conclusion. *Cf.* Hand, *The Commodities Clause and the Fifth Amendment*, 22 HARV. L. REV. 250, 251 (1909).

Subsequently, the decision in First National Bank v. Bellotti, 435 U.S. 765 (1978), which protected corporate freedom of speech against state action in reliance on the First Amendment incorporated into the Fourteenth Amendment, rejected the Harlan dictum. *See also* Near v. Minnesota, 283 U.S. 697 (1931); Fiske v. Kansas, 274 U.S. 380 (1927); L. TRIBE, AMERICAN CONSTITUTIONAL LAW § 11–2 (1988).

41. Hale v. Henkel, 201 U.S. 43, 74–75 (1906).

42. *E.g.*, Wilson v. United States, 221 U.S. 361 (1911); Bellis v. United States, 417 U.S. 852 (1974).

43. United States v. White, 322 U.S. 694, 698 (1944) (trade union defendant).

44. *See* Peters, *Common Law Antecedents of Constitutional Law in Connecticut*, 53 ALB. L. J. REV. 259 (1989).

45. Triplex Safety Glass Co. v. Lancegaye Safety Glass (1934) Ltd., [1939] 2 K.B. 395.

Canada: Reg. v. Bank of Montreal, (1962) 36 D.L.R.2d 45.

New Zealand: New Zealand Apple & Pear Mktg. Bd. v. Master & Sons, Ltd., [1986] 1 N.Z.L.R. 191.

Australia: *see* Ramsay, *Corporations and the Privilege Against Self-Incrimination*, 15 U. N.S.W. L.J. 297 (1992).

46. *E.g.*, United States v. Martin Linen Supply Co., 430 U.S. 564 (1977); American Tobacco Co. v. United States, 328 U.S. 781 (1946). *See* Note, *Double Jeopardy and Corporations: "Lurking in the Record" and "Ripe for Decision,"* 28 STAN. L. REV. 805 (1976).

47. *E.g.*, United States v. Hospital Monteflores, Inc., 575 F.2d 332 (1st Cir. 1978); United States v. Security Nat'l Bank, 546 F.2d 492 (2d Cir. 1976), *cert. denied*, 430 U.S. 950 (1977).

48. 201 U.S. 43 (1906).

49. 201 U.S. 43, 76 (1906). The Court also emphasized the importance of the economic interests at stake in further support of its conclusion: "Corporations are a necessary feature of modern business activity and their aggregated capital has become the source of nearly all great enterprises." The reference to "distinct corporate entity," and his previous reference to "the corporation being a creature of the state" in the discussion of the Self-Incrimination clause, illustrate again that reliance on the associational theory for attribution of constitutional rights to the corporation supplements, rather than replaces, the artificial person theory and its accompanying core corporate attributes.

50. 201 U.S. at 82 (McKenna, J.); *id.* at 78 (Harlan, J.).

51. Trustees of Dartmouth College v. Woodward, 17 U.S. (4 Wheat.) 518, 636, 642–44 (1819) (Marshall, C.J.).

A decade later, Marshall could confidently assert: "it is not denied that a charter incorporating a bank is a contract." Providence Bank v. Billings, 29 U.S. (4 Pet.) 514, 560 (1830).

52. 17 U.S. at 667 (Story J.).

53. *See, e.g.*, Fiske v. Kansas, 274 U.S. 380 (1927); Near v. Minnesota, 283 U.S. 697 (1931). *See* L. TRIBE, *supra*.

54. 435 U.S. at 792, 788. For a different view, *see* Watts, *Corporate Legal Theory Under the First Amendment*: Bellotti and Austin, 46 U. MIAMI L. REV. 317, 343 n.106 (1991).

55. 435 U.S. 765, 778 n.14, 792 (1978).

56. 435 U.S. at 824–26 (Rehnquist, C.J.); 435 U.S. at 809 (White, J.).

57. In *CTS Corp. v. Dynamics Corp. of America*, 481 U.S. 69 (1987), Justice Powell in effect retracted his characterization. *CTS Corp.* involved the constitutionality under the Commerce Clause of an Indiana statute regulating corporate takeovers.

Writing for the Court, Justice Powell said: " . . . state regulation of corporate governance is regulation of entities whose very existence and attributes are a product of state law." 481 U.S. at 89 (quoting Chief Justice Marshall's description in the *Dartmouth College* case of the corporation as an "artificial being" created by the state. Trustees of Dartmouth College v. Woodward, 17 U.S. [4 Wheat.] 518, 638 [1819]). Justice Powell also pointed to the portion of Justice Rehnquist's dissent in *Bellotti* quoting from the *Dartmouth College* case that the constitutional rights of a corporation were those "incidental to its very existence." This is the very passage that he criticized as "extreme." 435 U.S. at 825–26.

58. *See infra* ch. 10, notes 22 and 23.

59. 435 U.S. 765, 768–69, 778 n.14 (1978).

60. E. COKE, 2 FIRST PART OF THE INSTITUTE OF THE LAWS OF ENGLAND OR A COMMENTARY UPON LITTLETON 703, 736 (1st ed. 1628) ("person," "inhabitant"). *See also* 1 S. KYD, CORPORATIONS 15 (1793) ("person").

61. Rex v. Gardner, 1 Cowp. 78 (1755).

62. *E.g.*, United States v. Amedy, 24 U.S. (11 Wheat.) 392 (1826) ("person"); United States v. Northwestern Express Stage & Transp. Co., 164 U.S. 686, 689 (1897) ("citizens"). *See* W. COOK, CORPORATIONS §15a (4th ed. 1898) (reviewing nineteenth-century experience).

63. 15. U.S.C. §78(c)(a)(9) (1988); 15 U.S.C. §80a-2(8) (1988); 29 U.S.C. §152(1) (1988).

64. 1 U.S.C. §1 (1988); United Kingdom: The Interpretation Act, 1889 §19; Australia: Acts Interpretation Act, 1901 §22(1)(a).

65. In *Town of Brookline v. Gorsuch*, a subsidiary of Harvard University operating an electric power generation plant was held to qualify as "charitable" for purposes of the Clean Air Act. 667 F.2d 215 (1st Cir. 1981). Numerous other cases characterize corporations as charitable for tax purposes by reference to the identity of its shareholders. In these cases, the character of the shareholder was decisive, although it is evident that but for the attribution of the shareholders' status to the corporation, it would not qualify.

66. *E.g.*, Daimler Co. v. Continental Tyre (Great Britain) Co., [1916] 2 A.C. 307 (H.L.) (company held to be an enemy alien, although organized in England and conducting its business there, where its shareholders and directors were citizens and residents of Germany); *Abbey Malvern Wells Ltd. v. Minister of Local Gov't and Planning*, [1951] Ch. 728. (profit-making corporation operating a school held charitable and exempt from assessments when all shares were held in trust for charitable purposes).

67. Dewey, *supra*, at 655, 656. *See also* Smith, *supra*, at 283, 298.

68. *See* Horwitz, *supra*, at 176 (legal conceptions "do have 'tilt' or influence in determining outcomes"); Machen, *supra*, at 263; Schane, *supra*, at 594–95.

69. MacLaine Watson & Co. v. Department of Trade and Indus., [1990] 2 A.C. 418, [1989] 3 All E.R. 323 (H.L. 1989).

70. *See* A. CHANDLER, STRATEGY AND STRUCTURE: CHAPTERS IN THE HISTORY OF THE AMERICAN INDUSTRIAL ENTERPRISE 30 (1962).

Chapter 3

1. *E.g.*, Louis K. Liggett Co. v. Lee, 288 U.S. 517, 556, 589 (1933) (Brandeis, J., dissenting) ("The power to hold stock in other corporations was not conferred or implied. The holding company was impossible.") [footnote

omitted]; De La Vergne Refrigerating Mach. Co. v. German Sav. Inst., 175 U.S. 40, 100 (1899); Franklin Co. v. Lewiston Inst. for Sav., 68 Me. 43 (1877).

See W. COOK, STOCK AND SHAREHOLDERS, BONDS, MORTGAGES AND GENERAL CORPORATION LAW §315 (3d ed. 1894); 1 V. MORAWETZ, PRIVATE CORPORATIONS §431 (2d ed. 1886); W. NOYES, TREATISE ON THE LAW OF INTERCORPORATE RELATIONS, ch. 25 (1902).

2. See NOYES, *supra*, at §268; 1 MORAWETZ, *supra*, at §431.

3. See Blumberg, *Corporate Responsibility and the Social Crisis*, 50 B.U. L. REV. 157 (1970).

4. 175 U.S. 40, 54–55 (1899). *See also* People v. Chicago Gas Trust Co., 130 Ill. 268, 284, 22 N.E. 798 (1889) (gas utility held without power to acquire stock of another gas utility to expand its operations).

5. See People v. Chicago Gas Trust Co., 130 Ill. 268, 288, 22 N.E. 798 (1889); Louisville & N.R.R., 15 Ky. 25, 26 (1893) ("only a statute can confer the power to acquire stock of another corporation for the purpose of controlling the business or affecting management").

6. See J. HURST, THE LEGITIMACY OF THE BUSINESS CORPORATION IN THE LAW OF THE UNITED STATES 1780–1970 30–34 (1970), A. SCHLESINGER, JR., THE AGE OF JACKSON 334–39 (1945).

7. *See, e.g.* De La Vergne, 175 U.S. 40, 100 (1899); Buckeye Marble & Firestone Co. v. Harvey, 92 Tenn. 115, 118, 20 S.W. 427, 428 (1892).

8. Central R.R. v. Collins, 40 Ga. 582, 625, 630 (1869). Such statements are legion. *See also* Marbury v. Kentucky Union Land Co., 62 F. 335 (6th Cir. 1894) (Taft, J.); Tod v. Kentucky Union Land Co., 57 F. 47 (C.C.D. Ky. 1893) (Lurton, J.).

9. Thus, later in the century, courts were restating the doctrine to emphasize a lack of power to purchase stock for purposes of acquiring "control." *See De La Vergne*, 175 U.S. 40, 100 (invalidating purchase "for purpose of controlling their management"); *Buckeye*, 92 Tenn. 115, 118, 20 S.W. 427, 428 (invalidating acquisition to "enable to manage and control").

10. *E.g.*, N.Y. Act of Feb. 17, 1848, ch. 40, §8 ("It shall not be lawful for such company to use any of their funds for the purchase of any stock in any other corporation"); Ill. Laws of 1849 §8, at 89.

11. See First Nat'l Bank of Charlotte v. National Exch. Bank, 92 U.S. 122, 127 (1875) (Waite, C.J.). *See also* 1 V. MORAWETZ, *supra*, at §431.

12. Maryland and Iowa were two such jurisdictions. *See, e.g.*, Iowa: Traer v. Lucas Prospecting Co., 124 Iowa 107, 116, 99 N.W. 290, 294 (1904). Maryland: Booth v. Robinson, 55 Md. 419, 433–34 (1880). The Maryland decisions apparently rested on a misreading of the English decisions. *See* Booth v. Robinson, *supra*, at 434.

13. The New York statutes authorized corporate purchase of stock of "any corporation engaged in the business of mining, manufacturing or transporting

such materials as are required in the prosecution of the business of such company, so long as they shall furnish or transport such materials for the use of such company, and for two years thereafter and no longer." N.Y. Act of April 28, 1866, ch. 838, §3. *See also* N.Y. Act of June 7, 1890, ch. 564, §40.

14. Thus, Maryland banks were authorized to invest in stocks of corporations generally in order to provide capital, but this does not appear to include acquisitions of control. The state of Maryland also purchased shares of corporations, particularly banks, to provide capital. *See* Blandi, *Maryland Business Corporations 1783-1852*, in 52 JOHNS HOPKINS UNIVERSITY STUDIES IN HISTORY AND POLITICAL SCIENCE, at 19 (1934). In Pennsylvania, not only the state, but counties and cities invested in banks, canal, turnpike, bridge companies or railroads. *See* L. HARTZ, ECONOMIC POLICY AND DEMOCRATIC THOUGHT: PENNSYLVANIA, 1776-1860, at 46, 53, 82-104 (1948).

15. *See* DODD, AMERICAN BUSINESS CORPORATIONS UNTIL 1860 353-54 (1954).

16. *E.g.*, N.J. Act of Feb. 22, 1849 (railroads authorized to acquire stock of other railroads). For a review of the exceptions, *see* W. NOYES, *supra*, at §271; Compton, *Early History of Stock Ownership by Corporations*, 9 GEO. WASH. L. REV. 125, 132 (1940); Robinson, *The Holding Company* (pt. 1), 18 YALE REV. 390 (1910), (pt. 2), 19 YALE REV. 12 (1910). *See also* J. BONBRIGHT & G. MEANS, THE HOLDING COMPANY — ITS PUBLIC SIGNIFICANCE AND ITS REGULATION 58-65 (1932); Freedland, *History of Holding Company Legislation in New York State: Some Doubts as to the "New Jersey First" Tradition*, 24 FORDHAM L. REV. 369 (1955).

17. For a few years after the Civil War, the Pennsylvania legislature included the power in some special charters. However, the public outcry over the circumstances surrounding the enactment of the charters led to the adoption of a constitutional amendment in 1874 prohibiting special charters. *See* Louis K. Liggett Co. v. Lee, 288 U.S. 517, 556 n.32 (1933) (Brandeis, J. dissenting); J. BONBRIGHT & G. MEANS, *supra*, at 59-60.

18. Although Compton makes much of the exceptions, contending that they demonstrate recognition of the power to purchase shares well before the adoption of the New Jersey statute, his summaries of the exceptional charters and the restricted scope of the power, when granted, leave little doubt that these were not typical of the mainstream of American business. *Supra*, at 125-31.

19. *See* W. NOYES, *supra*, at §276.

20. *See* Dill, *Trusts — Their Uses and Abuses*, 54 CENT. L.J. 205, 207 (1901). Even Dill, who, as will be seen, was a leader in bringing about the revolution in New Jersey law, recognized the public policy problems presented by the development. He urged "publicity" as the "most effectual remedy" to retain public confidence and called for national legislation to require such disclosure. *Id.*

21. The important state court decisions holding the sugar and oil trusts illegal were: People v. North River Sugar Refining Co., 121 N.Y. 582, 582 (1890); State *ex. rel.* v. Standard Oil Co., 49 Ohio St. 137 (1892).

22. Although mere utilization of corporate forms could not avoid the Sherman Act, use of the parent corporation or the holding company to achieve industrial concentration was unchallenged.

23. *See* J. BONBRIGHT & G. MEANS, *supra*, at 337.

24. Act of Apr. 4, 1888, ch. 269, §1, 1888 N.J. Laws 385–86; Act of Apr. 17, 1888, ch. 295, §1; 1888 N.J. Laws 445–46; Act of May 9, 1889, ch. 265, §4, 1889 N.J. Laws 412, 414; Act of Mar. 14, 1893, ch. 171, §2, 1893 N.J. Laws 301.

25. James B. Dill, later counsel for Standard Oil, played an important role in the enactment of the statutes after 1888. For contemporaneous descriptions, *see* Steffens, *New Jersey: A Traitor State, Part II—How She Sold Out the United States*, 25 MCCLURE'S MAGAZINE 41 (1905); Keasby, *New Jersey and the Great Corporations* (pt. 1), 13 HARV. L. REV. 198 (1897). For more recent commentary, *compare* R. NADER, M. GREEN, & J. SELIGMAN, TAMING THE GIANT CORPORATION 43–44 (1976) and CONSTITUTIONALIZING THE CORPORATION: THE CASE FOR FEDERAL CHARTERING OF GIANT CORPORATIONS 42–51 (1976); *with* R. HESSEN, IN DEFENSE OF THE CORPORATION 68–71 (1979). *See also* Stokes, *Economic Influences on the Corporation Laws of New Jersey*, 38 J. POL. ECON. 551 (1930).

Hessen asserts that Nader and his collaborators confused Dill's role in the adoption of the later statutes with the enactment of the 1888 statute. He appears to be correct, but this misses the point. Because of its restrictive nature and the decades-old New York precedent, the 1888 statute was hardly momentous. The later statutes were the ones that opened the floodgates. *See* Steffens, *supra*.

26. 1896 N.J. Laws 313. *See* Stokes, *supra*, at 572–73 ("the law of 1896 was, therefore, openly and obviously a bid in favor of corporations").

27. *See* J. BONBRIGHT & G. MEANS, *supra*, at 68–72.

28. *See* Stokes, *supra*, at 574 *citing* G.H. MONTAGUE, TRUSTS OF TODAY 132 (1904).

29. *See* Stokes, *supra*, at 575 *citing* SPECIAL REPORTS OF THE CENSUS, DEBT AND TAXATION 166 (1907); W. COOK, STOCK AND STOCKHOLDERS, BONDS, MORTGAGES, AND GENERAL CORPORATION LAW 2604–05 (3d ed. 1894).

Dill, himself, took pride in the fact that "the revenue derived from corporations . . . practically abolished the necessity for state taxes" in New Jersey. Dill, *supra*, at 207 (1901).

30. Dill left no doubt as to the motivation for the New York action, stating: "New York out-Jerseyed New Jersey in so-called liberality to corporations. It amended its corporation act upon the theory that the greatest paper liberality would produce the greatest revenue." *See* Dill, *supra*, at 207.

This development, which has been aptly described as "law for sale" and "the race for the bottom," has been vigorously critized, notably by Justice Brandeis and Professor William Cary. *See* Louis K. Liggett Co. v. Lee, 288 U.S. 517, 566 (1933) (Brandeis, J. dissenting); Cary, *Federalism and Corporate Law: Reflections Upon Delaware*, 83 YALE L.J. 663 (1974). It is not without its defenders from lawyer-economists, who see it as a desirable development that allows market economics to provide corporate entrepreneurs and investors with the laws they prefer. *See* R. HESSEN, *supra*; R. WINTER, GOVERNMENT AND THE CORPORATION (1978). For a thoughtful review of the changing state corporation law over the nineteenth century, *see* Butler, *Nineteenth-Century Jurisdictional Competition in the Granting of Corporate Privileges*, 14 J. LEG. STUDIES 129, 161–63, and n.136 (1985) ("state action could not be effective in providing a 'responsible' corporation statute").

31. *See* Keasby, *supra*, at 200.

32. *E.g.* Robinson v. Holbrook, 148 F. 107 (C.C.D.R.I. 1906); Stockton v. Central R.R.N.J., 50 N.J. Eq. (5 Dick. Ch.) 52 (1892).

33. Public policy: *E.g.*, McCutcheon v. Merz Capsule Co., 71 F. 787 (6th Cir. 1896). Sherman Act: Northern Sec. Co. v. United States, 193 U.S. 197 (1904); United States v. Standard Oil Co. of N.J., 173 F. 177 (C.C.E.D. Mo. 1909), *aff'd*, 221 U.S. 1 (1911); *In re* Charge to Grand Jury, 151 F. 834 (E.D. Ga. 1907).

34. Special Message to Congress dated Jan. 7, 1910, 61st Cong., 2d Sess., H.R. Doc. No. 484, at 17 (1910).

35. *E.g.*, Brownsville Glass Co. v. Appert Glass Co., 136 F. 240 (C.C.W.D. Pa. 1905); Coy v. Title Guarantee & Trust Co., 157 F. 794 (C.C.D. Or. 1907); Pearce v. Sutherland, 164 F. 609 (9th Cir. 1908); Monmouth Inv. Co. v. Means, 151 F. 159 (8th Cir. 1906).

36. *See* J. BONBRIGHT & G. MEANS, *supra*, at 57.

37. *See* A. CHANDLER, STRATEGY AND STRUCTURE: CHAPTERS IN THE HISTORY OF THE AMERICAN INDUSTRIAL ENTERPRISE 30 (1962). *See also* J. BONBRIGHT & G. MEANS, *supra*, at 337 (the New Jersey statute was "a step the economic consequence of which has seldom been equalled in the entire history of business legislation").

38. *See* C. VAN HISE, CONCENTRATION AND CONTROL — A SOLUTION OF THE TRUST PROBLEM IN THE UNITED STATES 71 (reprint 1973) ("Since 1887, the holding company has been the dominant form of consolidation.") Van Hise provides detailed reviews of the growth and acquisition of monopoly power of Standard Oil, United States Steel, and American Tobacco companies, among others. *Id.* at 105–87.

39. This phenomenon is so well recognized that the Agricultural Foreign Investment Disclosure Act of 1978 dealing with foreign investment in the United States provides for an elaborate procedure to investigate tier-by-tier intercorporate links as far as the third tier. *See* 7 U.S.C. §3501(a) (1988); 7 C.F.R. §781 (1992). The provisions in the tax laws dealing with foreign tax

credits similarly cover even 10 percent-owned third-tier foreign subsidiaries. *See* I.R.C. §902; Treas. Reg. §1-902-1.

40. Writing in 1932, Bonbright and Means early recognized that for special regulatory purposes, regulation should extend further than the power to direct and should be broadened to include persons and corporations that could exercise a "material influence" over board decisions. *See* J. BONBRIGHT & G. MEANS, *supra*, at 9. Such reform statutes as the Public Utility Holding Company Act of 1935 and the Investment Company Act of 1940 substantially incorporated this suggestion, utilizing the term "controlling influence." As reviewed in Chapter 7, a number of foreign statutes have done the same, including legislation in the United Kingdom, the Federal Republic of Germany, Sweden, and the European Economic Community.

41. *See* J. BONBRIGHT & G. MEANS, *supra*, at 1–3, 339. For example, the Federal Trade Commission investigation of holding companies continued from 1928 to 1935 and resulted in the publication of a 101-volume study, FTC, Utility Corporations, S. Doc. No. 92, 70th Cong., 1st Sess. (1928). This study provided much of the political ammunition resulting in the enactment of the Public Utility Holding Company Act of 1935, utilizing pervasive enterprise principles for the restructuring and regulation of public utility holding companies, their subsidiaries, and affiliates.

Chapter 4

1. *See* W. COOK, CORPORATIONS §663 (4th ed. 1898).

2. *See* Stockton v. Central R.R.N.J., 50 N.J. Eq. (5 Dick. Ch.) 52 (1892).

3. *See* Erickson v. Revere Elevator Co., 110 Minn. 443, 444, 126 N.W. 130 (1910). After Professor I. Maurice Wormser coined the expression, "piercing the corporate veil," the expression became widely used. *See* Wormser, *Piercing the Corporate Veil*, 12 COLUM. L. REV. 496 (1912).

4. *See, e.g., In re* Horgan, 97 F. 319 (S.D.N.Y. 1899); Kankee & S. R. Co. v. Horan, 131 Ill. 288, 23 N.E. 621 (1890).

5. *E.g., In re* Rieger, Kapner & Altmark, 157 F. 609 (S.D. Ohio 1907); Montgomery Web Co. v. Dienelt, 133 Pa. St. 585, 19 A. 428 (1890).

6. Susan B. Anthony v. American Glucose Co., 146 N.Y. 407, 41 N.E. 23 (1895) (contract); Brownsville Glass Co. v. Appert Glass Co., 136 F. 240 (C.C.W.D. Pa. 1907) (patent royalty). *See* Brundred v. Rice, 49 Pa. St. 640 (1892) ("It is a stern but just maxim of the law, that fraud vitiates everything into which it enters. . . . there is nothing so sacred in a certificate of incorporation as to take it out of the reach of the maxim.").

7. *E.g.,* The Santa Barbara, 299 F. 147, 152 (4th Cir. 1924); Holbrook, Cabot, & Rollins Corp. v. Perkins, 147 F. 166 (1st Cir. 1906). *See* W. ANDERSON, LIMITATIONS OF THE CORPORATE ENTITY, A TREATISE OF THE LAW RELATING TO THE OVERRIDING OF THE CORPORATE FICTION §§239–43 (1931).

8. Hartwell v. Buffalo & L. R. Co., 19 Pa. C. 231 (1897) (construing PA. CONST. art. XVII, §5). However, at much the same time, the California Supreme Court decided to the contrary under a similar provision in the California Constitution. Knowles v. Sandercock, 107 Cal. 629, 40 P. 1047 (1895).

9. Commonwealth v. New York, L.E. & W.R. Co., 139 Pa. St. 457, 21 A. 528 (1891).

10. People's Pleasure Park Co. v. Rohleder, 109 Va. 439, 61 S.E. 794 (1908).

11. *See* First Nat'l Bank of Gadsden v. Winchester, 119 Ala. 168, 24 So. 351 (1898); Louisville Banking Co. v. Eisenmann, 94 Ky. 83, 93, 21 S.W. 531, 582 (Ct. App. 1893). *See* Fuller, *The Incorporated Individual: A Study of the One-Man Company*, 51 HARV. L. REV. 1373, 1375 n.8 (1978).

12. Because the doctrine would not have applied to partly owned subsidiaries, it would have had only a patchy impact. Corporations finding it useful to sidestep the doctrine could readily do so by tolerating a small minority interest in the subsidiary in question.

13. *E.g.*, Toledo R.R. v. Hamilton, 134 U.S. 296, 304 (1891); Central Trust Co. v. Kneeland, 138 U.S. 414 (1891). *See* 2 MACHEN, TREATISE ON THE MODERN LAW OF CORPORATIONS §§1076, 1081 *et seq.* (1908).

14. *E.g.*, Mortgage by parent does not impose lien on subsidiary's property: Central Trust Co. v. Kneeland, 138 U.S. 414, 423 (1891). Parent may not sue on subsidiary's cause of action: Fitzgerald v. Missouri Pac. R.R., 45 F. 812 (1891). Contracts of parent and subsidiary are not binding on the other: Richmond & Const. Co. v. Richmond, N.I.R.R., 68 F. 105 (6th Cir. 1895). *See* People v. American Tel. & Tel. Co., 117 N.Y. 241, 255, 22 N.E. 105 (1889). *See also* W. COOK, *supra*, at §664; Louisville Gas Co. v. Kaufman, 105 Ky. 131, 48 S.W. 434 434 (Ct. App. 1898) (sole shareholder does not destroy entity). This repudiated a decision five years earlier that cast doubt on the existence of the entity in the case of the so-called one-man corporations. *See* Louisville Banking Co. v. Eisenmann, 94 Ky. 83, 21 S.W. 531 (Ct. App. 1893).

15. *See* W. ANDERSON, *supra*, at §84.

16. Broderip v. Salomon, [1895] 2 Ch. 333 (Ct. App.), *rev'd sub nom.* Salomon v. Salomon & Co., [1897] A.C. 22 (H.L. 1896).

17. As reviewed subsequently in this chapter, this is particularly evident in the development of the doctrine of railroad "system" group liability in tort, which survived until the mid-1920's.

18. York & M.L.R.R. v. Winans, 58 U.S. 30 (1854).

19. Lehigh Mining & Mfg. Co. v. Kelly, 160 U.S. 327 (1895).

20. As reviewed in Chapter 2, the Court had earlier settled the issue of citizenship of corporations by reference to the state of incorporation.

21. For exceptions *see* Baltimore & Ohio Tel. Co. v. Interstate Tel. Co., 54 F. 50 (4th Cir. 1894) (parent/subsidiary); Lehigh Mining & Mfg. Co. v.

Kelly, 160 U.S. 327 (1895); Hatcher v. United Leasing Co., 75 F. 368 (C.C.D. Colo. 1896) (sister corporations).

22. Union Pac. Ry. v. Chicago, R.I. & Pac. Ry., 163 U.S. 564, 591 (1896), *aff'g*, 10 U.S. App. 98 (8th Cir.), *aff'g*, 47 F. 15 (C.C.D. Neb. 1891) (Brewer J.).

23. Phinizy v. Augusta & K.R. Co., 62 F. 771 (C.C.D.S.C. 1894).

24. Pennsylvania R.R. v. Jones, 155 U.S. 333 (1894); Chesapeake & O. Ry. v. Howard, 178 U.S. 153 (1900).

25. Pennsylvania R. Co. v. Anoka Nat'l Bank, 108 F. 482 (8th Cir. 1901) (shipper); Lehigh Valley R. Co. v. Dupont, 128 F. 840 (2d Cir. 1904) (passenger); Lehigh Valley R. Co. v. Delachesa, 145 F. 617 (2d Cir. 1906) (*per curiam*) (employee).

26. *Compare* Pennsylvania R. Co. v. Anoka Nat'l Bank, 108 F. 482 (8th Cir. 1901); Pennsylvania Co. v. Rossett, 116 Ill. App. 342 (1904); Wichita Falls & N.W. Ry. v. Puckett, 53 Okla. 463, 157 P. 112 (1916) (imposing liability) *with* Atchison, T. & S.F.R.R. v. Cochran, 43 Kan. 225, 23 P. 151 (1890); Stone v. Cleveland, C.C. & St. L. Ry., 202 N.Y. 352, 95 N.E. 816 (1911) (rejecting liability).

27. Davis v. Alexander, 269 U.S. 114 (1925).

28. 269 U.S. 114, 117 (1925).

29. Berkey v. Third Ave. Ry., 244 N.Y. 84, 94, 155 N.E. 58, 61 (1926). *See* W. CARY & M. EISENBERG, CASES AND MATERIALS ON CORPORATIONS 91 (5th ed. unabr. 1980).

30. *E.g.*, Conry v. Baltimore & O. R. Co., 112 F. Supp. 252 (W.D. Pa. 1953).

31. Mull v. Colt, 31 F.R.D. 154 (S.D.N.Y. 1962) (one hundred corporations operating two hundred cabs out of common garage and supporting facilities); Mangan v. Terminal Transp. Sys., Inc., 157 Misc. 627, 284 N.Y.S. 183 (Sup. Ct. 1935), *aff'd per curiam*, 247 A.D. 853, 286 N.Y.S. 666 (3d Dep't 1936), *motion for leave to appeal denied*, 272 N.Y. 676 (1937). *Cf.* Walkovszky v. Carlton, 18 N.Y.2d 414, 418, 223 N.E.2d 6, 10 (1966), *on remand*, 29 A.D.2d 763, 287 N.Y.S.2d 546 (2d Dep't), *aff'd*, 23 N.Y.2d 714, 244 N.E.2d 55 (1968).

32. 34 Stat. 584 (1906), 49 U.S.C. §1(8) (1982) (superseded).

33. 213 U.S. 366, 413, 415 (1909). *See* Marshall, *The Commodities Clause*, 17 J. POL. ECON. 488 (1909); Case Comment, *The Commodities Clause Decision*, 9 COLUM. L. REV. 523 (1909).

34. United States v. Lehigh Valley R.R., 220 U.S. 25, 272–73 (1911).

35. United States v. Delaware, L. & W.R.R., 238 U.S. 516, 526, 528–30 (1915).

36. United States v. Reading Co., 253 U.S. 26, 60–63 (1920).

37. United States v. Elgin, J. & E. Ry., 298 U.S. 492, 506, 512 (1936).

38. *See* Note, *The Commodities Clause: Its Application to Industrial Rail-*

ways, 50 HARV. L. REV. 322, 326, 332 (1936); Comment, *The Commodities Clause and the Regulation of Industrial Railroads*, 46 YALE L.J. 299, 311–13 (1936) ("difficulty of showing enough control to satisfy the court . . . is almost insuperable").

39. United States v. South Buffalo Ry., 333 U.S. 771, 785 (1948). The dissent challenged Justice Jackson's reading of the congressional history. 333 U.S. at 786.

40. Peterson v. Chicago, R.I. & Pac. Ry., 205 U.S. 364 (1907). *Cf.* Pullman's Palace Car Co. v. Missouri Pac. R.R., 115 U.S. 587 (1885).

41. Cannon Mfg. Corp. v. Cudahy Packing Co., 267 U.S. 333 (1925).

42. In fact, the lower court had asserted that on the facts before it, it would have held the parent liable for the subsidiary's acts, if necessary, to "prevent fraud" or "escape just liabilities." Cannon Mfg. Co. v. Cudahy Packing Co., 292 F. 169, 176 (W.D.N.C. 1923).

43. *E.g.*, Davis Improved Wrought Iron Wagon Wheel Co. v. Davis Wrought Iron Wagon Co., 20 F. 699 (C.C.N.D.N.Y. 1884).

44. Thus, the essence of partnership law is that the partners have united in a joint enterprise for profit and that each partner is the agent of the other partner. Although there are certain parallels between the partnership principle and the intragroup relationship, treating the group as a partnership would have meant a sweeping destruction of many dimensions of entity law.

45. An early decision rejected the partnership route to liability on the ground that corporations had no power to become partners. *See* White v. Pecos Land & Water Co., 18 Tex. Civ. App. 634, 45 S.W. 207, 208 (1898).

46. *See* RESTATEMENT (SECOND) OF AGENCY §14(m) (1958); Kingston Drydock Co. v. Lake Champlain Transp. Co., 31 F.2d 265 (2d Cir. 1929) (L. Hand, J.); Mobil Oil Corp. v. Linear Films, Inc., 718 F. Supp. 260, 266 nn.9, 10, 271–72 (D. Del. 1989) (the "use of the term 'agent' in this context is particularly unfortunate because it is easily confused with pure [common law] agency theory").

47. Whittle v. Vanderbilt Min. & Milling Co., 83 F. 48 (C.C.S.D. Cal. 1897).

48. United States v. Milwaukee Refrigerator Transit Co., 142 F. 247, 255 (C.C.E.D. Wis. 1905) (Sanborn, J.).

49. Harris v. Youngstown Bridge Co., 90 F. 322 (6th Cir. 1898). Although it accepted the lower court judge's concept of the applicable legal standards, the Circuit Court of Appeals reversed the circuit judge. It disagreed on the significance of such facts as that the capital was "small" and that no board meetings had been held for four years.

50. *E.g.*, Northern Pac. Ry. v. Dixon, 194 U.S. 338 (1904); Missouri, K. & T. Ry. v. Elliott, 102 F. 96 (8th Cir. 1900).

51. Cortes Co v. Thannhauser, 45 F. 730 (C.C.S.D.N.Y. 1891) (misrepresentation); Lalance & Grosjean Mfg. Co. v. Haberman Mfg. Co., 87 F. 563

(C.C.S.D.N.Y. 1898) (knowledge); Old Colony Trust Co. v. Dubuque Light & Traction Co., 89 F. 794 (C.C.N.D. Iowa 1898) (nominee).

52. *See, e.g.*, Higgins v. California Petroleum & Asphalt Co., 122 Cal. 373, 55 P. 155 (1898); Duval v. Hunt, 34 Fla. 85, 15 So. 876 (1894).

53. *Compare* Holbrook, Cabot & Rollins Corp. v. Perkins, 147 F. 166 (1st Cir. 1906); Columbus, S. & H.R. Co. Appeals v. Mercantile Trust, 109 F. 177 (6th Cir. 1901) (absence of substantial assets) *with* United States v. Reading Co., 183 F. 427 (C.C.E.D. Pa. 1910); Higgins v. California Petroleum & Asphalt Co., 147 Cal. 363, 81 P. 1070 (1905) (active corporations).

54. *See* Mesler v. Bragg Management Co., 39 Cal. 3d 290, 702 P.2d 601 (1985).

55. *See* BLUMBERG, THE LAW OF CORPORATE GROUPS: SUBSTANTIVE COMMON LAW, *supra*, at §§9.01-9.03, 18.01-18.02.

56. Arizona and Pennsylvania are two such states. *See In re* Reeves, 1990 U.S. Dist. LEXIS 11599 (D. Ariz. 1990); Culbreth v. Amosa (Pty) Ltd., 898 F.2d 13, 14 (3d Cir. 1990).

57. Thus, at least four books from 1927 to 1936 were devoted to the topic. *See* W. ANDERSON, *supra*; E. LATTY, SUBSIDIARY AND AFFILIATED CORPORATIONS (1936); F. POWELL, PARENT AND SUBSIDIARY CORPORATIONS (1931); I. WORMSER, THE DISREGARD OF THE CORPORATE FICTION AND ALLIED CORPORATE PROBLEMS (1927). Innumerable articles have also appeared in the legal journals.

58. *See* F. POWELL, *supra*, at chs. 2-4. A vivid characterization of the degree of "control" required under the "instrumentality" doctrine has been widely quoted: "Control, not mere majority or complete stock control, but complete domination, not only of finance, but of policy and business practise in respect to the transaction attacked so that the corporate entity as to this transaction had at the time had no separate mind, will, or existence of its own." Lowendahl v. Baltimore & O.R.R., 247 A.D. 144, 157, 287 N.Y.S. 62, 76 (1st Dep't), *aff'd*, 272 N.Y. 360, 6 N.E.2d 56 (1936).

59. *See, e.g.*, RRX Indust., Inc. v. Lab-Con, Inc., 772 F.2d 543, 545 (9th Cir. 1985); Pan Pac. Sash & Door Co. v. Greendale Park, Inc., 166 Cal. App. 2d 652, 333 P.2d 802 (1958).

60. Castleberry v. Branscum, 721 S.W.2d 270, 271-72, 272 n.3 (Tex. 1987) (contracts) (individual controlling shareholder).

Two Fifth Circuit opinions have endeavored to restate the *Castleberry* holding. Gibraltar Sav. v. LD Brinkman Corp., 860 F.2d 1275 (5th Cir. 1988); Pan Eastern Exploration Co. v. Hufo Oils, 855 F.2d 1106 (5th Cir. 1988).

61. TEX. BUS. CORP. ACT ANN. art. 2.21A (Vernon Supp. 1991).

62. *See, e.g.*, E. LATTY, *supra*; Radin, *The Endless Problem of Corporate Personality*, 32 COLUM. L. REV. 643 (1932).

63. Farmers' Loan & Trust Co. v. Pierson, 130 Misc. 110, 116-17, 222 N.Y.S. 532, 583-84 (Sup. Ct. Sp. T. N.Y. Co. 1927).

Chapter 5

1. Voting: MODEL BUS. CORP. ACT §33; DEL. CODE ANN. tit. 8, §160(c) (1991); N.Y. Bus. Corp. Law §612(b) (McKinney 1986).

Stock Purchase: MODEL BUS. CORP. ACT §1.40(6) (off. comment 3, at 44); GA. CODE ANN. §22-518 (Supp. 1982).

2. Cal. CORP. CODE §114 (West 1990). *See* H. MARSH, CALIFORNIA CORPORATION LAW §13.11 (2d ed. 1981).

3. Contract distinguished from tort: *e.g.*, Edwards Co. v. Monogram Indus., Inc., 730 F.2d 977 (5th Cir. 1984).

Substantive matters distinguished from procedure: *e.g.*, Energy Reserves Group, Inc. v. Superior Oil Co., 460 F. Supp. 483 (D. Kan. 1978).

Statutory matters distinguished from common law: *e.g.*, Town of Brookline v. Gorsuch, 667 F.2d 215, 220 (1st Cir. 1981).

4. As discussed later in this chapter, statutes of general application are those that regulate conduct without any express reference to corporate groups. Statutes of specific application are statutes expressly referring to corporate groups.

5. *See* Blumberg, *Intragroup (Upstream, Cross-Stream and Downstream) Guaranties under the Uniform Fraudulent Transfer Act*, 9 CARDOZO L. REV. 685 (1987).

6. Mobil Oil Corp. v. Commissioner of Taxes, 445 U.S. 425 (1980); Exxon Corp. v. Wisconsin Dep't of Revenue, 447 U.S. 207 (1980); ASARCO, Inc. v. Idaho State Tax Comm'n, 458 U.S. 307 (1982); F.W. Woolworth Co. v. Taxation & Revenue Dep't, 458 U.S. 354 (1982); and Container Corp. of Am. v. Franchise Tax Bd., 463 U.S. 159, *reh'g denied*, 464 U.S. 909 (1983).

7. Mobil Oil, 445 U.S. at 440–41; Container Corp., 463 U.S. at 179.

8. Exxon Corp., 447 U.S. at 219–20, 224–25, 440–41 (irrelevant that Exxon organized functionally into marketing, exploration, and production and conducted only marketing activities within the state, where the marketing was an integral part of a "highly integrated business"; "one must look principally at the underlying activity not the form of investment. . . . the form of business organization may have nothing to do with the underlying unity or diversity of business enterprise"). *See also* Mobil Oil, 445 U.S. at 440–41.

9. F.W. Woolworth, 458 U.S. at 466–70. ASARCO, Inc., 458 U.S. at 321–22.

10. Taylor v. Standard Gas & Electric Co., 306 U.S. 307 (1939).

11. Anderson v. Abbott, 321 U.S. 349, 356–63 (1944).

12. First National City Bank v. Banco Para El Comercio Exterior de Cuba, 462 U.S. 611, 623, 629–32 (1983).

13. Copperweld Corp. v. Independence Tube Co., 467 U.S. 752, 771–74 (1984).

14. Thus, the Supreme Court has acknowledged that "silence . . . in fed-

eral legislation is no reason for limiting the reach of federal law. . . . [T]he inevitable incompleteness presented by all legislation means that interstitial federal lawmaking is a basic responsibility of the federal courts." United States v. Little Lake Misere Land Co., 412 U.S. 580, 593 (1973). *See also* C.T. Carden v. Arkoma Assocs., 494 U.S. 185, 1023 (1990) (O'Connor, J., dissenting) ("application of statutes to situations not anticipated by the legislature is a pre-eminently judicial function").

Some English decisions, in a manner quite out of keeping with American law, refuse to apply enterprise principles to obvious utilizations of corporate structure to evade the objectives of labor and employment discrimination statutes. *See, e.g.,* Dimbleby & Sons Ltd. v. National Union of Journalists, [1984] 1 W.L.R. 67 (H.L.) (secondary boycott); Haughton v. Olau Line (UK) Ltd., 1986 I.C.R. 357 (C.A.) (sex harassment).

15. *See* BLUMBERG, THE LAW OF CORPORATE GROUPS: GENERAL STATUTORY LAW, *supra*, at §2.03.

16. *E.g.*, Town of Brookline v. Gorsuch, 667 F.2d 215, 221 (1st Cir. 1981) ("federal courts will look closely at the purpose of the federal statute to determine whether the statute places importance on the corporate form, an inquiry that usually gives less respect to the corporate form than does the strict common law alter ego doctrine"); Capital Tel. Co. v. FCC, 498 F.2d 734, 738–39 (D.C. Cir. 1974) (test of "alter ego under the strict standards of the common-law alter-ego doctrine which would apply in a tort or contract action" not applicable in statutory matters).

17. *E.g.*, Nationwide Mut. Ins. Co. v. Darden, 112 S. Ct. 1344 (1992); Estate of Cowart v. Nicklos Drilling Co., 112 St. Ct. 2589 (1992).

18. This is further illustrated by the experience of "piercing the veil jurisprudence." The application of the rigid rules of traditional "piercing the veil jurisprudence" as a transcendental doctrine routinely applied in very different fields of the law is one of the major weaknesses of the doctrine. The reliance on "piercing the veil" decisions in one area of the law, such as contract or substantive problems, to reach decisions in a very different area, such as tort or procedural problems, in which the law has very different objectives, has been much criticized. The lack of relevance of such indiscriminate utilization of "piercing the veil jurisprudence" is most evident in its application as developed for controversies between private individuals to questions of important public policy involving the construction and application of regulatory statutes.

19. In special areas such as labor, employment, and employment discrimination, American law uses the "integrated enterprise" standard for limited purposes. Similarly, "integrated enterprise" appears in isolated areas in the tax laws.

20. *E.g.*, Pullman's Palace Car Co. v. Missouri Pac. Ry., 115 U.S. 587 (1885).

21. "Control" has been termed a "complex and abusive concept" when

applied in other contexts to parties lacking the power to select the board or to give direct commands, but whose views operate as a constraint of decision-making. *See* Farrar, *Ownership and Control of Listed Companies—Revising or Rejecting the Concept of Control*, in COMPANY LAW IN CHANGE 39 (B. Pettet ed. 1987); E. HERMAN, CORPORATE POWER AND CONTROL, ch. 2 (1981).

22. 15 U.S.C. §79b(a)(7)(A),(B) (1988).

23. The Investment Company Act (ICA) is an anomaly. Although the ICA is distinctly more confined in its regulatory scope, it resembles pervasive legislation in many respects, and its statutory formulation follows those of the holding company statutes. It utilizes the supplemental concept of "controlling influence" and a presumption of control arising from ownership of twenty-five percent of voting securities of any class.

24. Rochester Tel. Corp. v. United States, 307 U.S. 125, 139–40, 145–46 (1939). *See also* Gilbertville Trucking Co. v. United States, 371 U.S. 115, 125 (1962).

25. "At least 50 percent" or "50 percent or less": I.R.C. §§246A, 279(i). "More than 50 percent": I.R.C. §§267(f), 957. "At least 80 percent": I.R.C. §§368(c), 1504(a)(2). "Voting" stock or "voting power": *e.g.*, I.R.C. §§267(f), 269. "Total value": *e.g.*, I.R.C. §§267(f), 957. "Total number": I.R.C. §368(c).

26. Section 482 gives the Commissioner of Internal Revenue the authority to reallocate income, deductions, and credits of "organization, trades, or businesses . . . owned or controlled directly or indirectly by the same interests in order to prevent evasion of taxes or clearly to reflect their income. . . ."

27. 29 U.S.C. §623(h) (1988); 21 NLRB ANN. REP. 14 (1956), *adopted in* Radio & Television Broadcast Technicians Local Union v. Broadcast Serv. of Mobile, Inc., 380 U.S. 255 (1965) (per curiam).

28. *See* Temp. Treas. Reg. under I.R.C. §367(b), §1.367(a)–3T(e)(3) (1990). An "integrated enterprise" standard was also used in 1917 for purposes of the World War I excess profits tax. *See* Treas. Reg. 41, art. 77.

29. A.L.I., FED. SEC. CODE (1980). Although the Code has not been enacted by Congress, as originally hoped, it has been frequently invoked by the courts. *See generally* 1 L. LOSS & J. SELIGMAN, SECURITIES REGULATION 278–85 (3d ed. 1989). Its standard on "control" has also been substantially utilized in A.L.I., PRINCIPLES OF CORPORATE GOVERNANCE: ANALYSIS AND RECOMMENDATIONS §1.05 (Proposed Final Draft 1992).

30. FED. SEC. CODE §202(29)(A),(B) (1980).

31. As of December 31, 1986, the number of shareholders of record of the fifty companies listed on the New York Stock Exchange with the largest number of shareholders ranged from a high of 2,782,000 to a low of 124,000. N.Y.S.E. FACT BOOK 26 (1987).

32. *See* Essex Universal Corp v. Yates, 305 F.2d 572, 580 (2d Cir. 1962)

(Clark, J., concurring) (28.3 percent represents working control). *See also* 4 L. LOSS & J. SELIGMAN, SECURITIES REGULATION ch. 5 (3d ed. 1990). However, this may change in the future with larger and more concentrated accumulations of shares in the hands of pension funds and other institutional investors.

33. *See e.g.*, Securities Exchange Act of 1934, 15 U.S.C. §§78c(a)(8) 781, 78m (1988); Federal Communications Act of 1934, 47 U.S.C. §219(a) (1988).

34. Cannon Mfg. Co. v. Cudahy Packing Co., 267 U.S. 333, 336 (1925).

35. International Shoe Co. v. Washington, 326 U.S. 310 (1945).

36. FED. R. CIV. P. 15 (statute of limitations), 33 and 34 (discovery), and 65(c) (injunctions).

37. *See* Taylor v. Standard Gas & Elec. Co., 306 U.S. 307 (1939); Pepper v. Litton, 308 U.S. 295 (1939); Consolidated Rock Prods. v. Du Bois, 312 U.S. 510 (1941); Comstock v. Group of Inst'l Investors, 335 U.S. 211 (Supp. 1992).

38. 11 U.S.C.A. §§101(2), 101(31)(B),(E), 547 (1988).

39. *E.g., In re* Vecco Constr. Co., 4 Bankr. 407, 409 (Bankr. E.D. Va. 1980); *In re* Interstate Stores, Inc., 15 Collier Bankr. Cas. 634, 640-41 (Bankr. S.D.N.Y. 1978); *In rA* Augie/Restivo Baking Co., 84 Bankr. 315, 329 (Bankr. E.D.N.Y.), *rev'd*, 860 F.2d 515 (2d Cir. 1988).

Chapter 6

1. Recent discussions include: F. EASTERBROOK & D. FISCHEL, THE ECONOMIC STRUCTURE OF CORPORATE LAW ch. 2 (1991); LIMITED LIABILITY AND THE CORPORATION (T. Orhnial ed. 1982); R. POSNER, ECONOMIC ANALYSIS OF LAW (3d ed. 1986); Dent, *Limited Liability in Environmental Law*, 26 WAKE FOREST L. REV. 151 (1991); Halpern, Trebilcock, & Turnbull, *An Economic Analysis of Limited Liability in Corporation Law*, 30 U. TORONTO L.J. 117 (1980); Hansmann & Kraakman, *Toward Unlimited Shareholder Liability for Corporate Torts*, 103 YALE L.J. 1879 (1991); Leebron, *Limited Liability, Tort Victims, and Creditors*, 91 COLUM. L. REV. 1565 (1991); Meiners, Mofsky, & Tollison, *Piercing the Veil of Limited Liability*, 4 J. CORP. L. 351 (1979).

2. *See supra* ch. 1 text accompanying notes 43 and 44.

3. This has been a major element in my previous contributions to this debate. More recently, in a comprehensive attack on the problem, Hansmann and Kraakman have rested much of their case for unlimited liability in tort on the limitations on exposure inherent in a pro rata regime. *See supra.*

4. *See supra* ch. 1, note 57.

5. This contention had some merit in the period of de facto limited liability in England because of a lack of adequate enforcement remedies. This period, however, came to an end with the adoption of the much strengthened procedures contained in the 1848 Act.

It should not go unnoticed that the present regime of limited liability, subject to the vague and unpredictable relief of piercing the veil jurisprudence, is itself responsible for a continual flood of litigation. LEXIS publishes several hundred decisions a year dealing with the issue.

6. Thomas v. Matthiessen, 232 U.S. 221 (1914); Pinney v. Nelson, 183 U.S. 144 (1901).

7. *See generally* 7A C. WRIGHT, A. MILLER & M. KANE, FEDERAL PROCEDURE AND PRACTICES §1770 (2d ed. 1986); H. NEWBERG, CLASS ACTIONS §§4.45 *et seq.* (2d ed. 1985). Separate actions would still be required in a forum with personal jurisdiction to permit shareholders to raise any personal defense.

8. Although the 1855 Act provided for limited liability for joint stock companies generally, limited liability did not become effective until 1856 for banks and until 1862 for insurance companies.

9. The Insolvency Act, 1986 §§213–15 (1986 ch. 45). *See also* Austl. Companies Act, 1981 §556; N.Z. Companies Act, 1955 §320(1).

10. The Insolvency Act, 1986 §214(7) (1986 ch. 45).

11. *See* Qintex Austrl. Fin. Ltd. v. Schroeders Austrl. Ltd., (1991) 9 A.C.L.C. (CCH) 109 (N.S.W. 1990). Chief Judge Rogers observed: ". . . there is today a tension between the realities of commercial life and the applicable [entity] law in [cases] involving conglomerates with a large number of subsidiaries . . . It may be desirable for Parliament to consider whether this distinction between the [entity law] and commercial practice should be maintained. This is especially the case today when the many collapses of conglomerates occasion many disputes." (1991) 9 A.C.L.C. at 110–11.

12. *See supra* ch. 5, note 39.

13. *See* O. WILLIAMSON, CORPORATE CONTROL AND BUSINESS BEHAVIOR 141–50 (1970); J. VAN HORNE, FUNDAMENTALS OF FINANCIAL MANAGEMENT 496–502 (2d ed. 1974).

14. United Nations, Transnational Corporations and World Development: Trade and Prospects 11, U.N. Sales No. E.88.II.A.7 (1988) (Figures are likely to be overestimated because of estimation problems.)

15. For example, *see* Vann, *International: A Model Tax Treaty for the Asian-Pacific Region*, 8 ASIAN-PAC. TAX & INV. BULL. 392 (1990) (calling for regional treaty for Australia and its trading partners to deal with the problem in tax matters).

16. Walkovszky v. Carlton, 18 N.Y.2d 414, 418, 223 N.E.2d 6, 8–9 (1966), *on remand*, 29 A.D.2d 763, 287 N.Y.S.2d 546 (2d Dep't), *aff'd*, 23 N.Y.2d 714, 244 N.E.2d 55 (1968). In the decision, the court made clear the distinction between investors and controlling shareholders participating in the business, stating: "[I]t is one thing to assert that a corporation is a fragment of a larger corporate combine which actually conducts the business. It is quite another to impose liability on shareholders."

17. Thus, the author's surveys of the largest one thousand American corpo-

rations indicated that the large American corporations had an average of forty-four subsidiaries each. *See* P. BLUMBERG, THE LAW OF CORPORATE GROUPS: PROCEDURE, APPENDIX ON DATA ON CORPORATE STRUCTURE (1983). As of 1976, a survey of 180 U.S.-based multinational companies with 10,845 subsidiaries showed that 8,059 subsidiaries, or about seventy-five percent, were wholly owned (survey based on Harvard Multinational Enterprise Project data). *See* J. CURHAN, W. DAVIDSON, & R. SURI, TRACING THE MULTINATIONALS 143 (1977).

18. *See* Hansmann & Kraakman, *supra*, at 1931–32.

19. Intragroup transactions to the benefit of the parent but that do not leave the subsidiary at a disadvantage do not violate existing fiduciary standards in Delaware and New York. *See, e.g.*, Sinclair Oil Co. v. Levien, 280 A.2d 717 (Del. 1971); Case v. New York Central R.R. Co., 15 N.Y.2d 150, 204 N.E.2d 643 (1965). Whether such a dubious result will survive future scrutiny remains to be seen. The American Law Institute recommends a general approach of fairness. A.L.I., PRINCIPLES OF CORPORATE GOVERNANCE: ANALYSIS AND RECOMMENDATIONS §5.10 (Proposed Final Draft 1992).

20. For the special purposes of particular statutes, however, wholly owned subsidiaries may be treated differently from partly owned subsidiaries. Thus, in the celebrated *Copperweld* decision, the Supreme Court held that a parent corporation could not conspire with its wholly owned subsidiary insofar as violation of the sections of the Sherman Antitrust Act, which makes conspiracies to monopolize unlawful, were concerned. For these special purposes, the Court relied on enterprise principles, stating that "a parent and a wholly owned subsidiary *always* have a unity of purpose or a common design." Copperweld Corp. v. Independence Tube Corp., 467 U.S. 752, 771–72 (1984).

Copperweld expressly reserved decision with respect to cases involving partly owned subsidiaries. For purposes of this particular statute, this question is more complex, and the law is still unclear, particularly in the case of less than 80 percent-owned subsidiaries.

21. *See supra* note 13.

22. *See* Leebron, *supra*.

23. *See, e.g.*, the original drafts of the proposed Council Regulation on the European Company and the proposed Ninth Directive on Company Law. C.E.E. Doc. No. XV 593 75-E, Doc. No. XI 215/77-E; BULL EUR. COMM. SUPP. 5/89; O.J.E.C. C 297 (1980), O.J.E.C. C 217 (1983).

Chapter 7

1. *See The Global 500, The World's Largest Industrial Corporations*, FORTUNE, at 176 July 27, 1992; United Nations, Transnational Corporations and World Development: Trends and Prospects (Executive Summary) 2, 5, U.N. Sales No. E.88.II.A.7 (1988).

For a review of the significance of corporate groups in the European Economic Community, *see* Gleichmann, *The Law of Corporate Groups in the European Community*, in REGULATING CORPORATE GROUPS IN EUROPE 435, 436–37 (D. Sugarman & G. Teubner eds. 1990).

2. *See* 2 GROUPS OF COMPANIES IN EUROPEAN LAWS (K. Hopt ed. 1982); F. WOOLDRIDGE, GROUPS OF COMPANIES: THE LAW AND PRACTICE IN BRITAIN, FRANCE AND GERMANY (1981); GROUPS OF COMPANIES (C. Schmitthoff & F. Wooldridge eds. 1991); REGULATING CORPORATE GROUPS IN EUROPE (D. Sugarman & G. Teubner eds. 1990); Hofstetter, *Parent Responsibility for Subsidiary Corporations: Evaluating European Trends*, 39 INT'L & COMP. L.Q. 576 (1990).

3. *See* Hofstetter, *supra*; Dobson, *"Lifting the Veil" in Four Countries: The Law of Argentina, England, France, and the United States*, 35 INT'L & COMP. L.Q. 839 (1986).

4. Salomon v. Salomon & Co., [1897] A.C. 22 (H.L. 1896). *See* L. GOWER, Gower's PRINCIPLES OF MODERN COMPANY LAW 97–100 (4th ed. 1979); Kahn-Freund, *Some Reflections on Company Law Reform*, 7 MOD. L. REV. 54 (1944) ("calamitous decision").

5. Maclaine Watson & Co. v. Department of Trade and Industry, [1990] 2 A.C. 418, 3 All E.R. 523 (H.L. 1989). *Compare* L. GOWER, THE PRINCIPLES OF MODERN COMPANY LAW 213 (3d ed. 1969) *with supra*, at 131–33 (4th ed. 1979). *Compare* D.H.N. Ltd. v. Tower Hamlets, [1976] 1 W.L.R. 852 (1976) *with In re* Southard & Co., [1979] 1 W.L.R. 1198 (C.A.), and *In re* Horsley & Weight Ltd., [1982] ch. 442.

6. The Companies Act, 1985 §§23(1), 143, 151, 229 *et seq.*, 330, 736(1); The Companies Act, 1989 §§21(1), 258. *Compare* EC Fourth and Seventh Directives on group accounts on which these provisions are modeled.

7. The Fair Trading Act, 1973, pt. V, §§57, 64, 65, 67 (ch. 64 of 1973).

8. *See* Statement of Standard Accounting Practice (England and Wales), Accounting for Results of Associated Companies, pt. 2.

9. City Code, Rules 8, 9. *See* 2 F. GORE-BROWNE, COMPANIES, ch. 29 (44th ed., A. Boyle ed. 1986).

10. The Income and Corporate Taxes Act, 1988 §§229, 308, 402, 410, 413(3), (7), 838(1), 840.

11. *Id.* at §§416, 747, 840.

12. The Employment Protection (Consolidation) Act, 1978 §§81(2), 153(4).

13. *See, e.g.*, Dimbleby & Sons Ltd. v. National Union of Journalists, [1984] 1 W.L.R. 67 and Haughton v. Olau Line (UK) Ltd., [1986] I.C.R. 357 (C.A.).

14. *See* Baxt, *The Corporate Veil in Tax Law—The Legal Perception of Companies as Separate Entities*, 1 AUSTL. TAX FORUM 239 (1984) (dealing with tax laws); J. Hill, The Juridical Person-Australia 4 (paper presented at XIII International Congress of Comparative Law 1990).

15. Briggs v. Jones Hardie & Co., Pty, (1989) 7 A.C.L.C. (CCH) 841, 863

(N.S.W. C.A.). Commentators differ over whether Australian law is readier to disregard the corporate entity and impose group obligations. *Compare* H. FORD, PRINCIPLES OF COMPANY LAW 708 (5th ed. 1990) ("no great readiness to disregard the corporate entity") *with* J. Hill, *supra*.

16. Income Tax Assessment Act, 1936 §§80G (losses), 160AFE (foreign tax credits), 160ZP (net capital losses), and 159 GZZA (controlled foreign corporations).

17. *See* Durnford, *The Corporate Veil in Tax Law*, 27 CAN. TAX. J. 281 (1979).

18. *See* B. WELLING, CORPORATE LAW IN CANADA ch. 3 (1984); T. HADDEN, R. FORBES, & R. SIMMONS, CANADIAN BUSINESS ORGANIZATIONS LAW ch. 9 (1984). In a more current survey, John H. Farrar describes that while Canadian courts are unwilling to adopt American authority on "piercing the veil" and pay lip service to British Commonwealth authority, there are signs of change, and Canadian law is in a "state of flux." Farrar, *Commentary, Fraud, Fairness and Piercing the Corporate Veil*, 16 CAN. BUS. L.J. 474 (1990).

19. Can. Stat., 1974–75, ch.33, §§2(2)–(5), 42.

20. R. v. Imperial Gen. Properties Ltd., [1985] 85 D.T.C. 5500 (Can.). *See* 1 L. HOULDEN & C. MORAWETZ, BANKRUPTCY LAW OF CANADA §B-20 (3d ed. 1989).

21. J. Hill, *supra*.

22. New Zealand Companies Amendments Act, 1980 §311B(5), 311C; New Zealand Companies Act, 1955, *as amended*, §§154, 158, 315A.

23. Law of Sept. 6, 1965, [1965] Aktiengesetz, BGB III 4121-1.

24. *See* Hofstetter, *supra*, at 582.

25. *See* Gleichmann, *supra*, at 435, 455.

26. *See* ch. 6, note 19.

27. *See* Gleichmann, *supra*, at 435, 454–55.

28. 95 BGHZ 330 (1985); *Tiefbau*, BGH ZIP 1989, 440z; NJW. *See* Hofstetter, *supra*, at 583.

29. *See* Birk, *The Group Enterprise as a Problem for German Labour Law*, in REGULATING CORPORATE GROUPS IN EUROPE, *supra*, at 355; Wiedemann, *The German Experience with the Law of Affiliated Enterprises*, in 2 GROUPS OF COMPANIES IN EUROPEAN LAWS, *supra*, 42–43.

30. Loi No. 67–563 of July 12, 1967 §101; Loi No. 85-98 of Jan. 25, 1985.

31. *See* 1 J. DALHUISEN, INTERNATIONAL INSOLVENCY AND BANKRUPTCY, pt.2, §3.02 (1983).

32. Cass. civ. com., 1982 Bull. Civ. IV, at 578. *See* Weissberg & Moissinac, *Piercing the Corporate Veil in France*, INT'L FIN. L. REV. 33, 35 (July, 1987).

33. Unlike the United States, the additional factor of fundamental unfairness or inequitable conduct to creditors does not appear to be necessary for imposition of liability.

34. Law of Oct. 28, 1982. *See* Rodiere, *Group Enterprises in French La-*

bour Law, in REGULATING CORPORATE GROUPS IN EUROPE, *supra*, at 305, 306–08.

35. *See* Hofstetter, *supra*, at 586.

36. The Swedish Companies Act, 1975, *as amended as of* 1980, ch 1, §2. *See* Rodhe, *Groups in Scandinavian Company Law*, in GROUPS OF COMPANIES IN EUROPEAN LAWS, *supra*, 142, 144–45.

37. Rodhe, *supra*, at 145.

38. Fourth Council Directive on Annual Accounts §§17, 58, No. 78/660, July 25, 1978, O.J. L222 (1978); Seventh Council Directive on Consolidated Accounts, art. 1, 83/349, O.J. L193, July 18, 1983; United Kingdom: The Companies Act, 1989 §21(1), 258.

39. *See* Gleichmann, *supra*, at 435.

40. 22 O.J. EUR. COMM. C 14, at 5 (1979).

41. Seventh Council Directive, 83/349/EEC, O.J. L193.

42. *See* Gleichmann, *supra*, at 435–36; *Corporate Law, Recent Developments—Nieuwdorp, EEC: 1. Law of Corporations*, 17 INT'L BUS. LAW. 35 (1989).

43. EC Merger Control Regulation (Antitrust), art. 3 (1), 4064/89 of Dec. 21, 1989, 33 O.J. EUR. COMM. (No. L 257) 14 [Antitrust Supp.], 4 Common Mkt. Rep. (CCH) 859, 860 (1990).

44. *E.g.* Imperial Chem. Indus. Ltd v. Commission, Case No. 48/69, [1972] E.C.R. 619, 662; Europemballage Corp. v. Commission, Case No. 6/72, [1973] E.C.R. 215, 242; Istituto Chemioterapico Italiano S.p.A. v. Commission, Case Nos. 6–7/73, [1974] E.C.R. 223, 253–55.

Chapter 8

1. United Kingdom Protection of Trading Interest Act, 1980 (ch. 11, 1980). Other countries with similar statutes include Australia, Canada, France, and Germany.

2. *See generally* M. JANIS, AN INTRODUCTION TO INTERNATIONAL LAW 241–50 (1988); RESTATEMENT (THIRD) OF THE FOREIGN RELATIONS LAW OF THE UNITED STATES §§213, 401 *et seq.* (1987).

3. *E.g.*, The Barcelona Traction Co. (Belgium v. Spain), 1970 I.C.J. 3 (1970).

4. Sumitomo Shoji Am. Inc. v. Avagliano, 457 U.S. 176 (1982). *Cf.* Compagnie Europeene des Petroles, S.A. v. Sensor Nederland, B.V., No. 82/716 (Dist. Ct. The Hague, Sept. 17, 1982), 22 INT'L LEGAL MATERIALS 66 (1983).

5. RESTATEMENT, *supra*, at §403.

6. RESTATEMENT, *supra*, at §§216, 414(2)(b), §414 comments a and b.

7. RESTATEMENT, *supra*, at 237 (Introductory Note to pt. 4, ch. 1).

8. *See* RESTATEMENT, *supra*, at §§403(2), 414(1), (2).

9. *See, e.g.* Uebersee Finanz-Korporation, A.G. v. McGrath, 343 U.S.

205 (1951); Clark v. Uebersee Finanz-Korporation, A.G., 332 U.S. 480 (1947). *Cf.* Daimler Co. v. Continental Tyre & Rubber Co., [1916] 2 A.C. 307, 336–48.

10. *See* RESTATEMENT, *supra*, at §402(1)(a); M. JANIS, *supra*, at 242.

11. *See* RESTATEMENT, *supra*, at §402(1)(c); M. JANIS, *supra*, at 245.

12. *See* RESTATEMENT, *supra*, at §18.

13. RESTATEMENT, *supra*, at §402 comment f. *See* United States v. Pizzarusso, 388 F.2d 8, 10 (2d Cir. 1968), *cert. denied*, 392 U.S. 936 (1968).

14. Compagnie Europeene des Petroles, S.A., 22 INT'L LEGAL MATERIALS 66.

15. *See* EEOC v. Arabian Am. Oil Co., 111 S. Ct. 1227, 1234–36 (1991).

16. 40 Stat. 41, (1917), 50 U.S.C. app. §§1 *et seq.* (1988). The President's authority was limited to actions determined by him to be "compatible . . . with the successful prosecution of the war." *Id.*, at §5.

17. Hamburg-American Line Terminal & Nav. Co. v. United States, 277 U.S. 138 (1928); Behn, Meyer & Co. v. Miller, 266 U.S. 457 (1925); Fritz Schulz, Jr., Co. v. Raimes & Co., 99 Misc. 626, 164 N.Y.S. 454 (City Ct. 1917) (rejecting *Daimler*).

18. [1916] 2 A.C. 307, 336–48 (H.L.).

19. 55 Stat. 839–40, 50 U.S.C. app. §5 (1982) [emphasis added]; U.S. Treas. Dep't Pub. Circular No. 30, 7 Fed. Reg. 2503 (Apr. 1, 1942); Uebersee Finanz-Korporation, A.G. v. McGrath, 343 U.S. 205 (1951); Clark v. Uebersee Finanz-Korporation, A.G., 332 U.S. 480, 483 (1947). *See* Kaufman v. Société Internationale Pour Participations Industrielles et Commerciales, S.A., 343 U.S. 156, 156 (1952) (under the 1941 amendments, the corporate veil can now be pierced if enemy officers or shareholders).

The Circular glossed over a major problem of statutory construction. Although the FWPA amended section 5(b) of TWEA to employ the "subject to the jurisdiction of the United States" standard, it unaccountedly failed to make any change in the statutory definition of a corporation in section 2 as a corporation organized under American law. In *Clark*, the Supreme Court recognized the problem but stretched to enforce the regulation, "harmonizing" the construction of section 2 to implement the change made in section 5(b). 332 U.S. at 488–89.

20. *See* Sommerfield, *Treasury Regulations Affecting Trade with the Euro-Soviet Block and Cuba*, 19 BUS. LAW. 861, 869 (1964).

21. *See* generally A. HERMAN, CONFLICTS OF NATIONAL LAWS WITH INTERNATIONAL BUSINESS ACTIVITY: ISSUES OF EXTRATERRITORIALITY (1982); Hirschhorn, *Controls on Exports*, in LAW & PRACTICE OF UNITED STATES REGULATION OF INTERNATIONAL TRADE, bk. 9 (C. Johnston, Jr., ed. 1989); EXTRA-TERRITORIAL APPLICATION OF LAWS AND RESPONSES THERETO (C. Olmstead ed. 1984); A. LOWENFELD, TRADE CONTROLS FOR POLITICAL ENDS (1983).

22. U.S. Treas. Dep't Pub. Circular, *supra*. Pres. Proc. No. 2914, 3 C.F.R. 100 (Dec. 16, 1950); 31 C.F.R. §§500-500.589 (1989). *See generally* 3 A. LOWENFELD, *supra*, ch. 1, §1.22, DS-71; Lee & McCobb, *United States Trade Embargo on China, 1949-1970; Legal Status and Future Prospects*, 4 N.Y.U.J. INT'L L. & POL. 1 (1971); Sommerfield, *supra*.

23. *See* Leigh, *The Long Arm of Uncle Sam—US Controls as Applied to Foreign Persons and Transactions*, in EXTRA-TERRITORIAL APPLICATION OF LAWS AND RESPONSES THERETO 47, 53 (C. Olmsted ed. 1984).

24. S.A. Société Fruehauf-France v. Massardy, [1968] D.S. Jur. 147, [1965] J.C.P. II 14274 bis, 5 INT'L LEGAL MATERIALS 476 (1966) (Cour d'appel Paris). *See* Craig, *Application of the Trading with the Enemy Act to Foreign Corporations Owned by Americans: Reflections on Fruehauf v. Massardy*, 83 HARV. L. REV. 579 (1970).

25. *See* Leigh, *supra*, at 53-54; Fazzone, *Business Effects of the Extra-Territorial Reach of the U.S. Export Control Laws*, 15 N.Y.U.J. INT'L L. & POL. 545, 571-72 (1983).

26. *See* generally Corcoran, *The Trading with the Enemy Act and the Controlled Canadian Corporation*, 14 McGILL L.J. 174 (1968); Fazzone, *supra*.

27. 39 DEP'T ST. BULL. 209 (1958).

28. *See* N.Y. Times, June 24, 1982, at A1, col. 5; Pattison, *Extraterritorial Enforcement of the Export Administration Act*, in EXPORT CONTROLS 87-88 (M. Czinkota ed. 1984). More recently, the 1992 American expansion of the Cuban Embargo to include foreign subsidiaries of American corporations was condemned 59 to 3 by the United Nations General Assembly. *See* N.Y. Times, Nov. 25, 1992, at A1, col. 8 (criticized as violation of international law).

29. *Sumitomo Shoji Am, Inc.*, 457 U.S. at 176.

30. *See* A. LOWENFELD, *supra*, at ch. 2, §5.62; Atwood, *The Export Administration Act and the Dresser Industries Case*, 15 LAW & POL'Y IN INT'L BUS. 1157 (1983); Kincannon, *The Dresser Case: One Step Too Far*, 5 N.Y.U.J. INT'L & COMP. L. 191 (1984); Note, Dresser Industries: *The Failure of Foreign Policy Trade Controls under the Export Administration Act*, 8 MD. J. INT'L L. & TRADE 122 (1984).

31. Protection of Trading Interests (U.S. Export Control) Order, 1982, *reprinted in* 21 INT'L LEGAL MATERIALS 852 (1982); *See* A. LOWENFELD, *supra*, at ch. 2, §5.61; Moyer & Mabry, *Export Controls as Instruments of Foreign Policy: The History, Legal Issues, and Policy Lessons in Three Recent Cases*, 15 LAW & POL'Y INT'L BUS. 1, 82 (1983); Nollen, *The Case of John Brown Engineering and the Soviet Gas Pipeline*, in EXPORT CONTROLS, *supra*, at 111-19.

32. Nollen, *supra*, at 132.

33. Compagnie Europeene des Petroles, S.A., 22 INT'L LEGAL MATERIALS 66.

34. *See* Moyer & Mabry, *supra*, at 148.

35. Compania Swift de La Plata, S.A. Frigorific s/convocatoria de acreedores, 19 J.A. 579, 151 La Ley 516 (1973). *See* Gordon, *Argentine Jurisprudence: The Parke Davis and Deltec Cases*, 6 LAW. AM. 320 (1974) (Gordon I); Gordon, *Argentine Jurisprudence: Deltec Update*, 11 LAW. AM. 43 (1979) (Gordon II); Rosenn, *Expropriation in Argentina and Brazil: Theory and Practice*, 15 VA. J. INT'L L., 277, 311–14 (1975). This discussion relies heavily on the valuable articles by Professor Michael W. Gordon.

36. However, this solvency did not survive. It was swallowed up by administration costs, inflation-indexing of claims, interest, and claims of the government for advances during the period of governmental intervention.

37. An English language version of the opinion appears in Gordon I, *supra*, at 334–40.

38. Law No. 20.557 (Nov. 7, 1973), 12 INT'L LEGAL MATERIALS 1489 (1973); Law No. 21.382 art. 20 (Aug. 13, 1976), 15 INT'L LEGAL MATERIALS 1364 (1976).

39. *See* Abraham & Abraham, *The Bhopal Case and the Development of Environmental Law in India*, 40 INT'L & COMP. L.Q. 334 (1991).

40. *In re* Union Carbide Corp. Gas Plant Disaster at Bhopal, India in Dec. 1984, 634 F. Supp. 842 (S.D.N.Y. 1986), *aff'd in part, rev'd in part*, 809 F.2d 195 (2d Cir.), *cert. denied sub nom.* Executive Comm. Members v. Union of India, 484 U.S. 871 (1987). The complaint alleged not only direct liability of the American parent company, but a sixth count sought to impose intragroup or enterprise liability on the parent for the acts of its Indian subsidiary. Complaint, Government of India v. Union Carbide Corp., No. 85 Civ. 2696 (S.D.N.Y. 1985).

41. (1989) 1 S.C.C. 674, (1989) 2 S.C.C. 540, (1989) 3 S.C.C. 38. *See* N.Y. Times, Oct. 4, 1991, §D, at 4, col. 1.

42. Thus, in the *Amoco Cadiz* oil spill litigation, a U.S. district court had imposed liability on the American parent for the spill involving a subsidiary's tanker. As in the *Bhopal* litigation, the judgment rested both on a far-reaching assertion of enterprise liability and on a finding of negligence directly by the parent. In its lengthy affirmance on appeal, the Court of Appeals for the Seventh Circuit did not find it necessary to discuss the lower court reliance on enterprise principles at all. *In re* Amoco Cadiz Oil Spill, 1984 A.M.C. 2123 (N.D. Ill. 1984), *aff'd*, 954 F.2d 1279 (7th Cir. 1992).

43. *See* R. BLANPAIN, THE BADGER CASE AND THE OECD GUIDELINES FOR MULTINATIONAL ENTERPRISES (1977).

44. *See* Loucks v. Standard Oil Co., 224 N.Y. 99, 111, 120 N.E.2d 198, 202 (1918) (Cardozo J.).

45. Deltec Banking Corp. v. Compania Italo-Argentina de Electricidad, S.A., 171 N.Y.L.J. 18, at col. 1, Apr. 3, 1974 (Sup. Ct.), *aff'd mem.*, 46 A.D.2d 847, 362 N.Y.S.2d 362 (1st Dep't 1974).

46. *See* BLUMBERG, THE LAW OF CORPORATE GROUPS: BANKRUPTCY, *supra*, at §17.23.5.

47. Tahan v. Hodgson, 662 F.2d 862 (1st Cir. 1981). I am grateful to Prof. Detlev Vagts for calling this case to my attention.

48. *See* Lowe, *Public International Law and the Conflict of Laws: The European Response to the United States Export Administration Regulations*, 33 INT'L & COMP. L.Q. 515 (1984).

49. RESTATEMENT, *supra*, at §437, reporters' note 1.

50. Société Internationale v. Rogers, 357 U.S. 197, 208–13 (1958).

51. [1972] 23 U.S.T. 2555, T.I.A.S. 7444, 28 U.S.C. §1781 (Supp. 1991); Société Nationale Industrielle Aerospatiale v. United States Dist. Ct. for the S. Dist. of Iowa, 482 U.S. 522 (1987).

52. Act against Restraints of Competition (GWB) §23(3). Organic Pigments, WuW/E 1613 (BGH May 29, 1979); Morris/Rothmans, WuW/E 3051 (Kammergericht July 1, 1983). *See* Kuhn, *Foreign Takeovers and Merger Control in the Federal Republic of German*, [1989] INT'L BUS. L. 399–400, *citing* Federal Cartel Office Guidelines (1975).

53. *E.g.*, Imperial Chem. Indus., Ltd. v. Commission, Case 48/69, [1972] E.C.R. 619, 622; Europemballage Corp v. Commission, Case 6/72, [1973] E.C.R. 215, 242; Istituto Chemioterapico Italiano S.p.A. and Commercial Solvents Corp. v. Commission, Case 6 and 7/73, [1974] E.C.R. 2223, 253–55.

54. Foreign Investment Review Act 1973–74, ch. 46 (1973), *as amended by* Investment Canada Act, Can. Stat. ch. 20 (1985); Dow Jones & Co. v. Attorney-General of Canada, 122 D.L.R.3d 731 (Fed. Ct. App. 1981), *aff'g*, 113 D.L.R.3d 395 (Fed. Ct. 1980).

55. *See* RESTATEMENT, *supra*, at §414, reporters' note 2.

56. COMPANIES (Acquisition of Shares) (N.S.W.) CODE; NCSC v. Brierly Invs. Ltd., 6 Austl. Co. L. Cas. (CCH) 995, 1015 (1988). *See* White, *Corporate Law: Recent Developments—III, Australia*, 17 INT'L BUS. LAW 33, 34 (1989).

57. Sweden, Laws 98, *cited in* RESTATEMENT, *supra*, at §414, reporters' note 2.

58. Seventh Council Directive on Consolidated Accounts, 26 O.J. EUR. COMM. (No. L 193) (July 16, 1983); 1 COMMON MKT. REP. (CCH) ¶1421. Statute for a European Company: Amended Proposal for a Regulation, BULL. EUR. COMM. SUPP. 4/75 arts. 196, 200, 203–10 (1975), BULL. EUR. COMM. SUPP. 5/89, COM (89) 268 final SYN 218.

59. 21 INT'L LEGAL MATERIALS 422 (1982).

60. Council Directive 77/187, 1977 O.J. (L61) 26.

61. *See* H. GROTIUS, DE JURE BELLIS AC PACIS 337 (Carnegie Classic No. 3, 1925 H. Kelsen trans. 1646 ed.) (Book II, ch. XI, §XIII); A. KUHN, LAW OF CORPORATIONS (1912 & 1968 reprint), *citing* Goldschmidt, UNIVERSAL-GESCHICHTE DES HANDELSRECHT 340 (1891); O. HOLMES, JR., THE COMMON LAW 30 (1881).

62. R.S. §4283 (derived from Act of Mar. 3, 1851, ch. 43, §3, 9 Stat. 635 (1851), 46 U.S.C. §183(a) (1988). *See* G. GILMORE & C. BLACK, LAW OF

ADMIRALTY, ch. 10 (2d ed. 1975); Donovan, *Origins and Developments of Shipowners' Liability*, 53 TUL. L. REV. 999 (1979).
63. Flink v. Paladini, 279 U.S. 59, 62–63 (1929). The issue of shareholder liability arose under the California constitutional and statutory provisions imposing pro rata shareholder liability.

Chapter 9

1. *See* 4 R. POUND, JURISPRUDENCE 192 (1959); E. WARREN, CORPORATE ADVANTAGES WITHOUT INCORPORATION 10 (1929).
2. *See* Hart, *Definitions and Theory in Jurisprudence*, 70 L. Q. REV. 37 (1954). *See also* H. KELSEN, GENERAL THEORY OF LAW AND THE STATE 99–100 (1949); Kelsen, *The Pure Theory of Law*, 50 L.Q. REV. 474, 496 (1934) [The legal] "Person is only the personificative expression for the unity of a bundle of legal rights and duties. . . ."); J. HALL, READINGS IN JURISPRUDENCE 444–45 n.1 (1938) ("A person [that is, a legal unit] is any entity to which the law attributes a capacity for legal relations.")
3. *See* Motta v. Samuel Weiser, Inc., 598 F. Supp. 941, 948–51 (D. Me. 1984) ("a right, to be enforced in a court of law, must have a 'holder' or 'bearer.' There must be a 'legal unit' to which the right attaches.") *See also* A. KOCOUREK, JURAL RELATIONS 76 ("[Legal] Personality is the sum total of the legal advantages and disadvantages of a person (persona) . . . [It] may be likened to a ledger account with credit and debt relations.")
4. Thus, some eighteenth-century applications for English charters to the Crown mentioned the existence of transferable shares, central management, and perpetual or long-term existence among the major reasons for seeking to incorporate. *See* A. DUBOIS, THE ENGLISH COMPANY AFTER THE BUBBLE ACT 1720–1800, 91–93 (1938). Limited liability was of relatively slight importance and, according to DuBois, was not even mentioned in the formal arguments in support of the applications for early corporate charters and was only mentioned intermittently thereafter. The first such references occurred in 1768 and 1784. *Id.* at 95–97.
5. *See* D. FEHRENBACHER, THE DRED SCOTT CASE 16 (1978); Flanigan, *Criminal Proceedings in Slave Trials in the Antebellum South*, 40 J. SO. HIST. 537, 537 (1974).
6. Anthony v. State, 9 Ga. 264 (1851). *See* D. FEHRENBACHER, *supra*, at 34; Flanigan, *supra*, at 538, 546 (Southern states were "astonishingly considerate of slaves' procedural rights in major criminal offenses.").
7. Tucker v. Alexandroff, 183 U.S. 424, 438 (1902) [citations omitted].
8. The Camanche, 75 U.S. (8 Wall.) 448, 476 (1869).
9. *E.g.*, The John G. Stevens, 170 U.S. 113 (1898); Tucker, 183 U.S. 424, 438; Homer Ramsdell Transp. Co. v. La Compagnie Generale Transatlantique, 182 U.S. 406 (1901).
10. The Little Charles, 1 Brock. 347, 354, 26 F.Cas. 979, 982 (C.C.Va.

1809) (No. 15,612) (Marshall, C.J.). *See* United States v. Brig Malek Adhel, 43 U.S. (2 How.) 210, 234 (1844) (Story, J.).

11. *Compare* The China, 74 U.S. (7 Wall.) 53, 61 (1868) *with* Homer Ramsdell Transp. Co., 186 U.S. 406.

12. Pennoyer v. Neff, 95 U.S. 714, 734 (1877).

13. Pramatha Nath Mullick v. Pradyumna Kumar Mullock, (1925) L.R. 52 Ind. App. 245 (Privy Council); 87 Ind. Cas. 305. *See* Duff, *The Personality of an Idol*, 3 CAMB. L.J. 42, 44–45 (1927). *See also* Gordon, *Legal Rights of an East Indian Idol*, 11 A.B.A.J. 431 (1925); Renton, *The Gods, The Judges, and the Laws*, 9 KINGSTON L. REV. 3 (1979).

14. *See* Duff, *supra*, at 44–45.

15. *See* C. STONE, SHOULD TREES HAVE STANDING? – TOWARD LEGAL RIGHTS FOR NATURAL OBJECTS 9 (1974).

The suggestion was not new. A half-century earlier, Gerard Henderson had suggested: "anything can be made a legal unit and the subject of rights and duties. . . . There is no reason, except the practical one why, as someone has suggested, the law should not accord to the last rose of summer a legal right not to be plucked." *See* G. HENDERSON, THE POSITION OF FOREIGN CORPORATIONS IN AMERICAN CONSTITUTIONAL LAW 166 (1918). An English scholar later observed that it was "absurd but not impossible to award legal personality to trees, sticks, or stones." *See* G. PATON, A TEXTBOOK OF JURIS-PRUDENCE §68 (1946).

16. Sierra Club v. Morton, 405 U.S. 727, 741–43 (1972).

Chapter 10

1. *See* A. BROMBERG & L. RIBSTEIN, PARTNERSHIPS §103 (2d ed. 1988); Crane, *The Uniform Partnership Act and Legal Persons*, 29 HARV. L. REV. 838 (1916); Jensen, *Is a Partnership under the Uniform Partnership Act an Aggregate or an Entity?*, 16 VAND. L. REV. 377 (1963); Rosin, *The Entity-Aggregate Dispute: Conceptualism and Functionalism in Partnership Law*, 42 ARK. L. REV. 395 (1989).

2. The Uniform Partnership Act, adopted in 1914, has been enacted by almost all states. 6 U.L.A. 1 (Supp. Pamph. 1992).

3. *E.g.*, Petroleum Corp. of Texas v. United States, 939 F.2d 1165 (5th Cir. 1991) (Texas law); Scott v. Edwards Transp. Co., 807 S.W.2d 75 (Sup. Ct. Mo. 1991) (en banc).

4. I.R.C. §§701, 703, 706(b), 707, 741–43 (taxation), 1 U.S.C. §1 (general), 11 U.S.C. §§101(37), (8)(A) (bankruptcy), 15 U.S.C. §77b(2) (securities), 29 U.S.C. §1002(9) (ERISA) (1988).

5. United States v. A & P Trucking Co., 358 U.S. 121, 124, 127–28 (1958). Criminal liability in the case rested on the attribution of the knowledge of employees. The Court had previously held that such employee knowledge could be attributed for criminal purposes to a partnership but not to the

individual partners. Gordon v. United States, 347 U.S. 909 (1954). Accordingly, the case involved the issue of imposition of criminal liability on a partnership whose partners had committed no crime.

6. The Motor Carrier Act punished any "person" who knowingly violated any of its provisions and defined "person" to include a "copartnership." 49 U.S.C.A. §§303(a)(1). As discussed, the general construction provision of the Code did the same "unless the context indicates otherwise." 1 U.S.C. §1 (1976).

7. 358 U.S. at 127–28.

8. Blau v. Lehman, 368 U.S. 403, 414–16 (1962).

9. Moffat Tunnel League v. United States, 289 U.S. 113, 118 (1933); Byam v. Bickford, 2 N.E. 687, 140 Mass. 31 (1885); State v. Sunbeam Rebekah Lodge No. 180, 169 Or. 253, 127 P.2d 726 (1942).

10. *See* 6 Am. Jur. 2d, *Associations and Clubs* §15. Although one can rationalize these cases by suggesting that the right to the name or insignia belonged to the members collectively, the fact is that the courts recognizing the right and granting relief did not find it necessary to do so.

11. *See, e.g.*, Moffat Tunnel League, 289 U.S. 113, 118; Brown v. United States, 276 U.S. 134 (1928).

12. *See* J. Crane, Partnerships §99 (2d ed. 1952); S. Worthington, Law of Unincorporated Associations and Business Trusts §64 (2d ed. 1923); Comment, *Liability of Members and Officers of Nonprofit Unincorporated Associations for Contracts and Torts*, 42 Calif. L. Rev. 812 (1954).

13. *See* Johnson v. South Blue Hill Cemetery Ass'n, 221 A.2d 280 (Me. 1966); State v. Sunbeam Rebekah Lodge, 127 P.2d 726.

14. *See generally* 1 T. Frankel, The Regulation of Money Managers — The Investment Company Act and the Investment Advisers Act 258–71 (1977), 4 *id.* 346–80 (1980); 2 L. Loss & J. Seligman, Securities Regulation 1008–13 (3d ed. 1989); Finnegan & Garner, *The Separate Account as an Investment Company: Structural Problems of the "Ectoplasmic Theory,"* 3 Conn. L. Rev. 106, 109 (1970).

A variable annuity is an annuity under a contract providing that the amount payable to the annuitant is to be determined by the actual investment results of the particular pool of assets dedicated to underwrite the contract. Equity investments predominate in the related portfolios, and with the inevitable fluctuation in equity values, the outcome is variable, unlike traditional insurance products with contractually guaranteed results. Variable policies respond to a concern with inflationary pressures.

15. Under the Act, "issuer" includes "any person" issuing a "security"; a "person" includes a "company"; and a "company" includes a "fund," a "special account" and an "organized group of persons." 15 U.S.C. §§80a-2(a)(8), (27) (1988); Investment Company Act Rules 0-1(a), 0-1(e)(2), 17 C.F.R. §§270.0-1(3), 1(e)(2) (1991). *See* Prudential Ins. Co. v. SEC, 326 F.2d 383 (3d Cir.), *cert. denied*, 377 U.S. 953 (1964). *See also* 4 T. Frankel, *supra*, at

346-79; Frankel, *Variable Annuities, Variable Insurance and Separate Accounts*, 51 B.U. L. REV. 173 (1971).

16. *See* Roth, Krawczyk, & Goldstein, *Reorganizing Insurance Company Separate Accounts under Federal Securities Law*, 46 BUS. LAW. 537, 546 n.36 (1991).

17. N.Y. INS. LAW §4240(a)(5), (12) (McKinney 1985).

18. I.R.C. §§501(c)(3) to (8); Treas. Reg. §1.501(c)(3)-1(b)(2).

19. Warth v. Seldin, 422 U.S. 490, 511 (1975); NAACP v. Alabama, 357 U.S. 449, 458-60 (1958). *See* 6A C. WRIGHT, A. MILLER & M. KANE, FEDERAL PRACTICE AND PROCEDURE §§1552, 1564 (1990).

20. O.J. EUR. COMM. (No. L 199/1) (July 31, 1985), E.C. Council Reg. No. 2137/85 (July 25, 1985). *E.g.*, United Kingdom: STAT. INST. 1989 No. 638 (1989); France: Loi 89-377 of June 13, 1989 on European Economic Interest Groupings, *amending* Ord. 67-821 of Sept. 23, 1967, §1. *See* EUROPEAN ECONOMIC INTEREST GROUPINGS (D. Van Gerven and C Aalders eds. 1990). *See also* Maclaine Watson & Co. v. Department of Trade & Industry, [1990] 2 A.C. 418; 3 All E.R. 523 (H.L. 1989).

21. Minton v. St. Bernard Parish School Bd., 803 F.2d 129, 131 (5th Cir. 1986); Maine v. Data Gen. Corp., 697 F. Supp. 23, 24 (D. Me. 1988); Pennsylvania Human Relations Comm'n v. US Air, Inc., 615 F. Supp. 75, 76 (W.D. Pa. 1985).

22. Benning v. Board of Regents of Regency Univs., 928 F.2d 775, 777 (7th Cir. 1991); Farias v. Bexar County Bd. of Trustees, 925 F.2d 866, 874 (5th Cir. 1991); Minton, 803 F.2d 129, 131.

23. Mt. Healthy City School Dist. Bd. of Educ. v. Doyle, 429 U.S. 274, 280 (1977) ("arm"); Moore v. County of Alameda, 411 U.S. 693, 713, 717, *reh'g denied*, 412 U.S. 963 (1973); Blake v. Kline, 612 F.2d 718, 720 (3d Cir. 1979) ("alter ego").

Chapter 11

1. These observations do not relate to the many small closely held corporations without subsidiaries that still proliferate in the economy, although they have long ceased to be predominant.

2. *See, supra*, ch. 7, note 44.

3. *See* Coase, *The Nature of the Firm*, 4 ECONOMICA 386 (1937); Coase, *Lectures on the Firm*, 4 J. LAW. ECON. & ORG'N 3 (1988).

4. Alchian & Demsetz, *Production, Information Costs, and Economic Organization*, 62 AM. ECON. REV. 777 (1972). *See* R. POSNER & R. SCOTT, ECONOMICS OF CORPORATION LAW AND SECURITIES REGULATION 12 (1960).

5. Jensen & Meckling, *Theory of the Firm: Managerial Behavior, Agency Costs and Ownership Structure*, 3 J. FIN. ECON. 305 (1976).

6. *See* O. WILLIAMSON, ECONOMIC ORGANIZATION: FIRMS, MARKETS,

AND POLICIES (1986); O. WILLIAMSON, ECONOMIC INSTITUTIONS OF CAPITAL-ISM (1985); O. WILLIAMSON, MARKETS AND HIERARCHIES: ANALYSIS AND ANTITRUST IMPLICATIONS (1975); O. WILLIAMSON, CORPORATE CONTROL AND BUSINESS BEHAVIOR (1970).

7. These are investments that have a much greater use inside the relationship than outside, thereby locking in the parties and permitting opportunistic behavior.

8. Professor Boulding expresses the limitation most vividly: "There is a great deal of evidence that almost all organizational structures tend to produce false images in the decision-maker, and that the larger and more authoritarian the organization, the better the chance that its top decision-makers will be operating in purely imaginary worlds. This perhaps is the most fundamental reason for suggesting that there are ultimately diminishing returns to scale." *See* K. Boulding, Richard T. Ely Lecture, 78th Annual Meeting, American Economic Association. Williamson makes much of this observation. *See* O. WILLIAMSON, ECONOMIC ORGANIZATION, *supra*, at 32.

9. *See* O. WILLIAMSON, MARKETS AND HIERARCHIES, *supra*, at 155-75; ECONOMIC ORGANIZATIONS, *supra*, at 154-58.

10. Hart, *An Economist's Perspective on the Theory of the Firm*, 89 COLUM. L. REV. 1757 (1989).

11. *See, e.g.*, Jensen & Meckling, *supra*, at 310-11.

12. I am grateful to Prof. Kurt A. Strasser for this useful analogy.

13. R. POUND, THE SPIRIT OF THE COMMON LAW 12-24 (1921); I *Id.*, JURIS-PRUDENCE 210-221 (1959).

14. I. MACNEIL, THE NEW SOCIAL CONTRACT: AN INQUIRY INTO MODERN CONTRACTUAL RELATIONS (1982); MacNeill, *Relational Contract: What We Do and Do Not Know*, 1985 WIS. L. REV. 483; MacNeill, *The Many Futures of Contracts*, 47 S. CAL. L. REV. 691 (1974); Green, *Relational Interests* (pt. 1), 29 ILL. (NW.) L. REV. 460 (1934).

15. A recent decision by the Supreme Court of Florida in a case involving contractor/subcontractor rights illustrates the inadequacy of traditional doctrine in conceptualizing this development. The majority attributed statutory lien rights of the contractor to the subcontractor under the label of "privity of contract" after finding a "common identity" between the owner and the contractor. A dissenting judge objected that the court had "essentially" reached its decision under the "alter ego" doctrine without compliance with the rigorous requirements of traditional "piercing the veil jurisprudence." Aetna Cas. & Surety Co. v. Buck, 594 So. 2d 280 (Fla. 1992).

16. *See* Easterbrook & Fischel, *The Corporate Contract*, in CORPORATION LAW AND ECONOMIC ANALYSIS 182, 192 (L. Bebchuk ed. 1989); Teubner, *Unitas Multiplex: Corporate Governance in Group Enterprises,* in REGULAT-ING CORPORATE GROUPS IN EUROPE 67 (D. Sugarman & G. Teubner eds. 1990). *See* Stewart, *Organizational Jurisprudence*, 101 HARV. L. REV. 371

(1987) (reviewing Dan-Cohen, *supra*); M. DAN-COHEN, RIGHTS, PERSONS, AND ORGANIZATIONS: A LEGAL THEORY FOR BUREAUCRATIC SOCIETY (1986).

17. The attribution of contract liabilities to a principal because of the acts of an agent in most cases arises because the principal has authorized the agent's acts, either expressly or by implication (actual authority), or has represented to third parties that the agent was authorized to act (apparent authority). There is, however, a small class of occurrences where a principal is bound even where the agent has neither actual nor apparent authority. In this class, the agent is said to have "inherent agency." This is no more than a conclusory statement, and there does not seem to be any satisfactory theoretical explanation as to why liability arises, other than that it appears appropriate on balance to do so. *See* W. SEAVEY, AGENCY §8F (1964); H. REUSCHLEIN & W. GREGORY, HANDBOOK ON THE LAW OF AGENCY AND PARTNERSHIP §26 (1975); RESTATEMENT (SECOND) OF AGENCY §8A (1958).

18. For a perceptive review of this development in German law, *see* Teubner, *Beyond Contract and Organization? The External Liability of Franchising Systems in German Law*, in THEORETICAL AND COMPARATIVE APPROACHES IN EUROPE AND THE UNITED STATES – DAS RECHT DES FRANCHISING (C. Joerges ed. 1991).

19. *See* Collins, *Ascription of Legal Responsibility to Groups in Complex Patterns of Economic Integration*, 53 MOD. L. REV. 731 (1990).

20. *See* BLUMBERG, THE LAW OF CORPORATE GROUPS: BANKRUPTCY, *supra*, §4.12.

21. *See* BLUMBERG, THE LAW OF CORPORATE GROUPS: SUBSTANTIVE COMMON LAW, *supra*, §13.05.

22. *See* BLUMBERG, THE LAW OF CORPORATE GROUPS: GENERAL STATUTORY LAW, *supra*, §13.13.

23. *See id.*, §16.05.

24. *See id.*, §18.02.4.

25. *See e.g.*, Farris v. Glen Alden Corp., 393 Pa. 427, 143 A.2d 25 (1958).

Table of Cases

Index

AFC0625 - 1

DATE DUE